There is no one better able to tell the story of the remarkable investment institution Vanguard than Charley Ellis. A brilliant writer, Ellis is the author of 17 books, including *Winning the Loser's Game*, the book that provides one of the most astute arguments supportive of indexing as an optimal investment strategy. He was also the founder of Greenwich Associates, providing strategic planning and analytic insights to financial services companies. He has written the definitive histories of the great investment firms Goldman Sachs and The Capital Group. In his book *The 7 Secrets of the World's Greatest Professional Firms*, he lays out exactly what it takes to succeed.

Perhaps most important, Ellis is the ultimate insider, not only of the investment industry but of Vanguard itself, where he served as a long-term director. He witnessed firsthand how the organization developed and grew and the decisions along the way that allowed Vanguard to gather over $8 trillion of the investment funds of individual and institutional investors. In these pages you will learn of the unwavering determination of Vanguard's founder, Jack Bogle, as well as the consummate business executives who followed and ensured that rapid growth could be accommodated effectively while preserving the unique culture of this iconic organization. This compelling inside story proves that it is really possible to build a dominant company by putting the client's interest first.

—Burton G. Malkiel
author of *A Random Walk Down Wall Street*

Inside Vanguard is a fun, engaging, and informative book! It provides a fascinating account of the leaders, vision, principles, personalities, conflicts, and market dynamics that led to Vanguard as a critical part of the investment landscape, how it arose, and where it is going. *Inside Vanguard* is a story told with a blend of both interesting anecdotes and focus upon key principles in a manner that only Charley can do!

—Narv Narvekar
CEO, Harvard Management Company

A master historian of investment management, Ellis recounts the story of Vanguard with characteristic fluency and insight. Ellis reveals the important first principles that gave rise to Vanguard and continue to fuel its success, while drawing engaging portraits of the firm's creative leaders through the decades. Readers curious about one of the most important and iconoclastic investment firms of the modern era will greatly enjoy *Inside Vanguard*.

—Robert Wallace
Chief Investment Officer, Stanford University

A riveting account of a firm and a mercurial founder that pioneered radical changes in the asset management industry. Fast-paced and incisively written, it provides unusual insights into how the success of a firm's culture is contextual to its time and corporate challenges. In Vanguard's case, the transition between two nearly opposite management cultures led to unprecedented achievements as it tackled exponential growth, technological change, and fierce competition

—Gumersindo Oliveros
CEO and CIO, KAUST Investment Management Company

Charley Ellis has written a fascinating book with numerous personal insights about the history of Vanguard that doubles as a treatise on how great organizations are built. I really enjoyed reading it!

—Seth Alexander
President, MIT Investment Management Company

Charley Ellis has done it again, presenting an engaging and insightful history of an institution which created the groundwork for many things that today's investors take for granted: passive investment vehicles, ETFs, low-cost alternatives, and a focus on the investor rather than the investment firm through low fees, good governance, and transparency. As in his excellent histories of Goldman Sachs and the Capital Group, Charley enlivens the story of Jack Bogle and the creation of Vanguard with the back stories of the people around Bogle who collaborated with him and challenged him in building one of the leading financial platforms serving both retail and institutional investors alike.

—Paula Volent, CFA
Vice President and Chief Investment Officer,
The Rockefeller University

INSIDE
VANGUARD

INSIDE VANGUARD

LEADERSHIP SECRETS FROM
THE COMPANY THAT CONTINUES TO REWRITE
THE RULES OF THE INVESTING BUSINESS

CHARLES D. ELLIS

New York Chicago San Francisco Athens London Madrid
Mexico City Milan New Delhi Singapore Sydney Toronto

1 2 3 4 5 6 7 8 9   LCR   27 26 25 24 23 22

ISBN   978-1-264-73483-2
MHID   1-264-73483-2

e-ISBN   978-1-264-73782-6
e-MHID   1-264-73782-3

This publication is designed to provide accurate and authoritative information in regard to the subject matter covered. It is sold with the understanding that neither the author nor the publisher is engaged in rendering legal, accounting, securities trading, or other professional services. If legal advice or other expert assistance is required, the services of a competent professional person should be sought.
—*From a Declaration of Principles Jointly Adopted by a Committee of the American Bar Association and a Committee of Publishers and Associations*

Library of Congress Cataloging-in-Publication Data

Names: Ellis, Charles D., author.
Title: Inside vanguard: leadership secrets from the company that continues to
    rewrite the rules of the investing business / Charles D. Ellis.
Description: New York : McGraw Hill, [2022] | Includes bibliographical references
    and index.
Identifiers: LCCN 2022022494 (print) | LCCN 2022022495 (ebook) | ISBN
    9781264734832 (hardback) | ISBN 9781264737826 (ebook)
Subjects: LCSH: Bogle, John C. | Vanguard Group of Investment Companies. |
    Chief executive officers—United States—Biography. | Mutual funds—United
    States. | Investments—United States. | Corporate governance—United States.
Classification: LCC HG4930 .E55 2023 (print) | LCC HG4930 (ebook) |
    DDC 332.63/27092 [B]—dc23/eng/20220524
LC record available at https://lccn.loc.gov/2022022494
LC ebook record available at https://lccn.loc.gov/2022022495

McGraw Hill books are available at special quantity discounts to use as premiums and sales promotions or for use in corporate training programs. To contact a representative, please visit the Contact Us pages at www.mhprofessional.com.

McGraw Hill is committed to making our products accessible to all learners. To learn more about the available support and accommodations we offer, please contact us at accessibility@mheducation.com. We also participate in the Access Text Network (www.accesstext.org), and ATN members may submit requests through ATN.

To the memory of David F. Swensen

and William R. Rukeyser

CONTENTS

CONTENTS

FOREWORD

The nineteenth-century Scottish philosopher Thomas Carlyle famously argued that "the history of the world is but the biography of great men." It is a temptingly elegant mental framework that taps into our deep-seated, human need for simple narratives with clear-cut heroes and villains.

After all, this is no archaic prism through which to look at the world. Even today, Hollywood constantly feeds and reinforces our desire for flawed yet brilliant protagonists who single-handedly change the course of history. Even modern-day incarnations of Batman shed the inconvenience of his sidekick Robin. But reality is always somewhat knottier. Knottier, yet more fascinating.

If great people can shape society, then society equally shapes great people. As Karl Marx observed in *The Eighteenth Brumaire of Louis Bonaparte*, his account of Napoleon's 1799 coup d'état: "Men make their own history, but they do not make it as they please; they do not make it under self-selected circumstances, but under circumstances existing already, given and transmitted from the past."

And as deeper examinations inevitably reveal, even the most titanic people and their most impressive accomplishments are inevitably the product of countless others that toil in the background. For every Napoleon, there is a Louis-Nicholas Davout or Jean Lannes, generals and marshals who often do the lion's share of practical empire-building.

The story of Vanguard often begins and ends with Jack Bogle. It is true that the money management giant was born largely through the sheer force of will of its founder, and congenitally injected with a dose of his messianic zeal. But to reduce the story of Vanguard to the story of just one man is deeply misleading.

It is hard to imagine someone better placed to write the true history of Vanguard than Charley Ellis, who combines the intimate knowledge of an insider with the incisive observations of an industry veteran. Some myth busting is the result.

As Ellis points out, Bogle was never shy about elevating the legend of "St. Jack" above the more complex reality. For example, Vanguard's founder would in later life see a kernel of his index investing proselytizing in his Princeton thesis on mutual funds. But that is quite the stretch if one reads more than Bogle's curated quotations and recalls that he was an equally ardent promoter of actively managed funds for the first quarter-century of his career.

Zealous Bogleheads—the moniker adopted by fans of Vanguard's loquacious founder—may bridle at Ellis's puncturing of some Bogleisms. But others may appreciate a more nuanced view of Vanguard's journey, whose extraordinary success owed much to Bogle's incendiary drive, but also to his many able colleagues and successors at the tiller.

Wellington's independent director Charles Root and Bogle's able assistant Jim Riepe were vital handmaidens to Vanguard's birth. The brainy "quant" Jan Twardowski was instrumental in the birth of its first index fund. Although initially an abject failure, it was pivotal in Vanguard becoming something more than a nondescript investment administration outfit. Without John Neff—the fund manager legendary both for the strength and durability of his stock-picking performance—Vanguard may not have survived the early lean years.

Bond chief Ian MacKinnon built up Vanguard's huge fixed income division, which has been essential to its success. Gus Sauter may have self-deprecatingly called himself the "head of the monkeys," but his importance to Vanguard's now-imperious indexing and quantitative investing efforts was enormous. Bill McNabb later steered Vanguard through the storm of the financial crisis with aplomb.

Arguably most importantly of all, Jack Brennan was the yin to Bogle's yang. The assiduous, publicity-shy Bostonian complemented the visionary, gregarious Philadelphian perfectly, but was also instrumental in many of Vanguard's most successful grand strategies, such as its mutually beneficial partnership with Primecap. The two men suffered a devastating, emotional fallout toward the end, but, quite simply, without Brennan Vanguard would not have become the disruptive giant it is today. He was Mark Antony to Bogle's Julius Caesar (or as Bogle later saw it, his Marcus Brutus).

Even this roll-call underestimates the many people who toiled under the mammoth shadow of Bogle to ensure Vanguard's success, and rarely if ever got the external fame they might have enjoyed at another organization—such as Jeff Molitor, whose steadfast refusal to allow a tech fund at the peak of the dot-com bubble burnished Vanguard's reputation for investment sobriety and care for clients.

Yet what they all wrought is nothing short of colossal. Even today, the magnitude of Vanguard is often underestimated because of its low-key nature and positioning, both culturally and geographically, on the outskirts of Wall Street and its braggadocious denizens.

At the time of writing, the investment group manages $8 trillion on behalf of over 30 million customers, which range from secretive sovereign wealth funds and sprawling pension plans to ordinary Americans, Australians, and Brits saving a little bit each month for their retirement. That makes it comfortably the second-biggest investment empire in the world, only outdone by BlackRock, which was built through a series of aggressive acquisitions rather than the steady organic growth of Vanguard.

Over the last two decades Vanguard has become synonymous with index funds, which indeed make up $6.2 trillion of its heft. Yet this obscures the fact that Vanguard also manages $1.7 trillion in traditional, actively managed mutual funds. This alone would make the company initially started as a clerical outfit one of the dozen largest asset management firms on the planet.

The central cause of Vanguard's success is not difficult to spot. Bogle often joked that he wasn't so sure about the Efficient Markets Hypothesis, Chicago professor Gene Fama's theory that markets are in practice unbeatable by active fund managers, which underpinned the first generation of index funds. But he was devoted to what he dubbed CMH—the Costs Matter Hypothesis—and helped hardwire it into Vanguard's DNA, both through its unique ownership structure and through the spartan example he himself continually set.

Today, Vanguard's innate frugality even shines through in its physical headquarters. Although the investment company is today so big and successful it has transformed the surrounding townships—entire business hotels exist around Malvern virtually solely to cater to Vanguard-associated visitors—the "ships" where its staff toil are dowdy compared to even third-tier Wall Street firms.

More pertinently, low costs mean that Vanguard can continually undercut rivals, whether in index or active funds. Weighted by assets, the current average expense ratio of Vanguard is just 0.09 per cent. In contrast, the industrywide average for traditional, actively managed mutual funds is about seven times higher, according to Morningstar.

In practice, being so much cheaper than virtually every one of its rivals—who have shareholders to please, who demand a certain profit margin and dividends—is for its clients the investing equivalent to beginning every soccer game a goal up on your opponents.

The advantage is particularly stark for dirt-cheap passive funds. S&P Dow Jones Indices, the benchmark provider, estimates that equity index funds as a whole have saved American investors a cumulative $365 billion in management fees since the mid-1990s. A large chunk of that is attributable directly to Vanguard. And even that ignores the de facto gains derived from index funds beating the vast majority of active funds over that time period.

Cheapness has periodically cost Vanguard's clients in terms of technical glitches and frustrations, caused by overly modest investments in technology over the years. But there are few signs that the occasional annoyances have impacted Vanguard's upward trajectory, and in 2020 the company inked a huge partnership deal with Indian IT giant Infosys that could transform its reputation as a technological laggard. Rivals will be watching carefully.

Nonetheless, great success—and the overwhelming prospect of more to come—raises many questions.

BlackRock is a global giant, but in the US mutual fund industry Vanguard is utterly dominant. It controls over a quarter of the domestic market share, almost as much as Fidelity, BlackRock, and Capital Group combined. Is there a point where Vanguard's success becomes problematic from a societal perspective? Can dominance—although well-earned and a boon to clients—at some point somehow become unhealthy and even harmful?

This is a question Bogle wrestled with in his last days as well. Although he scoffed at many of the theories lobbed out by academic and traditional investment groups about the vagaries of index funds, he admitted disquiet about the "reality that the indexing sector itself has many of the characteristics of an oligopoly." Although a rare oligopoly with seemingly positive results for consumers, the likelihood of this concentration only deepening in the coming years was not necessarily in the "national interest," as Bogle put it.

Of course, this needs to be seen in light of how Bogle spent his later years burnishing his own reputation even if it meant flinging some rocks at the company he founded. But he is not wrong. Vanguard's ballooning size will inevitably start dragging it into some of our age's most contentious issues. Ellis rightly notes—and backs it up with copious examples—that Vanguard is dedicated to "doing the right thing." But the reality is that the right thing is often in the eye of the beholder, and many issues are becoming increasingly polarized.

For example, some of the company's clients may think it should do its utmost to pressure energy companies to halt exploration—perhaps even some production—to ameliorate the climate crisis. In fact, they may think it has a fiduciary duty to do so, given that global warming could unleash a socioeconomic cataclysm. Other clients may think this preposterous, insist that Vanguard should support companies that are producing the essential ingredient of virtually all economic activity, and argue that it only has a fiduciary duty to maximize returns.

Even King Solomon would struggle to reconcile many of these conflicting and politically touchy arguments. Threading the balance between being an overly passive and active shareholder is likely to be one of the defining challenges for Vanguard for the next few decades.

Nonetheless, such is the curse of success. Vanguard is today one of the financial world's most consequential companies, and its future looks even brighter than its vibrant past, thanks to several ambitious, strategic gambits launched in recent years.

Vanguard has now set its sights on doing for the expensive and often substandard industry of financial advice what it did for investment management. Vanguard's Personal Advisor Service—which was launched by Brennan's successor Bill McNabb in 2015—already manages $243 billion.

Under Tim Buckley, now Vanguard's latest chief executive, the latest initiative is a move into private equity, through a partnership with HarbourVest. Although seemingly anathema to the company's mantra on the importance of cheap fees and transparency—concepts not commonly associated with the private equity industry—this is potentially another crucial plank in its advice and retirement business. And who knows, maybe Vanguard is quietly plotting to eventually bring the private equity phenomenon to the masses? Now that would be a revolution.

So, grab a bottle of cheap Cabernet Sauvignon—Bogle's favorite wine—and settle in to read Ellis's fascinating and fleshed-out tale of the Vanguard journey.

Robin Wigglesworth
Global finance correspondent, *Financial Times*

INTRODUCTION

The Vanguard Adventure

The Vanguard adventure began nearly 50 years ago with almost nothing: a few dozen people, mostly clerks, doing the routine work of administering 11 mutual funds that were losing assets as investors continued to reduce their investments. Vanguard had no role in either selling or investing, the two main parts of the mutual fund business; for these, it was entirely dependent on the organization that had, after an increasingly bitter fight, terminated the man who was the tiny entity's leader.

Today, Vanguard is the world's largest and most widely admired mutual fund organization—larger than its three main competitors combined—as it serves over 30 million investors and over $8 trillion in assets. At the same time, it is also one of the most rapidly growing.

Along the way, Vanguard has changed the fund industry and is well positioned to continue driving the industry to change again and again in the years ahead.

If you are one of those 30 million entrusting their trillions of savings and investments to Vanguard—as do I, my wife, children, grandchildren and our church—you will find strong confirmation of your decision to take advantage of Vanguard's low-cost, high-integrity commitment to advancing investment services. If you are new to Vanguard and its remarkable commitment to serve investors large and small, you will learn how its strengths developed—an all-American adventure story—and why it remains the investment industry's main agent of change, to the great benefit of many millions of investors.

The expressed values and explicit behavior of individuals seldom become the core beliefs of large organizations, particularly over several decades fraught with turbulence and change. But as Vanguard's adventure story unfolds, readers will see how the essence of Jack Bogle's original beliefs became the enduring DNA of today's Vanguard. They will see how a driven, creative, forceful entrepreneur, a self-described "small company guy," was outgrown years ago by the managerial challenges of explosive growth, bringing the need to develop an unusually effective organizational system with the many different managers and teamwork. Without Jack Bogle's creativity and unrelenting drive, Vanguard could never have been conceived, launched, or made successful in its early years. And it could never have reached the extraordinary success it has achieved without Jack Brennan's taking over as CEO when he did, followed by the contributions of his successors Bill McNabb and Tim Buckley.

At Vanguard's beginning, low fees were consistently the least important in a long list of the criteria by which investment managers were selected. But low fees became what Vanguard could offer to attract investors and their assets. Then, in an era of super-high interest rates, a new type of mutual fund was invented: money market mutual funds. These funds all invested in the same safe, short-term instruments: treasury bills, commercial paper, and the like. And since the funds were so much the same, one factor stood out: low fees. Low fees now mattered to investors. Focused on controlling operating costs, Vanguard had the industry's lowest fees and swiftly captured substantial market share and assets.

Before long, Vanguard used that visible edge to extend into both taxable and municipal bond investing. Again, investors noticed, and Vanguard assets surged. As assets increased, Vanguard could and did continue reducing costs and fees. Then the same formula and more good luck propelled the firm into equity investing: Vanguard offered an equity fund managed by John Neff, who achieved impressive performance *and* low cost. Vanguard's reputation rose among an increasingly appreciative and growing group of investors as it drove costs and fees lower and lower, while other mutual fund managers actually *increased* their fees.

Vanguard's low-cost, low-fee strategy was made possible by its unique structure: Vanguard was and is a *mutual* mutual fund organization; Vanguard is owned by the Vanguard funds—and hence indirectly by the investors in those funds—so there is no divided loyalty and no need to reward owners with increasing profits the way other mutual fund organizations are designed to do.

A powerful "externality" created an opportunity for Vanguard to build an enormous business in exchange-traded funds (ETFs) and index funds: the world of "active" investment management has, over the past several decades, changed in many ways that make it harder and harder for active fund managers to outperform the indexes. Most fail.

Part of the change has been a Darwinian process of driving inferior managers out of the business, so only the better managers have survived and can still compete. Another part of the change has been an extraordinary increase in both the quality and the quantity of information available to all investment managers and the speed with which information is distributed to investors. All professional market participants have powerful computer systems and Bloomberg terminals with modes to access and analyze all sorts of information instantly.

Volume of trading has increased enormously and, importantly, the fraction of trading done by professional experts has increased from below 10 percent (by small bank trust departments when banking was limited to single states and America had over 14,000 banks) to over 90 percent (led by hedge funds and aggressive active managers). As a result, the experts must trade mostly with other experts, who all know almost all the same superb information, at almost the same time, and so are mighty hard to beat. Costs and fees matter a lot and have been increasingly difficult to overcome. One result is that, over the long term, 89 percent of actively managed funds fail to equal—let alone beat—their self-chosen target market.

This means that Vanguard's index funds and ETFs have been able to grow enormously. In its array of actively managed funds, too, Vanguard's ability to negotiate low fees with managers gives investors a compelling advantage. So does its experience in selecting and monitoring active managers. Low-cost offerings have also enabled Vanguard to build an enormous business as a manager of 401(k) funds, which increasingly dominate the retirement industry.

Looking ahead, simply slowing the rate of reductions in its already low fees enables Vanguard to make game-changing capital investments of over half a billion dollars year after year in new kinds of value-adding services it can deliver to present and future investors, as it continues to change the investment services industry again and again. The Vanguard adventure continues.

PART ONE

Opportunities

CHAPTER 1

BOGLE'S BEGINNINGS

Jack Bogle was born into rapidly declining affluence.

His parents, William Yates Bogle Jr. of Montclair, New Jersey, and Josephine Lorraine Hipkins of Brooklyn, both born to wealth in 1896, married in 1924 and lived in a large home in Verona, New Jersey. Lorraine lost twin girls named Josephine and Lorraine at birth; in 1927 had a son, William Yates Bogle III, known as Bud; and then on May 8, 1929, a pair of twin boys, David Caldwell Bogle and John Clifton Bogle, whom she called Jack.

Named after his grandfather, Jack Bogle looked to his great-grandfather, Philander Banister Armstrong, as his "spiritual progenitor." While in the insurance industry, Armstrong gave speeches, wrote a book, *A License to Steal: How the Life Insurance Industry Robs Our Own People of Billions*, and tried to get readers to contribute $2.50 apiece to join the Policy Holders' Alliance and force insurance companies to "disgorge their [hundreds of millions of dollars] stolen from policy holders by dishonest laws, dishonest accountings, dishonest mortality, dishonest profits, dishonest forfeitures, and dishonest premiums."*

---

* However, in 1907 Armstrong was the president of Excelsior Fire Insurance Company when it was put into receivership by the New York State attorney general and the state superintendent of insurance. Allegedly, $137,500 of the $300,000 invested in the small company was never deposited and fictitious credits had been created instead.

3

The Bogles enjoyed a few years of high living, thanks to inheritance. Lorraine, her son Jack said, "was glamorous and charming, and everybody loved her."[1] William was sometimes called "the Prince of Wales," partly due to a resemblance but probably more because of his carefree spending. After crashing his Sopwith Camel biplane in England as a member of the Royal Flying Corps during the Great War, he worked in sales for American Brick, a company his own father had founded, and American Can, which had acquired another outfit his father had founded, the Sanitary Can Company, when it got into financial trouble in 1917. That way of life was stopped abruptly by the 1929 Crash. It wiped out William Bogle's inheritance and threw the Bogle family, including the infant twins, from affluence into increasingly serious financial troubles.

The young Bogle boys soon had to work to help out. At 10, Jack delivered newspapers and magazines and worked in an ice cream parlor. He recalled, "I didn't just get the job done, I was super responsible."[2] At 16, Jack and David crossed the first wage milestone: "We earned more than $1 an hour! I earned $1.04," sorting mail and canceling stamps at the Bayhead, New Jersey, Post Office. Financially, Jack learned to be conservative and would always be driven. "I don't think there is anything healthier than learning that you have to earn what you want to spend," he reflected many years later. "It's a great blessing. When you are working at a young age, dealing with the public, you learn about human relations. You learn about dealing with people. You learn about getting to work on time. You learn that sometimes bosses are really tough. And you learn the customer is always right." He also learned to create a self-protective fantasy world of his own enhanced perceptions, and to project them consistently and convincingly to others.

Jack Bogle always spoke warmly of both his parents. "Dad grew up a playboy, leading a Scott and Zelda social life. He tried to sell bricks, but one day said to himself, 'This guy doesn't want to buy bricks today.' So he went across the street to a bar." He soon became a heavy drinker. After a series of failures at work during the thirties and early forties, he was fired for the last time. His drinking got worse. He had to sell the home in Verona and the Bogles moved for two years, probably rent-free, into a house Lorraine's parents owned in Lakewood. Then, to cut costs further, they moved down to the Jersey shore.

By 1945 they were down to living in a two-room apartment on the third floor of a modest house in Ardmore, near Philadelphia. In a space between the two rooms were a coffeemaker and a hot plate. (Sometimes Bogle's story was modified to have the family living in what had been a garage, with young Jack sleeping on a dirt floor.) Usually, dinner was at a nearby Horn & Hardart, a chain known for vending dishes through the wall. Bogle quickly explained, "We didn't go to the automat part; we sat down for dinner."[3] Years later, he and his two brothers took turns giving their mother injections of Demerol to ease her pain from cervical cancer. "Day after day she worked in a small clothing shop. My God! The sacrifices my mother made!" said Bogle. "You can't imagine the burden she had."

In his late eighties, Bogle continued to cherish memories of his parents and see the world as he wanted to see it, saying, "I loved my father, still do. He did his best. I was Goody Two Shoes to my parents. My mother read to me *The Little Engine That Could*. There was nothing bad. I always thought we had a wonderful, wonderful background." After a pause, he continued, "I learned to save, to save for a bike." Another pause. "I do not like to spend money. Never have."[4]

While his twin focused on studies and was artistic, Jack and older brother Bud developed a compelling need to win—or at least beat each other. "We would always fight, and it was for real: dropping large rocks on each other or hitting each other with hammers," recalled Bud. "It was really weird, the violence. 'That which does not kill you,' as the Prussians say, 'makes you stronger.'" Bogle got stronger. "Having a challenged family life is a . . . you survive that or you don't," he reflected. "You survive that and you are stronger than a person who goes breezing through life thinking the world is their oyster. Taking a job when you don't have to is very different from taking a job because you need the money."

> "I do not like to spend money. Never have."

Bud Bogle learned hard lessons. As he recalled years later, he protected his younger brother Jack from "whatever kind of bad things my father got into, which was too much wine, women and song. I was the guy who had to find the damn bottles of booze and break them in front of him," while both father and son cried. "It was horrible. To see what was going on [at home] was too much for me." So he quit home and went to live in Connecticut with his mother's brother, Clifton Armstrong Hipkins, who worked on Wall Street. With Clifton's help, Lorraine arranged for her sons to get work scholarships to the 100-year-old Blair Academy. Bud graduated after one year, followed by Jack and David, after two years, in 1947. Blair was good for Jack and Jack was good at Blair—and then good for Blair. He would become Blair's all-time leading donor and a trustee for many years.

Looking back on his Blair years, Jack said, "I was a very introverted person. My brothers had more friends than I did, no question about it, and, in many ways, I kept to myself. I had a huge imagination and a lot of things I wanted to accomplish—and I accomplished them, including becoming captain of student waiters." His time at Blair, where academic demands were high, proved transformational. "Virtually everything I've accomplished in life began with my years there." Even 70 years later Bogle recalled, "I started with a miserable grade of 40 in Jesse Witherspoon Gage's algebra class. But my final grade of 100 was then thought to be the only perfect score he had ever awarded." Jack was particularly good at math problems and was at his best with a slide rule.

> "Having a challenged family life is a . . . you survive that or you don't," he reflected. "You survive that and you are stronger than a person who goes breezing through life thinking the world is their oyster. Taking a job when you don't have to is very different from taking a job because you need the money."

Graduating cum laude, Jack was voted "best student" and "most likely to succeed" by his classmates. But he was *not* valedictorian, falling short by only a fraction of a point; he was the salutatorian. Revealing the intense need to win that he would show again and again as an adult, Jack went to several of his instructors, urging them to reconsider his grades so he could graduate first in his class. He was unsuccessful. Late in life he still believed ranking second is not good enough and cited a crossword definition of "came in second" as "lost."[5]

Given the family's financial situation, only one of the three Bogle boys was able to go to college; the other two had to go to work to help support the family. It was understood that Jack, with his intense competitive drive and his record at Blair, would be the one to go—if he could get enough financial aid. He did; Jack entered Princeton with a generous scholarship that, with student jobs, would cover all his costs.

While Jack was at Princeton, Bud enlisted in the Marines and was stationed in Japan. The situation at home had gone from bad to worse. Shortly after his discharge, it fell to Bud to confront his father: "Your wife, my mother, and I can't take it anymore." Crying, Bud put his father on the train to New York City. Decades later, Jack Bogle characteristically airbrushed away the trauma, preferring to say only that "they separated."

As a scholarship boy at Princeton, Jack experienced his own separation. Princeton's exclusive eating clubs dominated campus social life. Belonging to the "right" club mattered greatly, and some members did not accept scholarship boys as equals. Jack became a member of the most prestigious Ivy Club, where he, being on scholarship, would be waiting on tables. In some ways he was "in," but in other ways he was not.

To earn what he needed to cover costs, Jack had two jobs. In addition to waiting on tables up to 30 hours a week (as he had at Blair), he worked in the athletic department ticket office—and later became manager. "I worked 40 hours a week." As a sophomore, his grades fell to Princeton's equivalent of a C average and he nearly lost his scholarship. He had to pull his average up to a B and the next year to a B+.

Jack then got a $40-a-week summer job as a stringer for the *Philadelphia Bulletin,* covering the police beat in the 10th and Jefferson Street precinct. When word of a house fire came early one Sunday morning, he called in a routine story without actually going to the scene. A savvy and suspicious rewrite man asked, "What color was the house?" Jack had no idea. But he learned another life-lesson: "No shortcuts! Tell the truth, the whole truth and nothing but the truth"[6]—even if that did sometimes involve a few carefully selected enhancements.

With his aptitude for mathematics, Jack was drawn to economics. Paul Samuelson's *Economics: An Introductory Analysis* was first published in Jack's sophomore year. "It opened my eyes to the world of economics, a world I never knew existed—economics as a body of law, quasi-scientific or even scientific."[7] (In 1993, Samuelson wrote the foreword for *Bogle on Mutual Funds: New Perspectives for the Intelligent Investor.*[8])

As a junior, Jack sought a topic for his required senior thesis. Being Bogle, he wanted something unique. He found it in *Fortune*'s December 1949 issue: an article titled "Big Money in Boston" examining the nation's largest mutual fund, the $100 million Massachusetts Investors Trust. In retrospect, "Big Money" seems a big misnomer. Seventy years ago, all mutual funds together held only $2 billion in total assets—only 1 percent of household savings. While the article said, "Mutual funds may look like pretty small change," it also saw "a rapidly expanding and somewhat contentious industry of great potential significance." Here was a chance for Jack to make his own way, do independent research, use both his writing and numerical skills, and make a mark. His 130-page thesis, "The Economic Role of the Investment Company," received a grade of 1+. (At Princeton, the grading system's top grade was a 1+ rather than an A+.) This meant Jack would graduate magna cum laude. As he later said, "I thought I was in heaven!"[9]

Sadly, his mother died in February 1951, the year of Jack's graduation from Princeton. His father died of a stroke later that same year in Bellevue Hospital. Both parents at their deaths were 55. Jack was 21. Even near the end of his life, his eyes teared up as he recalled those family years.

At Princeton, Bogle was already showing his vital characteristics—brains, guts, fearless independence, imagination, unrelenting persistence and tenacity, close-to-the-edge risk-taking, long-term vision, and a romantic view of his life and himself. They would come together over many years to make him one of the most successful entrepreneurs of his generation, with a direct impact on millions of individual investors and their families and a powerful impact on the mutual fund industry. Nearly seven decades later, Bogle would explain philosophically, "I'm personally part of the past now, but the future will be dominated by my ideas."[10]

No reader can leave Bogle's Princeton thesis without being impressed by the breadth and depth of the research poured into it by a young man studying a little-known group of outfits with a short history. As with any long undergraduate study of an emerging industry with a dynamic, yet-to-develop future, selected excerpts can seem prescient while some others can seem naive. Rereading his 1951 thesis many years later, he wrote, with a classic Bogle mix of professed modesty and a warm pat on his own back, "One might expect that retrospective reflection on an academic thesis written 64 years earlier—based as it was on a subject little known all those years ago—would bring emendations, corrections, apologies, and rethinking of the original work. But such an expectation would not be the case. The fundamentals set forth in my thesis have stood the test of time. . . . My first reaction was that I wasn't much of a writer! My second reaction was that it was pretty well written for a kid—and not the smartest kid in the world—who, when he began writing his thesis, was but a year beyond teen age."[11]

An objective evaluator would certainly agree that the thesis was well written, particularly for an undergraduate, and the research was unusually extensive. The text was balanced with original and relevant statistics, tables, and charts. But since Bogle frequently cited his paper from his later position as one of his industry's recognized thought leaders, it seems fair to evaluate his own mature evaluations rigorously. Overall, after 50 years of industry experience and with 20-20 hindsight, Bogle said, "I hit most of my targets with remarkable accuracy." Well, maybe not quite most. But that college paper laid the foundation for principles that later made Vanguard an appealing exception in its industry:

> **Serving investors with candor.** Jack Bogle would make Vanguard the model of candor and continuously urged the industry to change and come with him. How many investors know that over the long term of 15 years, almost 90 percent of actively managed mutual funds have had returns *below* that of their chosen market? The fund industry is not known for candor, but for consistently overemphasizing the positives while minimizing the negatives in its record.

> **Shareholders first.** "I was right in my citation" in the thesis that the industry's "ideal goal" would be to put the clients' interests first. Such idealism was far from industry practice and even from Bogle in his early years at the Wellington investment firm—but then became remarkably and uniquely central at Vanguard three decades later. As the older Bogle so often

scolded, the main focus at most fund families has been on the management company's business success and profits, instead of the clients'.

Index funds. "I hinted in the thesis at the powerful idea of indexing by saying 'funds can make no claim to superiority over the market averages.'" That hint was barely a whisper. Connecting that hint to the eventual surge in indexing over half a century later, after a very slow start, is a stretch, particularly for the man who devoted the first 25 years of his career to vigorously promoting and selling actively managed funds. As we shall see, he only backed into indexing to have something to sell without quite breaking the specific terms of a board of directors' decision, and only began to see success 15 years later.

Fees. Funds' costs for active investment management have only recently begun to come down after 50 years of increasing significantly. Since the era of Bogle's thesis, fee schedules have generally defied economic theory: for years, as volume surged, fees did not go down, they actually increased. Bogle's focus on costs came only years after he left his original employer and launched Vanguard.

Governance. Mutual funds have not taken a strong lead in corporate governance. Only recently have fund managers moved from complete passivity to show any interest in how the companies they invest in conduct themselves. It's notable that the leaders in good governance activity today are the leading indexers: Vanguard, BlackRock, and State Street.

Financing new businesses. Venture capital for new businesses has almost never come from mutual funds and, realistically, should not have, for good reasons: start-ups are illiquid, so they present great difficulty in pricing, particularly on a daily basis. They are too small to "move the needle" of major mutual fund companies. They require specialized investing skills and if successful, produce highly irregular investment returns.

During the industry's formative years in the forties, fifties, and sixties, mutual funds were in a scrappy, tough, sales-focused business that only later became extraordinarily profitable as individuals and institutions increasingly invested in its proliferating products. While moving in the direction young Bogle had expected as it gained scale and the trust of investors, progress has been slow and driven primarily by external pressures. This handed Bogle an opportunity to criticize his industry and Vanguard's competitors. Over the years, particularly toward the end of his career, Jack Bogle would be widely recognized as the industry's toughest critic.

A childhood experience like Bogle's—a drunken father, increasing financial dependence on relatives, kids taking whatever jobs they could get to help cover costs, a family moving down and down scale from smaller houses to two rooms for five people crowded together with an electric hot plate in the hallway— would have clobbered most kids. Not Bogle.

> **Over the years, particularly toward the end of his career, Jack Bogle would be widely recognized as the industry's toughest critic.**

Anything like his cardiac record—six heart attacks in his lifetime and, eventually, a heart transplant—would have driven most men off to the sidelines. Not Bogle.

A series of career reversals such as he experienced would have discouraged most executives into retiring and licking their wounds. Not Bogle.

Bogle was always different. In his stubborn "I am right—always" manner, he brought on himself most of the daunting challenges he would face as an adult, as well as his long series of remarkable successes. He was always a clever fighter, with more staying power and drive than those around him ever expected. He was not only gifted in quantitative analyses but was also a remarkably creative visionary and entrepreneur driven to "press on regardless," as he regularly insisted.

Before it was all over, Bogle would achieve extraordinary success. He would:

- Conceptualize, create, and launch against long odds what would become one of the world's largest, most admired and trusted investment organizations, serving more than 30 million investors and managing over $8 trillion of invested savings.

- Become one of the most famous and admired advocates for a set of once contrarian beliefs and principles that are increasingly accepted as investment gospel. A large group of devoted fans, calling themselves Bogleheads, met with him annually and now actively celebrate and promote—in books and a busy website—his core concepts of sensible, successful long-term investing.

- Become the largest donor and fundraiser and longest serving trustee for his secondary school, Blair Academy, where two major buildings are named for members of his family; provide funding for numerous Bogle Scholars; be a major donor to the Pace Center for Civic Engagement at Princeton University; and lead the capital campaign for the National Constitution Center in Philadelphia.

- Write 12 books, which he believed would "protect me from being forgotten"; receive honorary degrees from Princeton and 13 other colleges; be elected to the American Academy of Arts and Sciences; and for many years be an avid competitor in both squash and tennis.

In vain, his wife would plead, "Jack, you can't keep going on like this—you have to stop." But at nearly 90, he couldn't. Not Bogle. He still had something to prove. And, as he explained to a close professional friend, "If I stop, I will die!"[12]

CHAPTER 2

A MERGER MADE IN HEAVEN

Looking for his first real job after graduation, Jack Bogle got a lucky break: Walter McGessler, the manager of Jack's eating club at Princeton, bumped into Walter Morgan, a former club member who was in the mutual fund business. McGessler urged Morgan to consider hiring Bogle, citing his thesis on mutual funds. Reluctant to waste his own time—he thought most Princetonians were spoiled kids who wouldn't work hard—Morgan asked two of his senior people, A. Moyer Kulp and Joseph E. Welch, to meet Bogle as a favor to McGessler. When they did, they were impressed by the young man's observations on the industry and urged Morgan to read the thesis. Morgan did and was more than impressed; he urged all his employees to read it, saying, "He knows more about the fund business than we do!"[1]

Even though he was determined to hire Bogle, Morgan pretended to have doubts, telling him, "I don't know what we're going to do with you. We don't really need anybody." Bogle was equally cagey, making clear that others were showing interest and a major bank had made him a firm offer. This flushed Morgan out: "Jack, you'll never get anywhere in a *bank*! Banking is dull! Join us. We're a growing company where you'll eventually be one of the top guys."

Bogle was unsure at first. Financially conservative since childhood, he appreciated the stability of banking, but he was also ambitious and wanted the chance to exercise his creativity and entrepreneurial drive that an investment firm could provide. In 1951, mutual funds were beginning to win their battle for acceptance and had attracted a million investors, though the average investment was still only $3,000. He joined Morgan's firm, Wellington, on July 9, 1951. With total fund assets of only $194 million, Wellington had an industry market share of 6.2 percent.

Bogle shared his first assignment with Jim French, who had started a few days earlier and would later become the head of trading at Wellington. It was clerical: demonstrate the benefits of a dividend reinvestment program recently invented by Morgan *if* it had been used over the past 15 years by an investor committing $10,000. French had a new calculating machine. Bogle had a slide rule and bet he would be faster at working out the answer. Bogle won.

After a few months of such entry-level work, Bogle was advanced to what would become seven years of helping Walter Morgan write shareholder reports and letters to investors, often with multiple rounds of revisions to satisfy Morgan—a process Bogle would later require of many others. In a year or so, his role expanded into public relations, including speaking to salespeople and industry groups. He would specialize in terse but interesting "quotable quotes" on the stock market, mutual fund trends, and the economy. This was the beginning of Bogle's development into a master of press relations. He had an instinct for finding the most convincing way to organize data to make Wellington look good. Bogle became a strong "outside" man focused on sales and would stay that way, never engaging in research or portfolio management or fund operations as did the "inside" men of the mutual fund business.

Walter Morgan's toughness was hard earned over a lifetime. He had seen his grandfather lose his life savings to speculation in gold mines and other boondoggles and then did nearly the same thing himself when fresh out of Princeton in 1920. One such "investment" was in a wildcat oil scheme. Another was in a proposed merger of local utilities—with his position leveraged with 90 percent margin. The merger did not go through, so share prices fell sharply. To meet margin calls, Morgan had to borrow from his family.

Realizing he needed more than just an economics degree from Princeton to succeed, Morgan sought experience at the accounting firm Peat, Marwick, Mitchell & Company in Philadelphia, a job that paid $125 a month, and took finance classes at night. A few years later, turned down for a raise, he moved to Haskins & Sells, where he became a CPA, and later decided, with urging from his grandfather, to run his own business "even if only a peanut stand." He launched an accounting firm, Morgan and Company, to offer tax and investment advice "to mix whatever imagination and adventurousness I had with the analytical experience and accounting training I had gained."

In the 1920s, most investment companies or mutual funds were organized as "closed end" funds with a set number of shares traded in the stock market, much like any other publicly owned company. The price a seller could get depended not only on the asset value of the securities owned by the fund but also on what a buyer would pay. Along with the other risks of investing in securities, this added the risk of the shares trading at a discount from the fund's underlying value. To avoid this risk, the first "open end" mutual fund, Massachusetts Investors Trust, began in March 1924 with just 200 investors and an important innovation: investors could buy or sell shares any day the market was open at the exact closing per-share value of the portfolio of investments in the fund.*

During the Roaring Twenties, the stock market rose more than fourfold, attracting millions of people with no investment experience. Morgan found himself giving customer after customer the same advice: diversify, balance stocks and bonds, and take a long-term view. He decided to establish an open-end investment trust, knowing he would have to raise money by selling shares in small amounts to individual investors. To get the $100,000 minimum required by regulators to launch a new fund, he put up $25,000, obtained another $25,000 from a wealthy accounting client, and raised the remainder from family and friends. Most of the new capital came not as cash, but as shares of stock in various companies, many recognizable blue chips. In July 1929, Morgan opened his new fund for business just months before the Great Crash.

---

* Over 250 closed-end trusts had been formed to invest, with leverage, in corporate stocks and bonds or in real estate. Open-end funds, while new in the United States, were common in the United Kingdom.

Morgan initially called the fund the Industrial and Power Securities Company, which he thought was "a name that would fit the times, a name that called forth the imagery of American industry, one that would give investors a picture of the power of our growing economy, one that would promise investors what they wanted." Later he would dismiss it as "a name no one could remember." The fund was different from the typical mutual funds, which were mostly 100 percent invested in stocks. Morgan's fund—deliberately, given the recent investment losses he and his family had experienced in stocks—was a "balanced" fund, diversifying among blue-chip stocks and high-quality bonds. Morgan also avoided the debt leverage that was so often then used to boost returns at the numerous closed-end funds. Expecting outsize returns in a bull market, investors priced many closed-end funds at well more than 100 percent of their net assets. But as Walter Morgan understood, leverage works both ways: it magnifies both gains and losses.

> Morgan found himself giving customer after customer the same advice: diversify, balance stocks and bonds, and take a long-term view.

Fortunately, soon after launching the new fund, Morgan took the advice of the fund's two investment advisers, Brandon Barringer, head of investment management at Philadelphia National Bank, and A. Moyer Kulp, an investment banker and the man who later urged Morgan to hire Bogle, to reduce the fund's stock holdings from 75 percent of total assets to just 33 percent. While the average fund that year fell almost 90 percent as the market plunged that year, Morgan's fund, launched in July at $12.74 per share, lost a mere 45 cents a share in its first year of operations. In a particular stroke of good luck, Morgan had sold the stock of Curtis Publishing, then a business leader in Philadelphia, at $124 before the Crash. It would fall 96 percent to just $5 in three years. As a balanced fund, Morgan's had a large part of its assets in bonds that went up as interest rates went down, and in cash. Investors noticed. During the fund's first year as new investors were attracted by the good record, assets doubled. The next year, they increased another 53 percent.

But as the challenging 1930s wore on, Morgan's fund stopped growing. Realizing that distribution (sales) was critical to future growth and that the fund's name was forgettable, Morgan renamed it Wellington Fund in 1935, aligning the fund name with the name of the investment management company he had formed several years earlier. (He had studied and admired Arthur Wellesley, the first Duke of Wellington, and felt the name had "an almost indefinable air of quality about it that made it almost perfect as a name for a conservative financial corporation.") To capitalize on the fund's comparatively favorable history, he hired salespeople who merchandised it to securities dealers in Philadelphia, New York City, Hartford, and Boston, particularly capitalizing on contractual monthly purchase plans. Plans committing the investor to invest a "contractual amount of money each month for 10 years" were first proposed by Alvin J. Wilkins, the leading seller of Wellington Fund shares. By the end of 1935, the Wellington Fund had grown to $1 million (about $19 million in today's dollars). Raising cash before the 1939 German invasion of Poland, the fund handily beat the market from 1939 to 1944.

Thanks to the end of the Second World War, a continuing focus on sales, and a surging stock market, assets in the Wellington Fund reached $25 million. It needed a larger management organization. Morgan convinced Moyer Kulp to move up from investment adviser to full-time head of investments and promoted Alvin Wilkins to head of sales and Joseph Welch to executive vice president. The fund kept growing. By 1949, fund assets were $100 million, and, just two years later, $190 million. Wellington Fund had become America's fourth largest mutual fund, and Walter Morgan was a recognized leader in a scrappy, sales-driven industry.

In 1955, with assets at $600 million, Morgan made Bogle his assistant at Wellington Management Company, giving him a long leash but continuing to insist on perfection. Bogle would stay in that position for seven years. As he would later say, "I was clearly the kind of person who wanted to run whatever I had anything to do with. I may not have been innately bright, but I was determined." Within a few years, he was in charge of marketing. Morgan began to see Bogle as his eventual successor *if* he proved himself an aggressive leader.

But by the late 1950s, trouble loomed. In a bull market for stocks and a bear market for bonds, Wellington's balanced-fund concept was being eclipsed by the all-equity mutual funds. Clever as always,

Bogle developed what Wellington enthusiastically promoted as "The 6 Percent Solution." The "solution" was at best a euphemism and more nearly a semantic deception. It involved paying out 6 percent of the market value of the Wellington Fund each year in cash as though the 6 percent were a dividend. While some of the money needed for these big payouts did come from dividends or interest earned on bond investments, the rest came from taking capital gains. Dividends and gains were combined to create a cash pay-out to the fund's shareholders large enough to attract underinformed retail investors who wanted large distributions of spending money and were willing to be assured by salesmen that the payouts were "almost like dividends." Nearly one-third was really just a return of capital. Competitors complained, and in 1950 the National Association of Securities Dealers banned combining capital gains with dividends. But Bogle and Wellington kept making the payouts—which investors accepted—without explicitly claiming they were dividends. In the 1960s the payouts from capital gains grew to be almost as large as the payouts from dividends and interest.

> **Morgan began to see Bogle as his eventual successor *if* he proved himself an aggressive leader.**

"Each year," as Bogle later recalled, "Moyer Culp and I would get together and I'd ask, 'We'll get this much in incoming dividends and interest, so can you cover the rest with realized capital gains?' That worked for several years, but we knew it couldn't go on forever. We were draining the well of unrealized capital gains. Over the years, the capital gains got taken and taken until none were left to take. At just about the same time, the go-go performance funds were getting almost all the attention of both brokers and mutual fund investors." Bogle added euphemistically, "Wellington was not doing badly, but its performance was below par." Realistically, Wellington was positioned in the wrong part of the mutual fund market, had an inferior record, had retained investors with a corner-cutting deception, and was in what appeared to be a slow but terminal decline. When capital gains had all been used up, Bogle would later recall, "In 1970, I recommended, and the board reluctantly approved, a payout of 25 percent from surplus. . . . While I wasn't keen about the idea, it seemed to do the job."[2]

In the mutual fund industry, qualitative changes have been at least as important as the quantitative changes. Eighty years ago, mutual funds were not so much bought; they had to be *sold*. The selling was through stockbrokers, a tough crowd operating on relatively low incomes and focused on "what's in it for me?" Brokers typically directed only small accounts into mutual funds. With commissions at 40 cents a share—at least quadruple today's retail rates, if any—brokers could make more money by keeping larger investors in an actively trading account for individual stocks.

So mutual funds needed a strong financial incentive for both the salesman and his firm. This incentive came from a sales charge, typically 8½ percent, deducted from the investor's money. When the investor put up $100, only $91.50 actually got invested; the other $8.50—which was, of course, 9.3 percent of the dollars actually invested—went to pay the broker and his firm. (For larger purchases, the sales charge declined on a scale.)

Bogle was becoming convinced that his boss and mentor, devoted as he was to his own balanced-fund creation, was missing the market for mutual fund sales. Walter Morgan insisted that his focus on a single mutual fund was both smart merchandising and the key to profitability because it kept costs under control. In contrast, Bogle believed multiple funds would attract multiple types of investors, so he wrote a business plan that would eventually have the Wellington firm offering a full range of funds. Acceptance would mean overcoming Morgan's long-held double commitment to one fund and the balanced-fund concept.

With Wellington's funds lagging, Morgan finally accepted Bogle's entreaties to capitalize on market trends and offer an all-stock fund, at first called Wellington Equity Fund. Bogle became a fund officer for the first time as secretary of Wellington Equity Fund. The fund raised a then satisfactory $33 million in its initial offering and rose to $44 million in assets by the end of 1959.

Both the stock and bond markets had risen during the 1950s, so the mutual fund business prospered. With Wellington Management Company supervising more than $1 billion in early 1960, Walter Morgan took his firm public. Tough as ever, he was determined to retain tight voting control. He created two classes of shares: 867,800 A shares had one vote apiece, while 10,000 B shares (which only he and Joseph Welch owned) had 250 votes apiece. Of 3.4 million votes, 2.5 million—over two-thirds—would be cast by Morgan's and Welch's 10,000 B shares.

Over its first three years, the new Wellington Equity Fund handily outperformed the market, but in 1961, with the market down 8.7 percent, the fund plunged 25 percent. As the stock market recovered, the investment committee, cautious that the upswing might be short-lived, was too slow to reinvest cash reserves, so the fund underperformed again. Sales stalled. A Wellington Fund shareholder sued, claiming the Equity Fund's poor performance was hurting the larger Wellington Fund. Major change was needed.

The simple change to settle the lawsuit was to call the fund by a new name: Windsor. The much more significant change was to install a new portfolio manager in 1964: John Neff. In his 32-year run at Windsor, Neff would become known as the investment profession's investment professional. Hardly anyone had ever managed a large mutual fund so well for so long.*

Still, after the public offering, Wellington Management Company was troubled. Wellington Fund, which still produced 95 percent of the company's revenue, kept losing assets and market share.

On Labor Day weekend 1960, Jack Bogle, then 31, was playing tennis with his brother-in-law, John J. F. "Jay" Sherrerd, who was 30. Starting to serve, Bogle felt an acute pain, saw a flash of light, and suddenly looked drained.

"Jack, are you all right?"

"Jay, I have to stop a minute," whispered Bogle. "I think I just had a heart attack." The idea seemed absurd, so both men laughed and soon returned to play. (Bogle later recalled that he won.) Driving home, he felt worse, so his wife, Eve, drove him to the hospital. As Bogle recounted with a knowing smile, "I was in a decent amount of trouble." He stayed in the hospital for six weeks.

Over the next 35 years, Bogle would have five more heart attacks. One came while playing squash; he was revived by his opponent pounding on his chest. Another time, two doctors used

---

* Capital Group's Bill Newton had an even better record, but given his firm's "multiple manager" way of managing funds, his record was not known to the investing public.

CPR to get his heart beating again. "It's something that has made life rather difficult for me," he observed drily, "although I've always plunged into everything I had to do with great enthusiasm and concentration—and that ain't bad if you've got a malady. It's certainly better than doing nothing and just waiting for the Grim Reaper."[3]

With the launch of the new equity fund, Morgan began identifying Bogle as his likely successor at troubled Wellington Management Company. The new all-equity fund's poor early performance hurt sales badly. Overall, the parent company, with weak investment performance and a dated product line, was struck in a steady decline within a growing industry. This made its problems both worse and more visible. The firm was consistently losing market share. This was certainly not okay for a newly public company.

The business strategy of Wellington Management was in a stall, having already maximized sales in various clever ways and retarded redemptions as much as possible. Of Wellington Fund's inflows, a full 30 percent were from those unsavory 10-year contractual investment plans. In those plans, half of the investor's first year's "investment" actually went to pay the high sales commission needed to get stockbrokers to make the difficult, time-consuming sale of locked-in investment contracts. By allocating those brokerage commissions, Wellington could get some firms—but not the better ones—to press their salesmen to push sales of shares in Wellington Fund. But brokers could be pressed only so far, and now they were increasingly giving up on Wellington and turning to the "performance" funds that were so much easier to sell. In sum, Wellington had already maxed out its share of the hoary, hard-sell practices of the old-line mutual fund business.

As a young executive in the 1950s, Bogle had worked hard to master the arts of being an "industry contact" or "source" for the media. His effective model: be brief, be factual, different, provocative, and easy to understand; give pithy quotes; and above all, be readily accessible. As the years and citations accumulated, he became a credible name to both reporters and readers. Journalists learned to call Bogle first because he was so helpful and so consistently the industry iconoclast, always taking the side of the oft-abused everyday investors. Almost inevitably, media coverage was favorable to Bogle and so to Wellington.

As young Bogle was moving up through the ranks, Wellington, while large, kept going down. At the rate assets were disappearing, it would sink in just a few more years. As a "numbers guy," Bogle had been studying the trends and knew the firm must take action— the bolder the better—to fix its problems: dependence on one conservative balanced fund, no strong equity fund in the go-go era, a paucity of investment talent, and total dependence on mutual funds. As a hard-charging young leader with industry expertise, Bogle was certain that he was the right man at the right time to take the lead in making the right bold strategic move.

> **His effective model: be brief, be factual, different, provocative, and easy to understand; give pithy quotes; and above all, be readily accessible.**

Morgan told Bogle, whom he had advanced from administrative vice president to executive vice president in 1965, "Do whatever it takes to turn our company around." One possibility was to recruit a new team of highly talented fund managers, build a research team, create a strong investment record and then reposition Wellington as a can-do, contemporary investment organization. But that would be expensive, would easily take a decade and maybe even longer, and might not work. Wellington was generally tagged within the industry as a stodgy fund run by a stodgy organization. Philadelphia was not considered nearly as significant for investing as New York City, Boston, or Los Angeles. All-equity funds were surging in market share, and Wellington's only all-equity fund had stumbled badly. Reorganizing and repositioning Wellington was sure to be a difficult, risky, costly way to go.

However, with the right acquisition—particularly one that opened doors to the booming institutional business of managing large pension funds that were moving money out of bank trust departments in search of performance-oriented investment management firms—a strategic repositioning could be done quickly with fewer risks and at a far lower cost. As Bogle later said, "Brash, overconfident, and impetuous, I found a way to solve all our problems in one fell swoop in 1966."

If Bogle could not beat the performance funds, he could do even better by joining them through a merger. The major mutual fund organizations—Fidelity, Capital, Dreyfus, Putnam, Keystone, and others—were all too big, so he ruled them out. If he found the right investment management organization, ideally privately owned with a strong investment performance record, Wellington Management Company could use its publicly traded stock to make a carefully targeted acquisition. With the right acquisition, Bogle could reposition Wellington Management Company quickly at low risk *and* low cost—a dramatic leap into the future and a great personal triumph for young Bogle.

The retail opportunities were obvious. Wellington Management had built a strong wholesale distribution system for selling fund shares through retail brokerage firms. Wellington used its substantial volume of "near money" brokerage commissions to get favored fund treatment at major retail brokerage firms. To get more of Wellington's large brokerage commissions, these firms would make sure—by paying their brokers more and setting "must do" sales quotas—that their salespeople emphasized the funds of Wellington Management Company.

In the increasingly sophisticated stock market of the sixties, Bache & Co., a still-large but fading old-line "wire house" brokerage firm, was losing market share with individual investors and was unable to compete effectively for business with the surging institutions. Still, Bache was Wellington Management's leading distributor. The two firms were important to each other. Bache needed Wellington and its reciprocal commission business as much as Wellington needed Bache and its sales force.*

In late 1965, over lunch with John C. Jansing, the national mutual fund sales manager at Bache, Bogle shared some of his concerns about his firm. Deliberately casual, he said he was thinking of acquiring a mutual fund firm with investment talent and a record of superior investment performance that had what Wellington did not have—a pure growth fund with strong performance—and needed what Wellington did have: stock brokerage commissions that could

---

* Later Bache would get a major capital infusion from Prudential Insurance, recruit a large group of research analysts, and engage in block trading in an all-out but unsuccessful effort to penetrate the institutional business.

be directed to brokers in reciprocity for selling funds to individual investors, and a strong wholesaling sales organization that could get distribution through retail stockbrokers. The ideal acquisition target would have three key characteristics: strong investment talent; a hot investment performance record, particularly in recent years; and a weak sales organization, because that would make Wellington Management Company's strength in sales compelling.

Jansing knew just the firm: a Boston outfit with a sizzling investment record—and almost no sales. "If you are really thinking about doing a merger with a hot fund, there's a group up in Boston managing the Ivest Fund with a great investment performance but weak sales. They also have a good counseling business with wealthy individuals and institutional clients. It's run by four guys you'd be very comfortable with." Jansing agreed to make introductions to the Boston firm, named for its four principals: Thorndike, Doran, Paine & Lewis.

Bogle jumped at the opportunity. As he would say later, "Beauty is always in the eye of the beholder," and with no prior experience in acquisitions, he could see only great beauty. The Boston firm's Ivest Fund had the best five-year record of all mutual funds nationwide. Over six years, while the S&P 500 market index had nearly doubled—jumping up 94 percent—Ivest was up *four times* as much: 389 percent.[4]

Despite that sizzling record, Ivest had almost no sales results: only $17 million in the previous *year*. No vivid imagination was required to envision the immediate opportunities Bogle must have conceived in a merger. Wellington had powerful distribution; Ivest had great performance. Combining strength with strength, Bogle would transform Wellington Management in one single, decisive strategic action into a powerhouse with what he and others soon called "the merger made in heaven." The frosting on the cake was the Boston firm's solid investment counseling unit. This would give Wellington highly attractive entrée into the fast-growing institutional business of managing pension funds and endowments. With Wellington's sales prowess and prominence, and Ivest's performance record, Bogle was sure sales could easily be multiplied.

At 36, he saw no downside. He knew he was one of the best informed and hardest working young leaders in an industry with surging growth, major structural change. and great prospects. He was sure others—Walter Morgan, all the managers at Wellington, and the whole mutual fund industry—would soon see what he saw as *the* great strategic move.

Wasting no time, Bogle was soon negotiating merger specifics with Robert W. Doran and W. Nicholas Thorndike. From first meeting to merger, everything took only nine months and went smoothly. Bogle, as Bob Doran would later recall, was "very bright, very enthusiastic. He was vital, alive. These initial conversations were very, very positive." Years later Bogle would recall his own thinking: "Let's merge! We'll solve all our problems at once." But in retrospect he would bitterly observe, "If you're stupid as well as impatient, mergers are *always* bad for one side or the other."[5]

During the merger discussions, Walter Morgan, at 67, set the overall tone with his white hair, conservative nature, and genial stories of the hardscrabble mutual fund business of the forties and fifties. Confident externally and even more confident internally, Bogle was the classic assertive, optimistic, solo, alpha-male initiator. In contrast, Doran, by nature a collegial listener with an open-minded interest in others' thoughts and feelings, was comfortable with freestyle discussions that could lead a group of partners and friends gradually to consensus decision. To Nick Thorndike, a socially secure Boston Brahmin, Bogle must have seemed to be anxiously wanting a deal. Both sides could see the overall structure of a mutually favorable deal, but behind the alignment of financial interests were major differences in personalities, management concepts, and organizational cultures. Over time, these differences would not stay hidden.

> But in retrospect he would bitterly observe, "If you're stupid as well as impatient, mergers are *always* bad for one side or the other."

At TDP&L, as the Boston firm was known, the Morning Meeting—8:30 to 9:00 each weekday—had become a hallowed tradition. Morning Meetings began in 1958 as a gathering of four friends, who then worked at different firms, to share ideas and information. In those early days, most meetings were held in Stephen D. Paine's apartment where breakfast was usually turkey livers— the Paines owned a turkey farm—and scrambled eggs. Diners were always charged 30 cents. As the organization grew, Doran cared particularly about those meetings and their being "spontaneous, almost without form" so they would facilitate participants' learning from each other and reinforce the firm's culture of collaboration—not consensus or conformity. Today's Morning Meetings are held in a room with many-tiered seating and multiple screens showing financial information, current portfolio holdings, and market price trends. There is no hierarchy. Discussion is respectful and reasoned, with occasional touches of humor. Carefully selected clients and prospective clients are invited to sit in the back row and watch the experts exchanging insights. It's novel, fun, and makes a great impression.

"We never had a grand strategy, but if something came along, we were always game to take a peek," explained Doran. "Our firm persevered because [our] people adhered to a distinctive culture. At its core, ours is a story about how people decided to treat each other, and how that collective decision became the foundation of an enterprise."[6]

Suddenly, in the midst of merger discussions, a shadowy but colorful American dealmaker named Bernard "Bernie" Cornfeld of Investors Overseas Services, based in Switzerland to avoid taxes and selling mutual funds all over the world, declared he opposed the merger. IOS held 10 percent of Wellington Management's A shares in the offshore mutual funds Cornfeld controlled, so his support was important. Cornfeld threatened to sue to block the merger. So Bogle, who had never had a passport, got one and flew to Geneva.

Cornfeld was blunt: "This merger is ridiculous! The problem is not that they are SOBs. The problem is that they are no-good SOBs. If they fail to live up to your expectations, you won't get rid of them; they'll get rid of *you!*"[7] Bogle was troubled by Cornfeld and his rant, but not dissuaded.* Since nothing convinces the righteous like having to fight for an objective, when questioned about the merger being out of character for conservative Wellington, Bogle smiled knowingly and replied with confidence, "Everyone likes a deal." He pressed on regardless of how much he would later rue the day.

---

* Cornfeld's bluster about blocking the merger came to nothing. He was later convicted of financial fraud and sentenced to prison in Switzerland. Much of the money invested in the IOS funds was "flight capital" of tribal leaders in Africa and generals in China.

Just then, another merger opportunity came in from Bogle's friend and fellow Philadelphian Paul F. Miller, Jr., and Bogle's brother-in-law, Jay Sherrerd. The two had developed superb national reputations in investment research and portfolio management at Drexel Harriman Ripley, the result of a recent merger of two Establishment securities firms. Miller was increasingly obliged to devote most of his time to routine organizational management and wanted to get back to full-time investing. Seeing an opportunity, he went to Bogle's home one evening to propose they work together: Bogle would run administration and sales while Miller led investment research and management.

Bogle did not want to abort the TDP&L merger, but instead saw an exciting chance for a strategic double play. He proposed a bold twofer: bring Paul Miller on board to lead investing in Philadelphia *and* do the deal in Boston. Wellington would do both! While Miller had his own reservations about the Boston group, Bogle persuaded Miller to join with him in managing Philadelphia while Doran and Thorndike would manage operations in Boston. A press release announcing the new arrangement was prepared.

But Sherrerd was sure that, given their personalities, his best friend couldn't work with his brother-in-law and he did not want to lose Miller. "You both love to be the boss. Jack's a detailed, hands-on manager, Paul, and you're a policy guy who hates details. I can't imagine Jack telling you what to do or you telling Jack what to do."[8] Then Drexel countered with a major increase in Miller's compensation and the chance to run his own investment unit while shifting administrative tasks to others. Miller decided to stay where he was. The press release was never sent out. Eventually both Miller and Bogle appreciated Sherrerd's warning. As Miller later explained, "I think we would ultimately have had some real clashes." The merger with TDP&L went ahead and closed on June 6, 1966. Some participants later remarked that 6/6/66 might have been a devilishly unfortunate date.

Serious troubles were signaled in the first year after the merger when another heart attack landed Bogle in the hospital. "Even though he was hospitalized, he would still countermand decisions we were making back in the office," recalled Doran. "That was the start of the realization that our management styles were very different."[9] Bogle eventually agreed. The Boston group was, he said, "private, independent with a nonhierarchical structure, collegial, participative in its management style with shared decision-making, dialogue, and debate among peers, while the management style in Philadelphia was autocratic and hierarchical. I knew I wasn't tactful or diplomatic." In a stunning understatement, he observed, "Those different styles tended to clash."[10]

But that recognition came only years later. At the time of the merger, Bogle was so certain that there would be no major conflict that he agreed to have the 10,000 Class B shares—the shares with 250 votes each that were to be relinquished by Morgan and Welch—granted in units of 1,250 shares apiece to each of the four Boston partners. Combined with the 148,000 Class A shares, valued at $4 million, that they would also receive, each of the four Bostonians would have 10 percent voting control, while Bogle, with 4,000 B shares plus his own A shares, would control 28 percent.[11]

Walter Morgan wanted to maintain control for at least a few more years as the two groups got used to each other, so he proposed a voting trust to hold all the shares for five years, until April 1, 1971. This would give the directors ample time to see how the combination was working. After that confirmation, the voting trust would dissolve and Thorndike would become chairman of the management company board, Doran COO and Bogle CEO. Offices would be kept in both Boston and Philadelphia, and the four Boston partners would go onto the Wellington Management board of directors. The Boston group appreciated that plan and the long-term way Morgan was thinking ahead.

As Bogle lamented years later, "I had this naive idea that I could always persuade at least one of them to my position and that would give me 38 percent to the others' 30 percent." Bogle miscalculated and failed to foresee the jeopardy before him. The four Bostonians were a close-knit partnership of friends who would vote together, particularly as tensions and disagreements grew stronger—and collectively they had more votes. As Bogle would later observe: "Naive? Stupid might be more like it."

CHAPTER 3

TROUBLES BREWING

A s Bogle had intended, after the merger Wellington Management Company got more aggressive in sales and also changed its investment approach. "The merger was working well," recalled Bogle. "The best illustration was in Ivest Fund's sales, which got 70 percent of all our new sales in 1968." Ivest's assets surged from $1 million at the end of 1961 to $50 million at the end of 1966, and further grew to $340 million by the end of 1968.

Doran and Thorndike were surprised to discover that Philadelphia, contrary to their initial expectations, actually had considerable investment talent. Still, certain that an unstructured, interactive organization would be more successful at creative investing, they were keen to reorganize the compartmentalized structure in Philadelphia. At least one initiative would cause trouble. Doran went to the Philadelphia offices on a weekend and moved offices around to break up old patterns and increase collaboration. As he later recalled, "Understandably, when they came in on Monday, some people were quite upset."

One key move following the merger was to transform Wellington Fund, changing its mission from "conservation of principal, reasonable current income and profits without undue risk" to an ambiguous new mandate, "dynamic conservatism." Whatever its meaning, this approach resulted in a two-thirds increase in portfolio turnover, from a low of 15 percent of the securities replaced every year to 25 percent, and a shift in the proportion invested in equities from 55 percent to at least 75 percent of the fund.

New, aggressive funds were launched in rapid succession over the next several years: Explorer Fund invested in small growth companies; Technivest Fund used "technical" market indicators; and Trustees' Equity Fund, in stark contrast to its staid name, sought to capitalize on short-term market trends. John Neff's dual-purpose fund, dubbed Gemini, had been launched in 1967. Gemini Fund was a closed-end fund with an innovation: half the shares received *all* of the dividends, and the other half received *all* of the capital gains. Insurance companies gobbled up the "income shares" because under the then current tax code, 85 percent of intercorporate dividends were tax-free. However, early investors who bought the "capital shares" to get the anticipated benefit of two-for-one leverage suffered badly.* Those shares fell in the following years' bear market to a 40 percent discount from their depressed market value.

Wellington Management now had $2.6 billion in 10 funds, half in the struggling balanced Wellington Fund and 70 percent of the remainder in two more: Ivest and Windsor. To respond to shareholders' pleas for a way to switch out of Wellington Fund without paying yet another 8½ percent sales load, Bogle created a new fund, called W.L. Morgan Growth Fund. Initially named Morgan Growth Fund, Bogle added the W and L to settle a legal challenge from both Morgan Stanley and Morgan Guaranty Trust Company. As he later observed, "All these funds were managed in Boston. All were aggressive and all were a big hit with brokers. But all would soon fail to perform."

Revenues advanced from $151 million to $180 million. While Wellington Management Company's business, the *raison d'être* for the merger, was getting better, tensions and even animosities were developing as cultures clashed, and with time the stresses were increasingly personal. While publicly celebrating that the "new Wellington Management" was working even better than he could

---

* Though not me. Following up on Jay Sherrerd's observation of the low price Gemini Capital shares were later selling for, I bought in boldly and heavily margined my account, and saw the shares go from a discount to a premium as value stocks surged.

have hoped, Bogle was, as he later maintained, "becoming skeptical that the merger would be good for me personally."

Bogle proposed a bond fund. In 1970, America had only 10 bond funds. The Bostonians scoffed. "The stupidest idea I've ever heard of," declared Stephen Paine. "Bonds are yesterday!" "No! Bonds are tomorrow!" replied Bogle. At Bogle's insistence, an income fund with 60 percent bonds and 40 percent high-dividend stocks was launched as Wellesley Income Fund in 1970.[1] With Bogle continuing to press for an all-bond fund, Westminster Bond Fund would be launched in 1973. His prediction was accurate; by the year 2000, there were over 3,000 US bond funds.

Bogle's heart troubles struck again in 1967. He was away from work for six weeks that spring with a heart arrhythmia and the installation of a pacemaker at Cleveland Clinic. After he went into cardiac arrest there, a senior cardiologist thought he would never work again.

With his persistent heart problems, Bogle searched for the best cardiologist and found Dr. Bernard Lown at Boston's Brigham and Women's Hospital. Dr. Lown realized that Bogle did not have a common myocardial infarction, which is caused by closure of a coronary artery, but a massive heart rhythm disturbance. This diagnosis indicated that Bogle had only five or ten years to live. Yet Bogle was plainly vigorous and showing no deterioration. This was unusual. Lown put Bogle through a stress test, expecting him to last no more than seven minutes. Bogle lasted 18, showing—as in many areas of his life—a remarkable will to overcome and persevere. Then Lown was able to diagnose Bogle's exact problem: his heart was beating too rapidly to work effectively as a pump when he woke up in the morning or when he competed vigorously. At those times he was so tightly wound that he was releasing adrenaline, as he said, "like a prizefighter going into the ring." Lown prescribed strong medicine for those specific times and put Bogle on a novel regimen that worked well for the next eight years. During a follow-up visit, Bogle set a hospital record by performing 50 different exercise tests. He also returned to playing both tennis and squash. However, in that important first year following the merger, he was absent from the Philadelphia office for a considerable time and from the Boston office even more.[2]

Bogle stayed in the Boston hospital for a full month. This led to a particularly nettlesome misunderstanding. It began with the Bostonians asking about Bogle's health in the context of his being named CEO. They had reason to be concerned. Was it responsible to make him CEO of a public company when he might not be able to perform all his duties all the time? Moreover, if he would be confined in hospitals for long stretches and unable to carry out his duties as CEO, why burden him with all those administrative tasks and responsibilities? And since they would not put work ahead of health for themselves, how could they put Bogle in just such a position? So they asked difficult questions and suggested it would be better to wait before declaring publicly that Jack Bogle was CEO. Bogle saw those questions as insensitive and callous. After all, the decision that he would be CEO had already been made. It had been scheduled to be implemented right after the merger as part of the overall terms.

The tensions continued to increase and to spread to the Boston-dominated board of directors and to subordinates who worried about taking sides and getting caught in the politics. Bogle wasn't about to change his style—working hard, mastering the minute details, and taking decisive actions had taken him to the top of Wellington Management. He knew he was intolerant of others' opinions and considered his solo style a badge of honor. As fund board member Barbara Barnes Hauptfuhrer observed, "Jack's way is *the* way." And he had no interest in ever changing. Morgan took some of the blame, saying, "I taught Jack to be pretty tough—tough like I had been. Because I had owned almost all the stock, I could do any damned thing I wanted. But you can't do that when you have four or five guys who are virtually equal to you. . . ."

Misunderstandings added to the organization's structural problems. Leadership was divided between two historically proud cities some five hours and 300 miles apart. The groups were involved in two very different kinds of investment businesses. Retail mutual fund distribution was based on well-established *business* relationships between organizations (stockbrokers, mutual fund wholesalers, and fund management companies) with many small transactions; institutional investing centered on one-on-one long-term *professional* relationships between pension fund executives and portfolio managers. Fees, economics, and key success factors differed. Business opportunities differed. Profit drivers differed. Most important, effective leadership styles and management processes differed greatly. On many dimensions, the key success factors for the two units were nearly opposites.

The personalities differed, too. Bogle wanted to dominate decisions and persistently sought to dominate other people. He had no interest in "partners" or equals, despite the merger. His natural style in any meeting—one-on-one, with a small group, or with a large group—was always to take control, be the star performer, document his conclusions, make his case, and win his way. Keeping concentration on his version of his story, he was particularly good at blending charm and enthusiasm for his conclusion and his reasoning with repeated modest confessions of past mistakes and previous misjudgments.

"I knew I wasn't tactful or diplomatic," he said. "I am the kind of person who is either going to run something or not. I don't want committees. I don't want a lot of people involved. I don't want to get into an argument about the final decision once it is made." He dismissed the Bostonians' "collegial, participative style" of shared decision-making as lazy and irresponsible.

Being a mutual funds guy, Bogle naturally evaluated the "Boston Four" on the retail metrics that he considered the standards for success or failure. And they, being from the investment counseling world, evaluated Bogle by the institutional standards they knew best. Each side lost respect for the other. Adding to the problem, the board of directors of Wellington Management was dominated by Boston people, who were not inclined to respect a CEO from Philadelphia who, in turn, did not respect them. Geographic distance, differences in investment concepts—growth versus conservative, retail versus institutional, and others—were real differences, but the major differences were cultural. Bogle was authoritarian; Doran and Thorndike believed in consensus. As Bogle put it: "I'm self-confident. Sometimes to my own regret, I try always to tell the truth, I do *not* try to please."

As he recalled, "Wellington Management Company's board, dominated by Bostonians, and I were in a real power struggle. I wanted to control everything and so did they." Resentment over decisions made by one side, then reversed by the other side, festered into bitterness, and the vitriol emerged from behind closed doors to out in the open during meetings. Bogle was aggressive in sales and introducing new funds but conservative on investing. The Boston group was more aggressive on investing but more conservative, or less interested, in sales and introducing new funds. Where Bogle was always in a scramble for sales and new business, the Bostonians much preferred to have the business come to them. They believed this was more professional and developed better-quality business. They were also highly skeptical of cold-calling or soliciting institutional business. An obvious difference was in work habits: while Doran was usually at his desk by 7 a.m., the others in the Boston Four might start a workday at 8 and leave by 6:30. Bogle had always been a "rate buster" for long hours, coming in early and working late. And he had an acute interest in personally monitoring all the details of every matter.

> "I'm self-confident. Sometimes to my own regret, I try always to tell the truth, I do *not* try to please."

He held himself accountable for living out the image of John C. Bogle that he wanted all others to hold: a superior image of who he was and what he'd done. Bogle accomplished great things, but in a Faustian bargain with his own devil, he paid dearly for it because he always had to press on regardless. As he later put it, "We tend to live to the world's expectations. So if the world wants to call me Saint Jack, you try to behave more that way."[3]

Eventually the Bostonians decided Bogle must go. In a memo to the other Philadelphia directors, Charles Root, an actuary and an astute manager, and Robert Worden,[4] leader of a successful management consulting firm, reported, "Bogle [is] acknowledged . . . to be one of the most knowledgeable mutual fund experts extant [and] is also acknowledged by TDP&L to be a good deal smarter than any of them. Trouble is, Bogle has a dim view of [Thorndike's] management abilities and [Doran's] investment abilities,* and has been less than diplomatic in his handling of and communications with these two men—accentuated by geographic separation . . . Thorndike and Doran have decided they can't work with Bogle and would like to . . . heave him out."[5]

At 72, Walter Morgan decided to step aside as chairman of the mutual funds. Joseph Welch, only slightly younger than Morgan,

---

* Indeed. Bogle later said, "Any regrets? Sure! I somehow believed in permanently or consistently superior investment managers. Bad judgment. Bad decision. Stupid!"

also retired. So Bogle, in what would prove to be a crucial factor in the creation of Vanguard, was chosen as chairman of the single board of directors of all the different funds. That board was responsible only to the several funds, not to Wellington Management.

Behind the external appearance of smooth and orderly transition, internal stresses compounded. Bogle was so disturbed by the tensions that he was considering either resigning as CEO or launching a proxy fight for Wellington Management. In an effort to avoid a public confrontation, the funds' board asked two fund directors to help the two sides come to terms. They soon learned that would be a major challenge.

> We tend to live to the world's expectations. So if the world wants to call me Saint Jack, you try to behave more that way.

After a month, the two directors reported to the funds' board that the hostilities were so serious that they could blow up the company. Thorndike was highly critical of Bogle, saying he "finds it hard to trust or depend on others, doesn't like meetings to share ideas and gives directives by order rather than discussion." While recognizing Bogle's mutual fund expertise and his brainpower, Doran described Bogle as "out of touch with the ugly realities of the company and allows no forum for honest exchange."

When Doran and Thorndike met with Root in early December 1972 to inform him that the only solution was for Bogle to resign, Root lost patience. As he later said, "I, in effect, threw down the gauntlet. I said, 'You've got a great thing going for you. Don't mess it up! You've got to stop it.' . . . Then things kind of leveled off." Later in December, Bogle professed willingness to improve his relationship with Doran and Thorndike. In a memo to Root he wrote: "JCB, WNT and RWD all agree to forget past problems and make a Herculean effort to make the new arrangements work and to put aside personal differences for the good of the organization." A little later, Root would report that Doran and Thorndike, after making a major effort, had again decided they could not work with Bogle and that he should leave the company.

Meanwhile, Bogle continued to build his connections with the financial press corps by remaining immediately accessible and always quotable. And, of course, he loved the way the press put him in his favorite place: at the center of attention. Call by call, article by article, speech by speech, and quote by quote, he was building a personal brand, one of the best known in the business. He loved it.

On April 1, 1971, Morgan's voting trust terminated on schedule and the B shares were distributed as previously agreed. Then, for nearly two years, internal calm *appeared* to prevail. A longtime Wellington director, James F. Mitchell Jr., was approaching 70 and mandatory retirement. After his retirement, the Boston group would only need to persuade one director—Richard Corcoran, who was independent of both the Boston and Philadelphia contingents—to have effective control. The question was raised whether it wouldn't be wise to keep the same board together until the internal tensions had been overcome instead of trying to bring a new director up to speed on all the past discussions. Root, having anticipated the situation, said, "I've already asked him and he has agreed to stay on until the internal tensions are resolved, so it would be embarrassing to change now." Mitchell stayed on.

By the time James L. Walters joined Wellington as general counsel in January 1972, the Bogle-Boston friction was serious. Restructuring the funds with their own single board of carefully selected directors with Bogle as chairman was sometimes called "Bogle's escape hatch." Over the next few years, the prescience of that description would be proved. As the friction grew, Bogle requested that he, as CEO, be kept fully informed and asked Jim Walters to find ways for him to hold as much control as possible over the funds.

Next, Bogle discussed with Walters—apparently to test his expertise—the "internalization" provision in the 1970 Investment Company Act. Bogle was becoming convinced that the traditional management company versus investment company structure was lopsided and that, no matter what the theory was, the fund management company's interests always outweighed the investors' interests. He began exploring various possible redesigns. Before Walters joined Wellington, Bogle had pressed him on the concept of "mutualization" and whether the funds could manage their own administration. Of course, the Boston group did not favor such ideas and would have wondered: Could Bogle be laying the groundwork for an internal takeover?[6]

In 1973, Root recommended the independent fund directors hire their own legal counsel. They agreed and hired Richard B. Smith, a securities law expert who had served as an SEC commissioner and was a partner in Davis Polk & Wardwell, one of New York City's leading law firms. Root tried to get Bogle to move away from his "I'm right and they're all wrong" stance based on Bogle's misguided conviction that "sooner or later, they'll have to back down." Root expressed great doubt that the Bostonians would ever back down, particularly to Bogle.

Root was, in his own words, "thunderstruck" by the situation. Skeptical of the investment skills of the Bostonians, he believed Bogle had the leadership capability Wellington needed to succeed. Root came to a crucial recognition: the fund directors had the legal power to decide which investment management company to retain as manager of their mutual funds. Changing managers for pension funds had become common practice during the past dozen years, so why not change managers for mutual funds the same way to ensure the fund had the best manager? Root declared that if Bogle were fired, he would recommend to his fellow directors that the funds' board terminate its investment-adviser contracts with Wellington Management and select a new manager. This meant Bogle had the all-important trump card. Publicly owned Wellington Management could not survive without the income it was earning from managing investments for the various mutual funds.

Doran took the lead as spokesperson for the Bostonians. While tensions had been patched over before, they had come back to a rolling boil and now a permanent solution was needed. In Doran's view, morale was low: Bogle had not fostered a culture of teamwork and had "sapped the confidence of the top executives with an attitude that no executive had competence other than Mr. Bogle." As Doran explained, executives working under Bogle "were reminded of their limitations too frequently rather than spurred on to greater achievement" and that "the spirit of mutual trust had been damaged." Bogle's autocratic leadership had become inimical to the collegial, professional organization Wellington was trying to develop. For the future success of their company, Doran and Thorndike had concluded that Bogle really must go.

After adjusting for inflation, the great bear market of the mid-1970s was actually worse than the 1929 Crash. The Dow Jones Industrial Average fell 58 percent, bottoming out at 580 in October 1974. That dreadful market collapse put Wellington Management Company in serious financial trouble as assets fell nearly 25 percent and profits, nearly 30 percent. Far worse, the company's stock fell 80 percent, from $40 at the time of the merger to $8. Each of the four Bostonians' personal ownership value plunged from $1.5 million to just $185,000.

Doran told Bogle in February 1973 that Thorndike intended to assert himself more actively in management. Bogle was concerned, but Doran assured him that it was only natural for a senior executive to want a larger role, given the organization's difficulties and challenges. Bogle didn't buy that bland view. He suspected it reflected anger resulting from Bogle's decision—and the way the decision was implemented—to take Explorer Fund from Steve Paine when it lost 35 percent in a stock market that was down only 5 percent.

In August 1973, Bogle moved the mutual funds from Center City in Philadelphia to a suburban office complex called Glenhardie in Wayne, near enough to Valley Forge—"only" three miles away—that Bogle, in a clever marketing move, was later able to use Valley Forge as the firm's mailing address. On September 26, the four Bostonians met with Bogle at the Glenhardie offices. Doran told Bogle that they wanted more control over mutual fund activities.

Then, on November 14, Doran stunned Bogle: "Things are just not working out. I've talked to the others and we think it best if you left the company." Bogle again said he would not resign. Doran then told Bogle he had two options: leave completely, or leave the management company but continue with the funds in a strictly administrative role—the sort of work he did not enjoy and had delegated entirely to his able colleague James Riepe. Although Doran did not say so, Bogle would then become little more than a chief clerk. He could either fold his tent or he could fight. Bogle being Bogle, that decision was easy: fight!

Doran proposed a financial settlement for Bogle: a $20,000 annual annuity for 15 years with Bogle to sell his B stock back to the company at the then current market price of $6—not at a price premium for handing the Boston Four control of Wellington Management Company. Given the high interest rates at the time, the annuity's discounted present value would have been less than $150,000. Curiously, for an offer framed by financially experienced people, the proposed package was far too small for Bogle to consider it. He didn't. Bogle had no intention of taking money as part of a deal to resign and turn control over to the Boston Four, particularly if the company would be paying the money while they would personally get the benefit. "I've heard of few stupider things than that," burst Bogle. "I've done an effective job. I've gone the extra mile to assure communication and harmony with all of you." His anger drove him on: "I am tired and annoyed by all of this enough to say, 'Make me an offer in writing and have it signed by all four of you!'"[7]

Bogle insisted his management style and record as CEO had both been good, despite the difficulties. He argued that removing him would cause serious problems, "a material public relations problem as well as severe impact on Wellington employees, the regulating authorities, and the financial community."

Four days later, Bogle told Doran he would not resign as had been informally requested. Coleman Mockler, executive vice president of Gillette, a friend of Thorndike's, and a past board member of Ivest, agreed to approach Bogle on December 12, 1973, hoping to avoid having the matter go to the funds' board. But he could only repeat the prior offer, and Bogle told Mockler, "If they want to buy control of the company, they'll have to pay me out of their own pockets!"

The Bostonians took Bogle's counteroffer as either serious or at least as an opening to negotiations and started putting out the word that Bogle was on the way out. But Walter Morgan was adamant: "You can't fire *him*! He knows more about this business than all the people in Wellington Management put together!"

Bogle knew a formal termination would be on the agenda at the Wellington board meeting on January 23, 1974, *and* at the funds' board meeting the next day. To make his case, he wrote a 20-page memo to the independent directors, reviewing his achievements and advancing several creative proposals for the future, including mutualization.

Mutualization would have been seen as a radical change from the standard corporate structure of most mutual fund families. That standard structure had recognized the management company as the organizer, merchandiser and investment manager as well as the administrator of each fund in a family of funds. This view honored the history of mutual fund pioneers who had lived through the difficult thirties, forties, and fifties by being tough, sales-focused

small business entrepreneurs who just happened to be selling investment products called mutual funds. The management company's
proprietors, obliged by law to have a majority of fund directors be
"independent" of the management company, traditionally chose only
those close friends they could trust to go along with management and
to understand that doing so was why they had been selected.

Bogle had devoted more than 20 years to the hard-selling,
do-whatever-it-takes business model embraced by his mentor-
employer, Morgan. During those decades, his "press on regardless!"
mantra had been his daily guide as he focused on sales and profits.
Now, with his objective greatly changed—like a lawyer with a different client—he would make the strongest case he could for a *mutual*
mutual fund organization.

Bogle was convinced that so long as mutual funds were captives
of the management companies that had created and built them, the
power of the management companies would inevitably lead to higher
fees and therefore lower returns to investors. In his long memo, he
proposed a basic restructuring to get away from that conflict of interest by converting to a mutual form of corporation owned by the
several Wellington mutual funds. He estimated that could cut costs
by at least 40 percent.

Bogle's proposal had actually been fully worked out in a long
"highly confidential" memo three years before. It was simple and
decisive. The Wellington Group of mutual funds would acquire
Wellington Management Company for $6 million and thereby
acquire fixed and liquid assets of $4 million. The funds would then
act as their own investment manager and distributor *at cost*. The $2
million balance of the purchase price would be recovered in a single
year by *not* paying the 40 percent of management fees that had been
the annual profit of Wellington Management Company. Meanwhile,
the merger with Thorndike, Doran, Paine & Lewis would end, and
TDP&L would once again be an independent investment counseling firm with $1.6 billion in assets under management, and free to go
after institutional business.[8]

In his memo, Bogle added a series of reasons: mutualization
would be consistent with the public's increasing consumerism and
decreasing tolerance for conflicts of interest; it "would put to rest the

nagging question of the appropriateness of a publicly held investment management company which has become a profound problem." The cost savings to the funds would be "awesome," and mutualization would end the corporate problems with which the funds' directors had been struggling. In sum, it was the right thing to do, would provide substantial long-term cost savings to the funds' shareholders, could benefit Wellington's employees, and was clearly feasible.

On January 23, after a morning of routine business and lunch, Bogle presented his case. Fundamental and compelling as Bogle thought his proposal clearly was, it went nowhere. It was ignored. In fact, most participants could not see why Bogle had even bothered, unless he somehow hoped his proposal would be accepted by his adversaries, who would then have to decide they needed him and his reputation to implement it. All he got was an agreement to appoint four directors to a study group to consider his proposal. That study group never met.

Doran explained that a management decision had been made to terminate Bogle and said the decision required board approval. Thorndike, as chair of the meeting, offered the standard way out: "Well, Mr. Bogle, will you resign?"

That question was the final formality in the six-year, accelerating running feud between the Bostonians and the Philadelphians, separate warring groups within Wellington. Bogle knew he was at the tail end of his rope. If he chose not to resign, he knew the question had only one alternative: Bogle would be fired.

Saying he would consider the matter, Bogle, tough as ever, said the board should hear the reasons for his termination. Doran outlined the reasons, which were familiar to all the directors: Bogle's insistence on his own way, his inability to collaborate, and all the rest. When he finished his review of the reasons, chairman Thorndike repeated his question: "*Now*, Mr. Bogle, will you resign?"

Bogle then took out a 28-page document rejecting their offer of resignation and proceeded to read every page, concluding, "We are sitting here today more as a kangaroo court than as a board of directors, given the uneven, unfair, and ad hoc nature of events . . . and the advance commitments that have been made."

He rejected the request for his resignation for four reasons: it could cause irreparable harm to the company, and no case had been made that it was in the best interests of Wellington Management Company; dismissal was "in violation of elementary standards of fairness and of accepted standards of corporate practice"; the terms were "both unethical and illegal"; and the request, if accepted, would involve a "serious misuse of the company's corporate assets and a breach of fiduciary duty" by the board. Noting that earnings of Wellington had increased when most fund companies' earnings had been falling during recent turbulent markets, Bogle concluded by admonishing the other directors to "proceed with an open mind."

He wasn't done. "The process I have outlined might lend itself to a college fraternity or a social club, but it hardly comports with how a board of directors of a company responsible for $4 billion of other people's money should act. If it were not such a serious matter, it would be a joke."[9]

The words may have soared in Bogle's heart and mind, but they had no impact on the board's decision. Directors voted 10–1 to request his resignation in exchange for a slightly enhanced package: $60,000 a year until he found work and then $20,000 a year up to a total of $320,000.

Still, Bogle refused to resign.

On a quick second vote—10 votes in favor of termination and 2 abstentions, by Bogle and Neff—it was agreed that Bogle would be paid his current salary to advise the study group that never met.

In retrospect, the Bostonians had taken a substantial risk, whether they realized it fully or not, that Root's threat would become real. Doran would reflect back on that day and his thinking at the time: "We knew that the dismissal carried significant risk, but it was deemed the correct thing to do anyway. Certainly the funds' board had the authority to take extreme action against Wellington Management Company. They could have said: 'You've just fired Bogle, so we're going to fire *you*.' It could have happened, but we thought it was unlikely. The fact is, we just couldn't be sure what the independent directors of the funds would do."[10]

Neff, who had sided with Bogle, later said, "The measure of a man is how he handles himself when things aren't going well. That was Jack's finest hour. He couldn't have handled himself better."[11]

The board voted to elect Doran president and CEO and to continue for a time to pay Bogle his salary. As an investment executive,

Bogle now had nearly nothing. He had lost his company and his job. Why would any other fund company hire such a guy? He was known in the industry as a maverick, difficult to work with and even harder to work for. He had been wrong on his strategy of merger. He had been unable, as a manager, to work with Doran and Thorndike, and had been accumulating a reputation as a dogmatic hardhead who always had to be in charge and make all decisions.

> "The measure of a man is how he handles himself when things aren't going well. That was Jack's finest hour. He couldn't have handled himself better."

The meeting ended at midnight. Jack Bogle got home at 1 a.m. and told his wife that he had just been fired.

Eve was not surprised.

The next morning, January 24, 1974, Bogle was on the 6 a.m. train to New York City with Jim Riepe, his capable assistant, to press on regardless.

CHAPTER 4

AT WAR WITH WELLINGTON

Bogle and Riepe were on their way by train to a meeting of the Wellington mutual funds' board of directors in New York City, armed with a brazen proposal that would, if accepted, convert the previous day's painful personal defeat into a decisive victory. Bogle's opponents—"my enemies"—were a majority of the board of directors of Wellington Management. But they were only a minority of the directors of the board of the several mutual fund boards comprising the Wellington Group of Funds.

The funds' board had 11 fund directors: Bogle, Thorndike, Doran, and eight so-called independent or outside directors. Five of these had previously served as directors only of the Philadelphia fund boards and three had been directors only of the Boston funds. Bogle's vote-counting estimate of the split among those directors was 6–5 in his favor—himself and the five Philadelphia directors versus Doran, Thorndike, and the three Boston directors. Some of the Philadelphia directors feared that after Bogle's termination they would be dropped in favor of more Bostonians. That wasn't the Boston directors' only disadvantage. The night before the meeting, when Doran and Thorndike arrived in New York's Knickerbocker Club after driving through a heavy snowfall, no rooms were available, so they had slept on benches in the locker room.

At the meeting, Bogle learned his chances would improve significantly. His friend Charles Root proposed that, given their conflicted interests, Bogle, Doran, and Thorndike should not vote. The funds' board agreed, and Bogle's vote count improved significantly, to 5–3. But then the outlook changed again; director Bob Worden called Bob Doran to say he had decided, after a careful review of all the factors, to change his vote. This would have tied the vote count at 4–4, but that night Worden suffered a fatal heart attack. After a pause to acknowledge his passing, the maneuvering continued.

Root, a confirmed Philadelphian,[1] admired Bogle's abilities, was unimpressed by the skills of the Bostonians, and had the courage to form an independent opinion and hold onto it. He urged the fund directors to choose their own fund chairman and president and then select and contract with whatever investment manager the board might want. As Bogle recalled, "At that marathon 12-hour meeting, as chairman of each of the mutual funds, I proposed that we declare our independence from Wellington Management Company, mutualize our funds, elect our own officers and staff, and empower them to operate the funds on an at-cost basis." In an industry where the primacy of the management company had never been challenged, such a bold step would be without precedent. So the battle was joined and would be long and hard fought.

Bogle had prepared the ground with the directors of the funds, and when he took his mutualization proposal to them they were interested. This put Wellington Management Company suddenly on the defensive: it would soon be struggling to keep managing the mutual funds, the great majority of its business.

Root was focused on the legal power fund directors had: the power to decide which investment management company to retain as manager of their mutual funds. Given this "hire and fire" power—even if it had rarely been used by mutual fund boards—was it not at least conceptually irresponsible for a fiduciary board of directors *not* to consider all its options? Why not terminate Wellington and hire a new management organization?

As the board meeting was getting underway, an obvious question was whether Bogle should continue to hold office as the chairman of the mutual funds' board. Root had already made his position clear: keep Jack Bogle.

Bogle told the board: "This is *your* corporation. You were elected by the shareholders. You oversee the mutual funds on behalf of those shareholders. Wellington Management Company doesn't own and doesn't control the funds. You control them. This is a great opportunity for the funds to have their own voice. You do *not* have to fire me!"[2]

He pressed on with his mutualization proposal. Some directors were impressed by his courage, others by his unusual beliefs. Under his plan, the Wellington group of mutual funds would buy all the outstanding shares of Wellington Management Company and continue all its operations with one major change: operations would be conducted at cost. Bogle argued that all mutual funds were inherently and profoundly conflicted. In theory, fund management companies were supposed to serve the interests of investors as professionals and fiduciaries. But in practice they were run as businesses, maximizing profits for the owners of the management companies that sponsored, managed, advertised, and sold mutual fund shares to investors.

As Bogle explained to the fund directors, if the several mutual funds in the Wellington Group bought in all the stock of Wellington Management Company, Wellington—and only Wellington—would be organized as a mutualized mutual fund organization owned by the investors in those same mutual funds and governed solely by the funds' board.* That distinction could, with time and persistence, be converted into a decisive competitive advantage for the future Wellington.

Unfortunately for Bogle, all this was too much too soon for the fund directors despite their initial interest. They were properly conservative, none as daring nor as desperate as Bogle. They were deadlocked and unable to decide. Further study was a cozy way to avoid a difficult decision.

Before that crucial meeting of the funds' board was over, the independent directors had decided on a study of how the Wellington organization should be structured. It was to be done by Bogle, at his regular salary, plus directors Root, Barbara Hauptfuhrer, and Joseph Welch. After one meeting as a committee, they would be joined by

---

* While two other fund groups were internally owned in those days, both would soon shift to the traditional ownership structure including a management company that could be sold.

the full board of fund directors to study strategic options ranging from no change at all to the mutualization of the funds' services to acquiring Wellington Management Company.

As would only be understood many months later, that single board meeting reversed the power relationship. Bogle, exhausted by another "near death" experience, burst into sobs on the train back to Philadelphia with Jim Riepe. But they had not *lost*, he quickly insisted. Now, with the right moves, they could start *winning*.[3]

While the reasons Bogle gave the board for each step were plausible—"modernizing," "streamlining," "simplifying"—the main motivation, never stated, appeared in retrospect to be preparing the way for his campaign to convert all the funds into a mutual organization of mutual funds with himself in control. In March 1974, with help from Riepe, Bogle put out a 45-page confidential memo to the fund directors with a summary and conclusions on "The Future Structure of Wellington Group of Investment Companies," beginning with five goals: appropriate business independence, highest-quality investment services, optimum cost-effective administration, ability to attract and retain qualified people, and a corporate structure consistent with a future environment of consumerism and increasing regulatory surveillance. The report offered seven possible future structures, focusing on three as the least radical and the least disruptive. The emphasis was on one central objective: independence.

The memo showed how much could be saved by adopting option 2, internalizing administration costs and not paying Wellington's 40 percent profit. Option 3 would internalize distribution (sales) and would achieve even greater savings. The prospect of going no-load was clearly stated. Option 4 would have the funds acquire Wellington Management Company. The memo declared, "Our detailed studies demonstrate that it is economically desirable, organizationally feasible, and legally permissible." It added that the purchase price for Wellington Management would be quickly repaid through annual savings.

Riepe and Bogle's long memorandum concluded that "the funds have already begun the first step toward self-sufficiency" and "the remainder of this first step—internal administration by completing option 2—is small in terms of people, but large in terms of dollars and important in terms of concept."

Doran and Thorndike responded with strong arguments in a memo that ran nearly 100 pages. Their extensive analysis led to four major conclusions:

- The mutual fund and institutional investment advisory activities of Wellington could not be unscrambled without harm.

- Wellington had provided outstanding administrative services and highly credible investment performance.

- Savings paled compared to the risks of impaired returns.

- Internalization would not increase independence or diminish conflicts of interest. It would only make the funds substitute new conflicts for well-recognized and regulated ones.

Recognizing that Wellington Management was sure to lose at least some of its business with the funds, it sent a team of Doran, Thorndike, and Jim Walters to make presentations to the fund directors. Walters focused on one core proposition: if the fund directors took over more than fund administration, mostly bookkeeping, they risked violating their fiduciary duties by taking on responsibilities beyond their capabilities. This worried the directors and also concerned the directors' new special counsel, Richard Smith, who was understandably cautious in a fast-changing, unprecedented situation.[4]

After six months of discussion and analysis, the directors chose the least invasive changeover: administration. They voted to adopt option 2: internalizing administration costs. The choice made the organization unique. Importantly, it would put Bogle in control of shareholder communications. Still, he was disappointed. He had hoped to control not just administration but also distribution, his career focus. Administration was the part of the funds' business he had always been least interested in—close to "washing the dishes and sweeping the floors"—and where he had little experience. But at least it was a start.

The funds would be served by a new organization that would have a small staff of 28 accountants and clerks serving the mutual fund shareholders with administrative services and developing an arms-length relationship with Wellington Management. Bogle still had a job, so he said, "It was a victory of sorts but, I feared, a Pyrrhic victory."[5] The work the small new unit had ahead of it was limited to internal operations that Bogle would depend on Riepe to manage, while Bogle focused on strategy.*

Bogle was already looking ahead to the next step. This was option 3 from the Future Structure Study: internalizing distribution. "While not accepted now, it may well be only a matter of time, perhaps within two or three years, when it will be, given the truly massive challenge to be faced in fund distribution." As his memo had concluded, "Perhaps, then, the issue is not 'whether,' but only 'when' [the funds] will become completely independent," breaking the remaining formal ties with Wellington Management.

A crucial initial step had already been taken back when Bogle was still at Wellington. All the Wellington mutual funds had been reincorporated as Maryland corporations. In addition, the "Philadelphia" and "Boston" fund boards had been consolidated into one common board of fund directors. This had required three layers of time-consuming approvals. First, each of the respective boards had to agree on which directors would stay and which would go. Second, a vote of the shareholders of each mutual fund had ben required. Third, approval by the federal regulators at the SEC had been needed. Astute observers might have noticed what would become important: a solid majority of the combined board just happened to be consistently supportive of one person—Jack Bogle.

Disputes during the breakup with Wellington Management were both legal and emotional. One early fight was over the Wellington name. Both sides wanted it. When Bogle heard he could not, for regulatory reasons, use the Wellington name, he exploded. "This is the last straw. This is stupid. I'm out of here! I'm going to resign and

---

* Bogle's situation might be compared to that of Vice-Admiral William Bligh (1754–1817), who served under Captain Cook in 1776 and was the officer in command of HMS Bounty in 1789 when Fletcher Christianson and others mutinied. On April 28, Bligh and 18 loyal crewmen were put in a 23-foot launch with no charts and only one week's supply of food and water. After 47 days and remarkable celestial navigation, Bligh and his men reached Timor, 4,164 miles away. They had each lived on one-twelfth pound of bread per day for 25 days. Bligh would later serve under Nelson at Copenhagen in 1801 and was appointed Governor of New South Wales in 1805. Three years later he was arrested by Major Johnston and a contingent of 400 in another mutiny called the Rum Rebellion.

leave the whole business." Charles Root called him the next morning: "Forget the name! A name is *not* important. You can call your
new firm by any name you want and then make it the best name in
the whole mutual fund industry!"[6]

A few days later, Bogle's rage had faded. He was looking for an
answer to an important question: What name to use? By good fortune, an antique print dealer called on Bogle, a history buff, and sold
him four prints, each depicting one of Great Britain's major sea battles in the era of Nelson, Wellington, and Napoleon, including one
entitled "The Battle of the Nile." Following that battle and his decisive victory, Nelson's dispatch to the British Admiralty celebrated his
flagship: "HMS Vanguard dispatch at the mouth of the Nile." Bogle
immediately saw the significance of the traditional meaning of the
word *vanguard*—leadership of a new trend—and seized the name for
his small new venture. "We had considered a name like Mutual Fund
Service Company of America," he recalled. "By comparison,
Vanguard sure looked good. So our decision
was easy. But would shareholders approve?"

Yes, they would. As a first step, on August
20, 1974, the fund directors, persuaded—or
worn down—by Bogle's tenacity, unanimously
agreed to form a new firm to be wholly owned
by the mutual funds.[7] By the funds' board

*vanguard—
leadership of a
new trend*

decision, the new firm would administer the funds' affairs—option
2 of Bogle and Riepe's array of choices—but would be explicitly
precluded from providing either investment advisory services or marketing and distribution services.[8] Thus would begin the beginning of
Vanguard *and* a four-year running battle for control of each of the
major functions of the mutual fund business.

Vanguard was incorporated on September 26, 1974, just a few
weeks before one of the worst bear markets in US history at last
came to an end. Vanguard began its administrative operations on
May 1, 1975.

PART TWO
Vanguard Rising

CHAPTER 5

OUT OF
THE ASHES

At the outset in 1975, Bogle's fledgling Vanguard had only a minor, mechanical business administering barely $1.4 billion of assets in a midsize group of mutual funds that were steadily losing assets. The 11 Wellington funds had experienced net redemptions by shareholders for 40 consecutive months, a trend that would continue for 40 additional months until January 1978. Total net cash outflow totaled $930 million, or 36 percent of the funds' assets.

Bogle would recall the time as "the ghastly period of attrition."

Even worse, the fledgling company had no control over its future because the success of every mutual fund organization depended on two major functions: investing and selling. Vanguard had zero role in either. For both selling and investing, it was totally dependent on Wellington Management Company, the organization that had fired Bogle and left him adrift in an investment storm.

But Bogle, ferocious to succeed, declared that Vanguard's small size freed it to be flexible and innovative in developing its strategy. He later recalled, "Our challenge at the time was to build, out of the ashes of major corporate conflict, a new and better way to manage a mutual fund complex." The Vanguard Experiment, as Bogle described his new venture, was designed "to prove that mutual funds could operate independently, and do so in a manner that would directly benefit their shareholders."[1]

Bogle characterized Vanguard's early strategy as "a generous dose of opportunism" plus "a touch of disingenuousness"—surely euphemisms—plus the essential "heavy measure of determination." But all those words came to Bogle after long years of struggling to achieve success. For any realistic observer at the time, his next move was easily defined as folly.

Bogle had put Jim Riepe in charge of fund operations—supposedly Vanguard's core business—so Bogle could focus on business strategy and communication with fund shareholders and the media. He was searching for any way to get around, or under, or over, the constrictions of his agreement not to sell or manage mutual funds. Looking for innovations and innovators, he called Dean LeBaron, the creative head of an exciting young investment firm already known as a serial innovator: Batterymarch Financial Management. Both men's firms were small and unusual enough to be much talked about by members of the investment community. "I've heard a lot about you and your firm," opened Bogle. "We should get together to see if there might be a way we could work together."

"Sounds like a good idea," LeBaron quickly replied. "When?"[2]

They bonded on several levels. Both were mavericks and innovators. Both were self-described tightwads interested in minimizing costs. Both were good at attracting public attention and enjoyed the admiration. Both were bold entrepreneurs.

LeBaron was a pioneer in international investing, particularly in the emerging markets of China and Russia and the countries of South America that were starting to ease their taxes on foreign investors and loosen limits on repatriating profits. Accounting standards were notoriously lax in these markets and research reports by capable, objective securities analysts were nonexistent. Local insiders were sure to get all investment news, good or bad, long before outsiders.

Typically, LeBaron saw potential advantages behind all these obstacles. If Batterymarch could find ways to work around or even exploit problems that caused most institutional investors to stay out of Latin America, the firm would have little or no competition in a highly inefficient market. LeBaron decided Batterymarch would conduct its own primary market research and make itself a market leader. He recalled, "I urged Jack to diversify internationally in order to reduce investment risk, but he never felt comfortable with international investing."

Bogle's weak heart added to his hesitancy. "Jack said he was willing to go to Latin America, but I would personally have to take CPR training and travel with him in adjoining seats on the same planes, and sleep in the same room in hotels. I agreed, but we never actually went."

LeBaron respected Bogle for several reasons. One was the unusually high quality of directors attracted to Vanguard, particularly in an era when so-called independent directors were often no more than cronies of the people in power at the mutual fund management companies. He also liked the innovative concept that the mutual funds collectively owned Vanguard.

Bogle admired LeBaron's refusal to allow his institutional clients to allocate commissions on Batterymarch trades to their preferred brokers. He believed that if brokerage commissions were so high that they had "currency" value, that value should be captured by the pension funds his firm was managing. Institutional brokerage commissions in the early 1970s, before rates could be negotiated, averaged 40 cents a share versus 1 to 2 cents today and were widely used as "soft dollar" currency to pay for all sorts of services, almost always for the economic benefit of market insiders, not investors.

Bogle also respected LeBaron's policy that Batterymarch would "call 'em as we see 'em" when voting on proxy issues for companies its funds owned, never influenced by whether the company was also a client. Batterymarch voted against all directors who authorized greenmail—buying enough shares in a company to threaten a hostile takeover so the target company would instead repurchase its shares at a premium[3]—and also did so at every other company where they were directors. This resulted in a distressed call from the chairman of a Batterymarch client. "Dean, do you realize Batterymarch is voting against me?"

"Yes. We have a strict policy of voting against any director who, at any company, approves greenmail."

"If that's your final position, Dean, you're fired!"

"Understood."

LeBaron's cost consciousness delighted Bogle, as did his irreverent attitude toward conventional investment organizations. Both men felt management companies' fees were too high and that investment managers were overpaid, overly focused on their own compensation and too little focused on serving clients.

Both Bogle and LeBaron were facile with figures, so they knew that most active managers were not beating the market. Instead, the market, after costs of trading and management fees, was increasingly beating them. Adopting the simple strategy of "if you can't beat the market, join it," both were intrigued with the new idea of market-matching index funds. Academic studies, and a recent *Newsweek* article by Nobel Laureate Paul Samuelson,[4] gave strong theoretical support to indexing. (Index funds carefully replicate the capitalization percentage weightings of all the stocks in an index of a major stock market, such as the Standard & Poor's 500 Index, by adjusting those weightings as prices change. Index funds can also seek to track segments of the market, such as growth stocks or small-cap stocks.)

> **Both men felt management companies' fees were too high and that investment managers were overpaid, overly focused on their own compensation and too little focused on serving clients.**

Batterymarch and a few other firms had developed index funds for the institutional market, even though they stretched financial regulations.* In those days SEC regulations required a qualified senior officer to sign off on every trade, which was impossible for index investors. SEC chairman John Shad told LeBaron, "It is illegal, but we'll let it go on. You're well intentioned but probably misguided."

No firm was offering an index mutual fund to individual investors, but both Bogle and LeBaron thought a retail index fund for individuals was an idea whose time had come.

Bogle was sure he had seen a crucial opportunity. An index fund needed no company or industry research to estimate future earnings and no expensive portfolio manager deciding which stocks to buy or when a new portfolio strategy was required—or even permitted. Once a stock market index had been created by a third-party

---

* The first institutional index funds had been offered as separate accounts by Wells Fargo Advisors (a subsidiary of Wells Fargo Bank), State Street Bank, and American National Bank, and all three were gradually signing up pension funds.

organization, an index fund simply and obediently reproduced it in a basket of securities. Indexing could be a breakout strategic move for Vanguard. Bogle was determined to get approval from his board of directors to launch First Index Investment Trust—the first index mutual fund.

"You're well intentioned but probably misguided."

He surprised the board in September 1975, just four months after Vanguard's launching, with a strong pitch to create this new kind of mutual fund—a passively managed fund guaranteed never to beat the market. Industry opponents soon derided the concept as the "the pursuit of mediocrity" or a "formula for a consistent long-term loser." Who would want to settle for just average? Who would ever aspire to be *passive*? Bogle, as usual, led with the numbers. In seven of the 10 years from 1964 to 1974, the S&P index beat more than half of the active managers and over the full decade it outpaced 78 percent of them. Three-quarters of stock mutual funds had failed to keep up with the market! That meant that, in the competition for investment performance, an index fund would be a "top-quartile" *winner.*

Introducing the first retail index fund as "first mover" appealed to Bogle. As with other strategic moves in those early years, he would meet strong resistance from his board. Only his creativity, his stubborn persistence and his facility with numbers would win the day. He carefully centered his case on a language technicality crafted for his specific purpose: an index fund would not need any investment *management.* An index fund would only need basic *administrative* capabilities. With skillful execution or trading, it would replicate an independently established stock market index like the S&P 500. By this logic, an index mutual fund would—if only just barely—avoid violating the limitations of Vanguard's narrow mandate; Vanguard would now have a mutual fund *without* "investment management."

After months of consideration, Vanguard's directors formally agreed in May 1976 to move forward with an SEC filing of First Index Investment Trust. Difficult as it may have been to sell the fund directors on indexing, that was far from the highest hurdle Bogle would face. Next, he had to sell Wall Street on his new fund idea; this would be much more challenging.

Despite Bogle's heady hopes, investment bankers were not at all excited about the opportunity to underwrite the new fund. They had many good reasons: Vanguard was an unknown firm and certainly not an important client for Wall Street. The great bear market of 1973–1974 had drawn the Dow Jones Industrial Average down by nearly 50 percent, and far worse after adjusting for rampant inflation. Retail investors remained shell-shocked. Indexing meant "settling for average," hardly a compelling selling proposition. Worse, the new fund would be offered with an 8½ percent load or sales charge. This cost *guaranteed* that investors would start out significantly behind the market and could never, ever catch up.

Having won the approval to launch an index fund, Bogle's first move was to call a man who knew all the Wall Street barons: Wellington's long-serving senior trader, Jim French. "Frenchy, I need your help. Which Street firms can we get to underwrite an index fund?"[5] After some thought, French gave Bogle a list of firms that were proven "friends of Wellington" and had strong retail distribution.

Bogle's second call was to Vanguard's Jan Twardowski, a young "quant" (mathematically focused) investor who would be in charge of the actual indexing. Twardowski said he would need to have sufficient capital in the new fund to be able to replicate the S&P market index. The more the merrier.

It took Bogle all winter and all spring to organize the initial public offering. Finally, he persuaded Dean Witter to lead the underwriting, with three other firms, aiming for an IPO of $150 million in the spring of 1976. To drum up demand among stockbrokers, Bogle covered the major centers like Boston, New York, Los Angeles, and Chicago, while Riepe was assigned to smaller cities like Detroit, Sacramento, Buffalo, Minneapolis, Austin, and Memphis. Both men learned that the demand for the new fund was, well, limited.

Based on the lack of interest, the original goal of $150 million was reduced to $75 million.

As they met with more brokers, nearly all of the questions they received were negative. "Why should we sell a fund that's never going to beat the market?" "Where is the excitement in a fund that has no focus, requires no skills, has no charismatic portfolio manager, and buys everything?"

That $75 million sales goal was cut again to $40 million.

A Minneapolis broker printed posters and sent them out to active managers. Below a picture of Uncle Sam based on patriotic wartime recruiting posters was a clear statement: "Index Funds Are Un-American!" Brokers asked yet more questions: "Index funds are having tough times selling into the institutional market, so why do you expect success at retail?"

When the fundraising target was reduced to $20 million, the question for Vanguard changed to a worried query for Twardowski: Is this amount too small for accurate index replication?

At $20 million and then at $15 million, Twardowski's assurances changed to a conditional positive: "We would need to sample the smaller stocks rather than deliver full replication, but that should not make a major difference in fund performance."

"Are you sure?"

"Pretty sure," came the hopeful response.

The IPO was a flop.

In August 1976, Bogle's index fund raised less than 10 percent of the originally intended amount—only $11.4 million.[6]

Bogle had been wrong: wrong on product design and wrong on selling strategy and wrong on timing—in retrospect, by 10 long years.

This amount of assets was much too small to earn enough in fees to cover operating costs and too small to invest proportionally in all 500 stocks in the S&P index. The problems were obvious in retrospect: most retail investors had never heard of index funds. First Index Investment Trust's name had no sex appeal for brokers or investors. With a front-end sales load deducted from an investor's invested assets, the fund could never overcome that initial handicap, and it also had a high expense ratio (the management fee paid by fund shareholders), particularly for an unmanaged mutual fund. It was a surefire loser.

While it was a highly visible commercial failure, soon dubbed Bogle's Folly, Bogle would years later claim it to be . . . "an *artistic* success." In a history of Vanguard's indexing, Bogle euphemistically described the seriously disappointing amount raised as "the seed capital we needed" and added, "We were ecstatic at the crucial fact that we now had our index fund."[7]

Even if nobody else did, Bogle saw that it was at least a start. It cracked the board's prohibition against Vanguard's managing investments. Cleverly, Bogle soon merged another fund Vanguard administered, Exeter Fund, into the index fund, thus increasing its assets by $58 million and, with market appreciation, to nearly $90 million. With this merger, the fund was large enough to own at least some of all the 500 different shares in the S&P Index. After six long years, assets lumbered up to $100 million in 1982. One unexpected marketing problem: in those years, unlike most, about three-quarters of actively managed equity funds outpaced the S&P 500 and therefore also beat First Index. Eventually, in a rising market, the S&P resumed outperforming most actively managed funds, and the index fund's assets finally climbed to $1 billion in 1988—12 years after its launch.

Part of Bogle's positive lens on reality had long been to think ahead and strive to innovate; another was his amazing ability to look back on experience through rose-colored glasses. He certainly did this with indexing, and after indexing finally became mainstream, he took greater personal credit. By 1996, after Bogle's retirement as CEO, Vanguard had 19 domestic index funds holding a total of $24 billion. Its international index funds held another $2 billion. Vanguard was home to nearly 60 percent of the industry's total index fund assets.

Bogle's next strategic move would eventually disrupt the core of the mutual fund business: sales, or distribution. He wanted to drop the traditional 8½ percent sales commission (load) and go no-load by offering shares directly to investors. This would roil the brokerage industry and, more importantly to Bogle, escape dependence on Wellington Management for distribution.

Bogle had been unrelenting for years in his drive to reduce the fees Vanguard paid to Wellington. In each confrontation, his two linked objectives were the same: to get a better deal for Vanguard and to punish Wellington for unseating him. Fees paid to Wellington were too high, he declaimed. Wellington's incremental costs for Vanguard were so low that a fee reduction was "obviously" called for. Wellington should offer Vanguard the lower fees paid by pension funds for similarly large accounts. And later, once Vanguard took on all the intensive work of distribution and investor service, the "only" thing Wellington Management contributed was portfolio management. Whatever his particular argument, Bogle always had extensive quantitative evidence to polish his case.[8]

J. P. Morgan famously opined that for every major business decision, there were almost always two reasons: a good reason and the real reason. Bogle's real, unstated motivation was getting even. Damaging Wellington was deliberate. He seemed not at all worried about weakening the investment manager Vanguard still depended on. Over time, Bogle got Wellington to make more than 200 small or large cuts in in fees paid by Vanguard.

Bogle's push to go no-load was a stunning break with the mutual fund industry and painful to Wellington Management Company. The 8½ percent sales charge paid to brokers who pushed customers to buy funds was the mutual fund industry norm 50 years ago, and Wellington Fund depended on it. In addition, Wellington paid out substantial commissions to brokerage firms to buy and sell securities for the funds. By directing these lucrative trades to certain brokerage houses, Wellington sought a quid pro quo arrangement from the same brokers to favor Wellington's funds when selling to investors.[9] Such behind the scenes "customers be damned" reciprocal "soft dollar" relationships were pervasive in the mutual fund industry.

> J. P. Morgan famously opined that for every major business decision, there were almost always two reasons: a good reason and the real reason.

None of this was outside the range of accepted practice of the time. That made Bogle's proposal to switch to no-load seem particularly radical. No-load funds were not widely offered except by large investment counseling firms, which did not see themselves as mutual fund firms but rather as investment advisers for institutions and wealthy families. These firms, including T. Rowe Price, Loomis Sayles and Scudder, Stevens & Clark, used their no-load mutual funds only as an administrative accommodation, a convenient, low-cost way of meeting the demand for investment services for such small accounts as the grandchildren of valued clients. A few of these investment counseling firms had been welcoming almost any investor who wanted to invest in their no-load mutual funds, but the major mutual fund organizations continued to impose sales loads.

The risks of Bogle's plan were obvious and large. Angry retail brokers would almost certainly stop selling the Wellington mutual funds. They might even urge their customers to switch out of the Wellington funds, which were already shrinking, into other firms' load funds, accelerating redemptions and loss of assets and revenues. And what if Vanguard gained little or nothing in new sales if individual investors didn't flock to it when it dropped the sales loads?

Later Bogle claimed, "I had always had an affinity for the no-load business," despite his two full decades of being out in front forcefully advocating Wellington's traditional, hard-sold load funds. Now, he argued that future trends favored going no-load: investors were becoming wealthier and more knowledgeable and sophisticated, and surely would realize the benefits of no-load funds.

Over the course of two days, February 7 and 8, 1977, after many doubts and long debates, the funds' directors increasingly saw merit in Bogle's case. They eventually accepted his tenuous argument that, since no-load funds would not be sold through traditional sales channels but bought directly from Vanguard, they didn't violate the board's prohibition on distribution. Finally, at 1 a.m., the funds' board voted 8–5 to eliminate all sales loads and reposition the Vanguard funds as no-load. This would make Vanguard a no-load distributor *if* investors would bring their business to Vanguard—*if* "pull" marketing would replace traditional "push" marketing and *if* the hoary maxim that mutual funds are not bought, they're sold, could now be reversed.[10]

"Innovations in investment management were always for the sellers, not the buyers of investment services," recalled Bogle. "I had always been close to our wholesaling sales force at Wellington. Each year, I'd say to them, 'Tell me what you want—but you all have to agree—and I'll work it out with Mr. Morgan.' We knew our dealers felt that they had been let down so often that we really had nothing to lose by going no-load. We held a press conference at 10 a.m. Our 20 wholesalers all lost their jobs that day so they, and the 100 broker dealers they worked with most closely, were of course angry. Robert 'Stretch' Gardiner, the head of Reynolds & Co., made various threats, and Dreyfus ran full-page ads saying, 'No load? No way!' But in practical terms such as business lost, we felt no bumps at all when we went no-load. In a month, everything had quieted down."[11]

After the directors' decision to take over mutual fund distribution, some legal and regulatory issues remained. Vanguard's plan required an exemption from the Investment Company Act, and that resulted in a shareholder's request for a hearing. He did not want the Wellington Fund to pay any part of the cost of distributing other funds.[12]

There were broader issues requiring SEC approval. An administrative hearing on these issues—the longest such hearing ever held—began in January 1978 and lasted five weeks. Hearing Judge Max Regansteiner's decision laid out the basis for Rule 12b-1, approved in May 1979, which for the first time allowed mutual fund complexes to add a new fee onto a fund's management fee to be used to compensate brokers for *not* advising their customers to change from one mutual fund to another. Ironically, some called Bogle "the father of the 12b-1 fee," an added fund cost that he spent much of his career railing against, and a fee that Vanguard has never charged.

Vanguard had filed a request with the SEC to allow it to spread the low cost of distribution across all its funds, instead of burdening a newly launched fund's return by obliging it to absorb the entire cost of its own distribution when its assets were still small. In April 1981, the SEC decided mutual fund companies could use shareholders' assets to help pay the costs of distribution, resolving the issue in the shareholder's hearing. The SEC also affirmed Judge Regansteiner's decision to allow Vanguard to allocate costs to the various funds, primarily in proportion to asset size. In another major break, Vanguard got permission to use the term "no load" in describing its offerings. The final 12b-1 rule required funds relying on 12b-1 *not* to call themselves no-load, another win for Vanguard.

The first Vanguard fund to go no-load in 1977 was the Warwick Municipal Bond Fund—a 6 percent load on a municipal bond fund had clearly been too much; muni funds normally returned much less than equity funds. A seminal change came with a law enabling mutual funds to pass through the tax exemption on municipal bonds to their investors.[13] Bogle made two complementary moves. First, he cleverly structured the Vanguard municipals offering in three different maturities: short, medium, and long term. Investors could choose the maturity they wanted. This choice was well received. Second, the Warwick fund led the way in an important break away from Wellington. The fund directors, at Bogle's persistent urging, decided to retain Citibank as the fund's investment adviser, rather than Wellington Management. While the bank's performance would, in a few years, lead to its termination as manager, the split expanded Vanguard's independence from Wellington Management.

With interest rates over 10 percent and banks restricted by regulation to paying 5¼ percent on certificates of deposit, money market mutual funds were surging. Vanguard launched its Prime Money Market fund in 1975—four years after the first such fund, Reserve Fund, was launched—with Wellington Management managing the Prime Money Market portfolio. As Vanguard's low fees became more widely known, its money fund's assets surged.

Net Assets of Vanguard Money Market Funds (Millions)

1975	$5
1976	$5
1977	$9
1978	$28
1979	$190
1984	$2,423
1989	$14,768

Though introduced as the simplest sort of investing, money market funds would become a surprising triumph at Vanguard. Confirming modest initial expectations, the money fund attracted only $5 million in 1976, largely from investors already using Vanguard. On this small base, the fund nearly doubled to $9 million in 1977. As rising inflation pushed interest rates higher on money market instruments, money poured out of low-paying bank certificates of deposit and into money funds invested in those higher-yielding instruments. Then interest rates exploded as Paul Volcker's Federal Reserve fought to break up the even greater damage high inflation *and* expected further inflation were inflicting on the economy. As the table above shows,

Vanguard's money fund assets reached $28 million in 1978 and *sextupled* to $190 million in 1979. They then multiplied an astounding 12 times in five years, to $2.4 billion in 1984. The surge was not over. In the next five years, money market assets zoomed up to $14.8 billion in 1989 and became Vanguard's largest product, nearly one-third of the assets at Vanguard.

In addition to the money market funds, Wellington Management had been managing 90 percent of Vanguard's fixed-income fund assets. Jim Riepe and Jack Bogle agreed the time had come to bring all fixed-income investment management in-house. The case was easily made to the Vanguard board of directors: given the rapid growth in money market assets and in bond assets, both taxable and municipals, Vanguard could save investors significant money by managing these "plain vanilla" assets in-house and at cost—well below the conventional fees charged by Wellington Management and other managers.* Bogle argued that money market funds didn't require investment management as traditionally defined. As fixed-income assets continued to increase, Vanguard's cost advantage would grow rapidly.

Low fees became even more of a competitive advantage as Vanguard's assets increased and its fees per thousand dollars decreased. Since money market funds all invested in much the same short-term instruments and since costs rose only slightly as assets ballooned, fees soon made a clearly visible, compelling difference in net returns. Investors increasingly turned to Vanguard. By 2022, Vanguard managed more than $250 billion in money market assets.

Bogle liked to say, "In investing, you get what you don't pay for."

Riepe agreed to recruit an experienced bond manager who could manage both money market funds and bond funds. He did not need to go far. He found his man in the fixed income department of Philadelphia's Girard Bank: Ian A. MacKinnon, who was responsible for $3 billion in fixed income assets. When MacKinnon joined

---

* Disputes between Bogle and Wellington Management were not limited to investment management fees. Another was over the "Valley Forge" building. Bogle wanted a long-term lease that would have obligated Wellington Management to keep a significant percentage of its assets tied up in the building. After extensive negotiations, a five-year lease was accepted.

Vanguard late in 1981, he had to share an office with the auditors and work from a small desk with a wall phone nearby. He was soon joined by Robert F. Auwaerter, and together they organized a fixed-income management unit responsible for $1.7 billion in assets. MacKinnon's unit would eventually manage $62 billion in 39 deliberately plain vanilla portfolios. In 1995, Vanguard was second only to Fidelity in total assets managed, with $180 billion. It was increasing its assets twice as fast as major competitors and was serving 3 million shareholder accounts and adding 3,000 new accounts every day. Wellington Management continued to manage Vanguard's high-yield bonds and mortgage-backed securities, as well as preferred stocks—categories that demanded more research.

> "In investing, you get what you don't pay for."

In marketing, Vanguard's compelling competitive advantage was low fees. "In bond and money market funds, Vanguard's expense ratios are anywhere from 50 to 100 basis points lower than our competitors' fees," MacKinnon noted. "Let me tell you, there's no better way to start your investment day than with a 0.5 percent to 1 percent head start. There's no need to sacrifice quality or strategy to boost yield."[14]

As assets rose, Vanguard's costs rose only slightly, so over time the cost of management per dollar invested went down and down again—eventually to just one basis point (one-hundredth of 1 percent) for some money and bond funds, dramatically lower than the competition. Among equity fund investors, higher fees were often somewhat perversely seen as indicative of more capable management and higher returns to come. Money fund investors would not ignore Vanguard's lower fees. The powerful virtuous cycle accelerated. As Vanguard kept adding assets, its fees kept declining, attracting even more assets.

Sophisticated investors told their friends to try Vanguard. Many investors feel the relationship they have with investment organizations is remarkably significant; once investors have an established relationship, they tend to do more business with that same organization. Investors attracted by low fees to Vanguard's money funds would often expand that relationship to include long-term bond funds, which also had low fees. And, if bonds, why not equities?

Once again, Vanguard was lucky. As the stock market turned in the early 1980s, what would become the best and longest bull market in US history began to gather momentum. John Neff's Windsor Fund, by then distributed exclusively by Vanguard, produced clearly superior results year after year, and his many fans working on Wall Street invested their own money in Neff's fund and told others what they were doing and why. (See Chapter 7.)

Meanwhile, Wellington Management was still getting battered. It remained investment manager for 11 Vanguard mutual funds and still had the institutional investment business of TDP&L, the Bostonians. But assets were down, and profits even more so. Worse, the collegiality that had been so central to the Bostonians had been severely shaken by their negative experiences.

> "There's no better way to start your investment day than with a 0.5 percent to 1 percent head start. There's no need to sacrifice quality or strategy to boost yield."

Time and again Bogle did exhaustive homework to build a convincing case that reducing fees paid to Wellington was the one best answer to whatever he had identified as the problem this time, making it hard for his directors to persist in disagreeing with him. As Bogle took away one part after another of Wellington's business, he was seriously threatening Wellington and his one-time "merger made in heaven." As a public company, Wellington's future rate of earnings growth was essential to its market valuation. But in building up Vanguard, Bogle was depriving Wellington Management of important business and profits.

Meanwhile the stock market was still way down from its peak, depressing Wellington's investment management income from fees based on assets. As investors lost confidence in Wellington's future earning power, its share price fell, and then fell again. The stock would actually drop almost 90 percent from a high of nearly $50 to a low of nearly $5. For the Bostonians, who had sold their company for stock, the price plunge was personally painful. They all realized it could get even worse. "It was just awful," Doran would later observe. "We were fighting to retain everything we had, and Bogle was fighting to take it away. Our assets were shrinking while revenues and our stock price were declining."

Without growth, it would be hard for Wellington to attract the new talent that every investment organization needs. If investment performance were ever subpar for two or three years, as often happens for even the best active managers, an easy case for termination of the Wellington-TDP&L merger could be made. It would link disappointment in investment performance with the disruption in Wellington Management's economics and the obvious weakness in its organizational structure revealed by Bogle's serial fee negotiations. If a few major institutional clients left—and their contracts all had "90-day notice of termination" clauses, making exit relatively simple—the impact would be hard to endure. If more than a few left, it could become a stampede.

Bob Doran, with help from others and several drafts, produced an internal memo titled "Looking Ahead" about the organizational values and culture he envisioned for Wellington. If it had come from almost anyone else, it might have been dismissed as just platitudes, but his partners knew from experience that Doran cared deeply, so they paid attention. As years had passed, those core values—mutual respect, pursuit of professional and business excellence, and providing opportunities for people to develop skills—were patiently nurtured into a compelling cultural reality for the Wellington organization.

Despite the acrimony between Bogle and his Wellington adversaries, individual friendships between some senior executives of Wellington and their former colleagues now at Vanguard continued and would, when opportunity came, facilitate rebuilding the working relationship between the two firms. (See Chapter 12.)

At Vanguard, Bogle and Riepe had achieved their ultimate strategic objective: an integrated, self-sufficient investment management organization that was now in control of distribution, client services, and investment management. Vanguard, to use its favored nautical terminology, was free to develop and implement a "blue water" strategy, full steam ahead.

Bogle enjoyed opening Vanguard's annual management retreat with surprise announcements to spur innovation. In 1992, his theme was the firm's "sacred cows." Of a dozen that he believed others thought were inviolate, he focused on three that he wanted to challenge:

- Vanguard would not be a technology leader.

- Vanguard would not provide custom-tailored investment advice on asset allocation.

- Vanguard would not need to match the fee waivers some competitors offered large new customers.

While he had just recently told *Forbes*, "Technology is too expensive; we can't afford to be the technology leader," he now declared, "We can't afford *not* to be technology leaders, so with our asset base growing by tens of billions, we are going to be the leader." But this didn't happen while he was CEO.

Bogle had grave doubts about Vanguard or any other firm being able to select active managers who could outperform the indexes, but with index funds gaining acceptance and asset allocation increasingly the focus of investment advice, he had now become convinced that offering advice could work. Again, however, Vanguard would not start giving advice until 1996, after Bogle's departure.

For what he liked to call a shot across the bow of competitors, Bogle announced that Vanguard would offer those investing $50,000 or more in Vanguard's four different US Treasury securities funds an expense ratio of only 0.10 percent, a price reduction of more than half. As Vanguard's record-keeping technology advanced, beginning in 2000—eight years after Bogle's first "shot across the bow"— Vanguard began gradually adding reduced Admiral pricing for more funds, and with lower minimum investments. Years later, Admiral shares had an average asset-weighted average expense ratio of 0.11 percent. This was half the Vanguard average and 80 percent lower than the 0.63 percent ratio of competitors. With these reductions, investors increasingly took notice and moved to Vanguard.

CHAPTER 6

THE COST-FEE NEXUS

At Boston Consulting Group in the 1960s, founder Bruce Henderson made a strong case for basing an organization's long-term strategy on low costs, arguing that they would enable the firm to charge lower prices. In doing so, the firm would gain market share and increase volume so much that the combination of lower costs and higher volume would enable it to become profitable. Repeated in a virtuous cycle, lower and lower costs would make possible lower and lower prices—that would lead to higher market share and larger volume, enabling even lower prices because the cost per unit of production would be lower.

Low fees for investors, Vanguard's central proposition, depend on low operating and fund management costs. Reducing, removing, and managing costs shows up over and over again as the company's primary management focus.

Bogle earned a reputation for frugality and a relentless focus on lowering the cost of investing. Vanguard investors admired his drive to reduce costs, knowing they would benefit with higher returns. His friend, Princeton economics professor Burton Malkiel, told this story when introducing Bogle before the Newcomen Society in 1992:

> Once Jack had to stay at New York's expensive Plaza Hotel for a meeting. When his turn in the check-in line

came up, he informed the desk clerk he wanted the cheapest room possible. The clerk suggested an economy single at $250, but Jack insisted that was way too high. After Jack rejected a number of other suggestions, the exasperated clerk indicated sarcastically that there was a windowless former broom closet next to the elevator shaft for $89. Jack quickly said, "I'll take it."

As the bewildered clerk was searching for a key, Jack turned to a gentleman waiting in line behind him and apologized for holding up the line. The gentleman, who turned out to be a Vanguard shareholder, said, "Oh, that's perfectly okay. You're Mr. Bogle aren't you? Cheap! Right?"

Bogle not only insisted on cheap hotel rooms; he also flew coach, wore off-the-rack suits long after they were showing their years, avoided the social circuit, and drove cars of a certain age, all as part of the penny-pinching image he cultivated for himself and, by extension, for Vanguard. He established the importance of low cost and increasingly offered low fees at Vanguard long before anyone else in the industry thought low fees could be important.

Of all the many beliefs about the investment management business, at least until recently, the strongest and strangest has been that fees are *not* important. Fees are widely perceived to be low. So why would being "lower than low" make sense as a business strategy? Who would notice? Who would care? Superior performance was every investor's obvious objective, and the relevant clichés were plentiful: "You get what you pay for." "You wouldn't choose a brain surgeon just because he charged less." "Do you really want a manager who is less than the best?"

Bogle knew that conventional certainties can become seriously misleading over time as business changes compound. The new investor already had the assets, so the manager was providing only returns. If, say, the returns on a balanced fund averaged 7 percent, the fee described as "only 1 percent" of *assets* was actually a full 15 percent of *returns*; 15 percent is clearly not "only 1 percent." Add another 1 percent of assets for transaction costs (commissions and market spreads between price to buy and price to sell), and an active manager must recover nearly 2 percent of assets—which means achieving nearly 30 percent higher returns than the market average. Could this be achieved repeatedly in a stock market dominated by equally well-informed competitors, equally well-armed with technology and talent, and all competing to identify and exploit *any* pricing error—making such opportunities remarkably difficult to find and quick to disappear? Bogle had studied the performance records of mutual funds and said: No!

Most fund management companies were *increasing* their management fees, particularly by adding on 12b-1 fees of 0.20 percent to 0.40 percent. Vanguard kept *lowering* its fees, attracting more attention and much more in assets. Yet for many years, Vanguard did not attract direct price competition because competitors were for-profit businesses, not "mutual" organizations. By 1995, Vanguard's average expense ratio had been reduced to 0.30 percent while its average competitor's had *increased* to 0.92 percent. The difference would matter.

Thanks to internal cost discipline—travel coach, stay in bargain hotel rooms, simple meals, no entertainment, moderate pay, little advertising—and tough fee negotiations with its external investment managers, Vanguard almost axiomatically had the lowest costs of operation. Cost consciousness is obvious in the spartan offices of senior managers. Simple, functional, and "standard issue," they are all gray, modest in size, and surrounded by cubicles used by the managers' direct reports. Vanguard was staking out a strategic corner of competitive advantage; for decades none of the other mutual fund companies would want to match its low fees.

From the point of view of the investor, if indexing can deliver almost all of the market's return (minus just a few basis points) at no more risk than the market itself, what does the typical mutual fund based on *active* investing offer? While there are winners every year in the contest to beat the market, over a decade or longer the record is sharply different—and instructive.

Even though each fund is free to select the particular market segment in which it will specialize—large or small companies, growth or value focus, and dozens more—*and* is free to assemble the team it wants, to select the research resources it values most

> Vanguard was staking out a strategic corner of competitive advantage

highly, to select the stocks it likes best and avoid those deemed less attractive, the grim reality is that over the past 15 years, a stunning 89 percent of actively managed mutual funds failed to keep up with their chosen target index. Managers who were in the winning 11 percent in one year were unlikely to stay there in succeeding years. Those funds that fail to match their benchmark lose far more than the few successful funds gain for shareholders. Adding insult to injury, investors in mutual funds notoriously do noticeably worse than the funds they invest in because they tend, as a group, to buy their funds high and sell them low.

Major long-term changes in the structure of the stock market and the overwhelming dominance of today's market by professional investors and computers have slashed the odds of any active manager's outperforming an index from *high* 60 years ago to *low* today. After the substantial costs of active management—over 1 percent of assets for fees and nearly 1 percent for transaction costs*—beating the market has gotten persistently harder in almost all the major markets around the world. (China, where stock market activity is still dominated by individual trades, continues to be an exception—until institutions inevitably begin to dominate.) The challenge isn't to locate an excellent manager. There are now so many excellent active managers that the real challenge is to find an active manager who is significantly *better* than excellent. Today almost all buying comes from expert professionals and almost all selling is to expert professionals. This is extraordinarily different from past markets dominated by part-time individual amateurs and ponderous institutions. The "willing losers" are almost all gone.

The near-equality of excellent investment talent reflects the remarkably near-equality of excellent information. Large securities firms that might have had only a dozen analysts 50 years ago now have 500 or more industry and company analysts, economists, commodity experts, portfolio strategists, and others in regional offices all over the world, gathering insights and information they distribute via the internet to their institutional clients everywhere. Every

---

* Almost entirely the spread between bid and ask prices, which can be particularly large when surprising positive or negative information provokes many investment managers to take sudden action.

professional has superb computer power, as well as Bloomberg terminals that enable users to organize any useful data in whatever way they like, on 345,000 desks worldwide. The SEC requires public companies to make diligent efforts, whenever giving any one investor significant information, to ensure that same information is simultaneously available to *all* investors. In sum, among the professionals, almost everyone knows almost everything at almost the same time.

What might an investor do to avoid the trap of costs exceeding benefits? Reduce costs! Index funds and ETFs are two ways to deliver cost-effective value. Another way is to carefully select active managers and contract with them to provide their investment services at unusually low fees. This win-win arrangement is now used to select managers for dozens of actively managed Vanguard funds.

Among the professionals, almost everyone knows almost everything at almost the same time.

Vanguard offers its active managers four major benefits: substantial assets will be accumulated if the manager performs; all shareholder services are provided by Vanguard; a Vanguard relationship allows managers to significantly diversify their business; and Vanguard investors' assets are more persistent or stable than those of the average mutual fund. Vanguard is more than happy to pay a successful manager a handsome incentive for outstanding results. Of course, there are significant penalties for underperformance as well.

Vanguard strives to provide superior indexing *and* superior active management. Either way, it is focused on providing investors with low-cost access to long-term investment managers and on guiding clients toward sound investment policy planning and staying on plan for the long term.

Even individually small cost savings add up. Many fund companies report and pay dividends four times a year. To minimize costs, Vanguard has semiannual dividend distributions for some funds. Each reduction in distribution frequency can save $50,000 to $100,000. Similarly, after analyzing mailing costs, Vanguard cut an eighth of an inch off the form for voting proxies and saved $40,000 a year for its investor-owners.

The most pervasive cost consciousness at Vanguard is in the vigorous use of technology to reduce the number of people required to deliver good service to investors. But at least one source of significant savings involved little technology and *more* people. Years ago, instead of increasing the permanent service staff to handle peak call-volume days, Vanguard developed a flexible response capability that both increased service capacity in the near term and reduced costs over the long term. Conceived by Jack Brennan, then chief operating officer, and dubbed the "Swiss Army" by Bogle after the defensive force that has protected that small country's independence for more than 500 years, the program was a successful response to a service failure.

Back in April 1987, with interest rates rising, the municipal bond market took an unexpected nosedive. Municipal bond markets are quite thin, so any rush by investors to buy or sell can quickly send prices up or down. Falling prices can provoke still more selling, which is what happened in 1987. Clients responded by suddenly wanting to switch from long-term municipal bond funds to short-term money market funds. While most fund managers charged a redemption fee, Vanguard (and Dreyfus) did not, so they got hit with almost all the anxiety selling. With some municipal bond prices off by as much as 20 percent, more than 27,000 calls poured into Vanguard's 800 phone lines from worried investors.[1] Bond manager Ian Mackinnon recalled, "It was like being in a traffic accident. Your mouth gets dry. You don't feel pain because you're in a state of shock."[2] Vanguard was not able to keep up with its standard of answering 90 percent of calls within 45 seconds.

Brennan was determined to prevent a recurrence and to do so cost-effectively. Call volumes vary for many reasons: market breaks, but also weather, tax season, and more. Peak to trough call volume generally varies 2 to 1. Brennan's solution: cross-train hundreds of crew members—including himself; James H. Gately, head of the individual investor group; Gus Sauter, head of indexing; and Jack Bogle—to serve as an on-call ready reserve of trained people who could staff the phones whenever needed—but *only* when needed. The training consisted of two days in a classroom and five weeks on the phones, with a two-day annual refresher. The Swiss Army met three Vanguard objectives: minimize costs, maintain high client service standards and, importantly, keep senior leaders in touch with retail clients.

The hard test of Vanguard's Swiss Army came just six months later, when the Dow Jones average dropped 22.6 percent in a single October day, the most before or since. Call volumes took off; the army was ready. Vanguard kept up with the surging demand for service, and smiles of satisfaction were everywhere among the crew. In times of investor anxiety, as Brennan has said, "First, you have to be there. Second, you have to provide good information, and third, you have to meet the client's request."[3]

One request during his service on the client phone lines tested Gus Sauter's sense of humor. The investor calling in wanted an actively managed fund and opined that index funds could be managed by a *monkey*. Sauter replied amiably, "I guess you're talking to the head of the monkeys."[4]

While systematically reducing or eliminating costs, Vanguard has also found a way to augment returns in a conservative way. By lending securities, Vanguard earns cash that goes straight back to investors. Vanguard lends securities to carefully selected dealers that want to sell those securities short, usually for their own risk-mitigation purposes. The dealers must always put up more than 100 percent in high-grade collateral, so Vanguard incurs no risk. As Bill McNabb, then head of the 401(k) business, told the *Financial Times*, "Everything we do [in lending securities] is 100 percent collateralized with maturities shorter than our own money market fund. So [the program] is run very conservatively. The extra income can, on occasion with certain index funds, offset management fees *entirely*. In such cases, the net cost of skillful management to investors: zero."

Another creative way to reduce cost is by changing service providers when one becomes unwilling to respond to business changes. Vanguard's original deal with Standard & Poor's was based on a fixed fee for the S&P 500 index fund. When that fund grew beyond all expectations, S&P realized it had made a big mistake and wanted more money. Vanguard refused to change the contract terms. Then Gus Sauter introduced an ETF version of the S&P fund. S&P claimed the ETF was a different customer, so it had a right to a higher fee. When Vanguard again refused, S&P's then parent company, McGraw-Hill, sued and won. But that was not the end of the story.

Sauter had earned his MBA at the University of Chicago, a flourishing academic center for quantitative analysis of investment markets. As a leading alumnus, he had been asked to serve on the Chicago business school's board of advisers. He knew that, decades before, Merrill Lynch had offered $50,000 to support what would become the school's Center for Research in Security Prices, or CRSP (pronounced crisp). Merrill Lynch had wanted contemporary proof that stocks were better long-term investments than bonds. That was then still a contentious proposition, although it had been argued at least since Edgar Lawrence Smith's 1924 book *Common Stocks as Long-Term Investments*, the bible of the 1920s roaring bull market.

Guided by corporate finance professor James H. Lorie, a gaggle of graduate students collected, organized, validated, and entered onto IBM punch cards the daily prices of more than 1,000 stocks over 8,650 days of trading—nearly 9 million entries. The center was successful at proving that stocks substantially outperformed bonds over time.* So Merrill Lynch got value for its money, and quantitative analysts found the data useful, particularly for research articles. But CRSP data was not marketable in the way Standard & Poor's data was because it had not been converted into an index that could be tracked, minute by minute, throughout the trading day. Sauter had a win-win opportunity in mind.

CRSP was not at all known to individual investors, Vanguard's main market. So before confronting S&P, Sauter did his homework. He commissioned a survey of investors to learn how much they cared that the index fund was tied to the S&P index. As he expected, most didn't care at all. They valued Vanguard as a low-cost fund manager but felt that any reputable index was as good as any other.

Sauter's proposal to Chicago's Dean Ted Snyder was compelling. Vanguard would advance the school 100 percent of the cost of converting the CRSP data into a first-rate continuous index, with the work to be done by two faculty members at $750 a day each. To use the index as the Vanguard fund's benchmark, Vanguard committed to paying an annual royalty that, while considerable, was low relative

---

* Ironically, the University of Chicago, generously endowed by John D. Rockefeller, had put most of its own endowment into bonds. As a result, the endowment underperformed its peers, dropping from second to tenth in assets.

to those imposed by S&P and provided the Chicago business school with a substantial annuity.[5]

And that's how the Vanguard S&P 500 Index Fund became the Vanguard 500 Index Fund.

Advertising was long one of the most obvious ways Vanguard minimized costs. It did almost no advertising—Fidelity spent more than 10 times as much on media ads. Jack Bogle had a personal solution for the advertising gap: get favorable newspaper, magazine, and cable TV stories about Vanguard, particularly in the *New York Times*, the *Wall Street Journal*, *Money*, *Forbes*, *Barron's*, CNN, and CNBC.

The secret to Bogle's success with the media was no secret at all. When many investment people avoided the press, he embraced it. Bogle was an active, skillful player, in the game every day. Financial reporters got to know that he answered phone calls and had facts to support his opinions about what was best for investors. He proclaimed that the investment management industry, highly profitable for insiders, all too often failed the individual investor by charging high fees while claiming but not actually delivering superior results: "Mutual funds charge fees that are too high." "Sales charges are excessive." "Managers are greedy and focus on the short term." "Advertising is misleading." "Somewhere along the road, the industry has lost its way." Reporters cited Bogle as a maverick, the conscience of the mutual fund business, an iconoclast. Some chided him for his love affair with controversy. As part of his persistent campaign, Bogle would offer, in several books and many articles and speeches, not only a tough critique of shoddy procedures, but also basic guidelines for success that every investor could understand and use.

> Reporters cited Bogle as a maverick, the conscience of the mutual fund business, an iconoclast.

Bogle's status as an industry icon was good for Vanguard's business. It also made Jack Bogle impervious to anyone else's management or control. Call by call, article by article, and quote by quote, he built a personal brand, one of the best in the business. In Jack Brennan's view, Bogle's press coverage was "worth millions" to Vanguard every year. Few people in business achieve name recognition and admiration that make them public celebrities—and in finance, very few. Jack Bogle made himself one. He loved it and defended it. When the *Washington Post* cited both Bogle and Warren Buffett as leaders who had set high standards of faithful services to investors, Bogle protested that the *Post* had mentioned Buffett more.

Whether others always liked it or not, Bogle had always been the most visible and recognizable spokesperson for Vanguard. That personalized and differentiated the firm, especially in the early stages. He complained in retirement, "They won't use me." That bothered Bogle on three levels: he would work without cost to Vanguard; he would have loved to do it; and he knew that Vanguard knew that. He felt they were hurting him and the firm he had founded by denying him the opportunity. What he could not, or would not, see was that his need to be independent and outspoken had tarred him as a loose cannon with opinions that were often in opposition to those of Vanguard's senior management. He had decried ETFs as temptations to trade too much. He went public with "concern" about index funds becoming market dominating and somehow causing harm. (See Chapter 18 for a discussion of these issues.)

Jack Bogle became one of the most widely recognized people in American business. He enjoyed the whole process. No matter how his wife might plead that he retire at 70 or 75 or even 80 or 85, he pressed on regardless. The focus of his unrelenting drive became perfecting his public reputation as the centurion of the everyday investor. He was consistent and plain spoken. In a fearless, curmudgeonly style, he held the attention of large audiences who delighted in anticipating what he might say and enjoyed hearing him out. Time and again, his audiences learned from him and learned to trust him. As more and more reporters paid attention to Bogle, he compiled and, every few weeks, mailed out to reporters and others packages of his recent speeches and articles with a page or so of Xeroxed handwritten commentary reinforcing his key points and correcting any errors he had seen in articles about him. Eventually, Bogle no longer needed to be CEO or even at Vanguard to be widely recognized and respected as an insightful observer to be reckoned with.

As the stock market plunged in 2008, financial firms terminated tens of thousands of employees to cut costs. Not Vanguard; while shaving millions of dollars from its cost structure, it terminated not one crew member (as its employees are known).

How did this retention fit with cost management? The need for crew did not drop comparably with the market. Clients still needed lots of service, maybe even more. Moreover, Vanguard senior management believed loyalty down would win loyalty up. Layoffs were averted by redeploying crew to other duties and project work. The result: unusually low turnover, unusually high morale, and continued dedication to serve clients.

Jack Brennan said, "Low cost is not the same as *cheap*. Our leaders understand that a focus on cost does not mean don't spend. It means spend wisely. We must be comfortable being—no, we must relish the opportunity to be—the lowest-cost, highest-value provider of investment services in the world."[6]

Lower pricing is more important in absolute dollars to larger investors. Larger investors are also less costly to serve per dollar invested. That's why owners of Vanguard's Admiral shares (and recently, all index fund shareholders) enjoy lower expense ratios. To the extent that it attracts larger investors, Vanguard gains advantages of scale, allowing it to reduce overall expense ratios, benefiting investors of all asset sizes.

> "Low cost is not the same as *cheap*. Our leaders understand that a focus on cost does not mean don't spend. It means spend wisely. We must be comfortable being—no, we must relish the opportunity to be—the lowest-cost, highest-value provider of investment services in the world."

"You define yourself more by *why* you do things than by *what* you do," said CEO Tim Buckley. "We try to look at every decision in terms of what we should do and what we should not do. We are always asking, 'How could each new idea work to reduce cost or increase service value or both?' We seek efficiency to increase our effectiveness in serving clients. For example, a bill-paying service that Jack Brennan loved as a personal convenience attracted only 4,000 customers. This was not an adequate number of users to achieve significant scale advantages, so it was terminated."

Pressing too hard on any one dimension can, of course, have unintended negative consequences and even do serious harm. Both speed of response and accuracy can fall short when Vanguard is growing so rapidly. Finding the right balance between minimizing cost and optimizing service is a perpetual challenge. Response time and errors are both tracked. Customer complaints are taken seriously.

With Jack Bogle's focus on *not* spending, unintended but serious consequences emerged years ago in two all-important areas: computer-based technology and compensation. In both areas, as we shall see, Jack Brennan and his management team took the lead in changing the course.

Senior managers and members of the Vanguard crew, aware that one of the major advantages of being in the investment industry was above-average compensation, were wondering. They liked the Vanguard mission of serving everyday investors with good service at low cost. They respected Bogle for "walking the talk" and being so personally committed to Vanguard's being *the* low-cost industry leader. They were fine with small, plain offices. They liked eating meals in the Galley, Vanguard-speak for the company cafeteria: simple food, plenty of variety, quick, and low cost.

Brennan liked to tell job candidates, "If knowing you'll never have extraordinary wealth would bother you, don't come to Vanguard. If you do come to Vanguard and do well here, you'll earn a very good income versus your peers and friends in other areas of our economy."[7] Still, increasing numbers of Vanguard people were concerned that they were not being paid all that well. Some worried that they were not only servicing investors (which they liked) but also somehow subsidizing the organization (which did not feel right). They wondered whether they were accepting less than they might earn in other investment organizations. Should they stay at Vanguard, potentially for their whole careers, as Brennan was always urging? Were they making a mistake? Brennan listened carefully, particularly in his "skip level" lunches with younger managers who reported to the senior managers who reported to him (see Chapter 10).

"I'm always glad to steal any good idea from anyone at any time," Brennan said with a big smile as he reflected on a great idea he saw first at S.C. Johnson, maker of Johnson Wax at Racine, Wisconsin. Invited to be the CEO's personal assistant when he graduated from Harvard Business School, Brennan saw firsthand something he really liked: the Johnson family was sharing part of the earnings of their company with the people who worked there, and that generosity attracted the better workers in the area to make their careers with S.C. Johnson.[8]

Brennan worked out the mechanics and made a compelling case for how profit sharing could be made to work for a mutual organization like Vanguard. Bogle quickly approved, and on December 21, 1984, sent a memo to all employees describing the Vanguard Partnership Plan.

MEMORANDUM

At our Christmas Party, I announced that the Board of Directors had approved the implementation of a new Profit Sharing Plan— the Vanguard Partnership Plan—designed to allow each and every Vanguard employee to share in Vanguard's growth and success.

Your Directors and Senior Management have decided to establish this Plan at this time because it offers the potential to provide benefits both to Fund shareholders and to our employees. Given Vanguard's unique structure, it is sometimes difficult to measure our true performance on an absolute and relative basis. We tend to focus on *asset growth*, which is an important measure, but one which does not tell the entire story about how Vanguard has performed during the year.

Unlike conventional companies, we do not have a "bottom line" which would allow us to measure our profits and our performance in a formal way. To address this problem, the Board of Directors has approved a formula for measuring "profits" for Vanguard . . . based largely on our expense-ratio performance relative to that of major competitive mutual fund complexes. Essentially, we use their expense ratios as a proxy for our revenues; we then subtract our expenses; the net amount remaining is our "profit."

We believe that by focusing on profits rather than simply on asset growth, we can heighten our employees' awareness of the importance of cost control and productivity improvement. In the competitive environment in which we work, it is important that we run a "tight ship" while providing the highest quality service in the industry.

We believe further that Vanguard's success in providing quality service and operational efficiency depends on our ability to attract and retain high caliber employees at every level of the company. This requires a sound compensation program, and the new Plan offers the opportunity for extra compensation—*if we earn it.* We are especially aware of the value provided by our longer-term employees, and the Plan is heavily weighted to reward Vanguard people who have been with us for periods ranging from more than two years to more than ten years.

Finally, our shareholders *do* benefit from Vanguard's unique structure and our at-cost operation. It seems only fair that you, the people who provide these benefits, share in the wealth created by our efficient, cost-effective operations. The Vanguard Partnership Plan is our attempt to do that.

The determination of each year's partnership payout starts with a three-year base of assets under management, relative fund performance, client wealth generation, and the cost savings to investors determined by comparing Vanguard's average operating expense to mutual fund industry averages. Each individual's payout is determined by a blend of tenure with Vanguard and job grade.

Since inception, Partnership Plan units awarded to crew members have increased in value at a brisk pace, averaging over 15 percent a year, including declines in 2002 and 2008. This has significantly increased many crew members' compensation. By further aligning the interests of crew, company, and clients, the Vanguard Partnership has measurably intensified loyalty. Turnover always increases cost, so expenditures that reduce turnover are best understood as wise investments. At Vanguard, there's practically no turnover among senior managers.

CHAPTER 7

ACTIVE INVESTING

anguard is committed to encouraging investors to recognize the importance of developing a long-term investment plan and staying with that plan. Vanguard is deliberately conservative about investing and regularly warns investors about paying too much attention to short-run market movements. These tenets are consistent with its dedication to keeping costs low without sacrificing value, quality, or performance.

Seldom does one person, particularly one who is not the founder or the CEO, make the decisive difference in the crucial early decade of a major company, but John Neff certainly did. Without Neff in those difficult early years, Vanguard would not have attracted the favorable attention of savvy investors who moved their money to get access to Neff's remarkable ability to outperform the market averages—and recommended that their family, friends, and business associates do the same.

Over 31 years, from year-end 1964 through year-end 1995, Neff's Windsor Fund beat the market 22 times. Each dollar invested in 1964 multiplied over *55 times*. Windsor's total return outpaced the S&P 500 index by more than 2 to 1—$10,000 invested with Neff would have compounded over those years to $564,637. What made his "best in the business" performance so noteworthy was that Neff's consistent priority was not only to achieve gains, but always to avoid loss and manage risk. On a risk-adjusted basis, his performance achievement was even more remarkable.

As the money poured into Windsor Fund, its assets and earnings surged. For fledgling Vanguard, those earnings were like mother's milk—vital to living and gaining strength. That's not all: investors attracted by Neff's Windsor Fund also noticed Vanguard's other offerings, particularly its low-cost money market and bond funds. Investors initially attracted by Vanguard's low fees on its fixed-income products saw Neff's record and often added an equity investment in Windsor Fund.

> What made his "best in the business" performance so noteworthy was that Neff's consistent priority was not only to achieve gains, but always to avoid loss and manage risk.

John Neff was born on September 19, 1931. His mother and father divorced when he was 4, and he would not see his father again for 14 years. John and his mother moved in with her parents in Grand Rapids, Michigan. Young John was an independent thinker determined to hold to an opinion; on his first-grade report card he was cited as "pugnacious." His mother claimed he would "argue with a signpost." In fifth grade, he got a demerit for "poor self-control." His self-confidence flourished alongside his inclination to flout convention. From age 11, John earned all his own spending money. In the summer of 1944, at 12, he caddied days and delivered newspapers nights to earn $40 a week (over $600 today).[1]

After two years as a Navy seaman without ever stepping on board a ship, Neff mustered out and went to the University of Toledo on the GI Bill. As he recalled, "An inventory of my skills on entering college revealed a relentless curiosity, facility with numbers, an ability to express myself and firm discipline. Although I finished high school awash in ordinary grades, college became a lark. My grades rarely fell below A, and I was graduated summa cum laude."

At Toledo, Neff met professor Sydney Robbins, a disciple of Benjamin Graham and David Dodd, whose book, titled *Security Analysis* but widely and reverently called "Graham and Dodd," became the bible of the emerging profession of investment research and management. During two courses with Robbins and with his strong encouragement, Neff got hooked on investing.

Unable to get a position in New York even with Robbins's endorsement, Neff took an offer from Cleveland's National City Bank in 1959 as a research analyst at $4,200 a year. As he would observe, "To say I loved my new challenge would understate my enthusiasm. I had hit the jackpot. Every detail fascinated me." Before long he was also earning a graduate degree at Case Western Reserve and had built up a personal investment account of $100,000.

Noticing that a senior auto analyst at National City drove a dilapidated old car, Neff intuited correctly that analysts at regional bank trust departments were not particularly well paid. He started looking for "another job with better pay" and focused on three mutual fund organizations: Dreyfus, National Investors, and Wellington. As Neff recalled, "The opportunity seemed broad enough and there was nowhere interesting to go at National City Bank . . . so I packed my bags and headed to Philadelphia."

The situation he found there after joining Wellington Equity Fund, later renamed Windsor Fund, was far from promising. "When I arrived in 1963, the Windsor Fund was in worse shape than I had anticipated," he remembered. "The team in charge had lost its sense of direction." In 1962, a tough year for many investors, the S&P 500 had been down 8.7 percent. Windsor was down by nearly three times as much: 25 percent. As the markets recovered with a gain of 22.8 percent, Windsor gained only 10 percent. With shareholders bolting for the exits, more money was flowing out of the small $75 million fund than was coming in. More ominous, Windsor was beginning to tarnish the reputation of the company's flagship $2 billion Wellington Fund. Having gone public just three years before, Wellington Management was worried about the adverse impact on its share price.

Neff studied Windsor Fund's record of investing and found several problems. Committee decision-making resulted in missed opportunities. Stocks were purchased at high prices that would plunge if optimistic expectations were not fulfilled. Market prices had become unmoored to the book value of the companies. Far too little fundamental research was being done. Windsor was asking for trouble and getting it. Neff's analysis won the respect of his seniors and, less than a year after arriving, he was put in charge as Windsor's first solo portfolio manager.

"Keep it simple" was Neff's motto. It would never change. But close observers would also celebrate his intricately detailed expertise on individual companies and industries.[2] Whether the market was up, down, or indifferent, he followed a durable and disciplined checklist of investment requirements:

- Low price-earnings ratio

- Fundamental growth in excess of 7 percent

"Keep it simple"

- Dividend yield protection (and enhancement, in most cases)

- Superior relationship of total return to price paid

- No cyclical exposure without a compensating low P/E multiple

- Solid companies in growing fields

- Strong fundamental case[3]

Neff was glad to articulate the logic behind his checklist:

> Rather than load up on hot stocks with the crowd, we took the opposite approach. Windsor didn't engage in the market's clamor for fashionable stocks; we sought to exploit it. Our strength always depended on coaxing overlooked, out-of-favor stocks to move up from *under*valued to *fairly* valued. We aimed for easier and less risky appreciation, and left "greater fool" investing to others.
>
> This strategy gave Windsor's performance a twofold edge: (1) excellent upside participation and (2) good protection on the downside. Unlike high-flying growth stocks poised for a fall at the slightest sign of disappointment, low P/E stocks have no favorable expectation built into them. Moreover, indifferent financial performance by low P/E companies seldom exacts a penalty. Hints of improved prospects trigger fresh interest. If you buy stocks when they are out of favor and unloved, and sell them into strength when other investors recognize their merits, you'll often go home with handsome gains. . . .
>
> Absent stunning growth rates, low P/E stocks can capture the wonders of P/E expansion with less risk

than skittish growth stocks. An increase in the P/E ratio, coupled with improved earnings, turbocharges the appreciation potential. Instead of a price gain merely commensurate with earnings, the stock price can appreciate 50 percent to 100 percent.

In Windsor's neck of the woods, the prospects for increasing an out-of-favor company's P/E ratio from, say, 8 times to 11 times always proved more promising than lining up in hopes of comparable percentage advances by companies that started with lofty P/E ratios. For a growth stock with a starting P/E ratio of 40 times earnings, comparable expansion would have to propel the P/E to almost 55 times earnings—to say nothing of sustaining it.[4]

Even Neff had below-market returns for two to three years in a row, and he might find today's market much harder to outperform given the increasing dominance of the stock markets by professionals. But Windsor's disciplined edge was usually formidable, and particularly powerful over the longer term.

Self-confident and repeatedly successful, Neff liked Vanguard's incentives for managers. Here's how he explained how a manager with confidence in his abilities would think: "Fairness to shareholders meant low transaction and investment management fees, coupled with incentives for exceptional performance and penalties for dismal performance. We met these hurdles at Windsor. Unlike funds that received fixed annual percentages of the assets under management, performance governed Windsor's compensation. Similar incentives and penalties are scarce because most managers lack confidence in their ability to do well."[5] Like some other Vanguard managers, Neff's incentive compensation depended partly on his fund's performance against a benchmark index.

In 1991, late in Neff's long run, Windsor Fund had an expense ratio of only 0.37 percent, a full 110 basis points less than the average stock fund. A major competitive advantage was locked in each year.

Neff was unusually well informed. Wherever he was and whatever he had going on, his habit was to read every page of the *Wall Street Journal* each day—and reread all those same pages on Saturday. He was blessed with a powerful memory. As the years went by and his knowledge accumulated, his expertise on specific companies and industries became an increasingly formidable competitive advantage.

Any student of actively managed equity investing has seen the evidence that the major markets around the world have become increasingly "professionalized" and therefore harder to beat after management costs and trading expenses. The number of people earning their living as analysts, fund managers, economists, market makers, and the like has gone from fewer than 5,000 in 1960 to more than half a million—and perhaps one million—all over the world. Every major firm—and some have 30,000 or more employees—expects everyone in its internal information network to begin and end the day with half an hour of receiving, answering, and sending email and text messages. As network theorists know, as the number of nodes increases arithmetically, the useful value of a network rises geometrically. Time available for making investment decisions that can take advantage of new information has dropped decade by decade from six months to six weeks to six days to six hours to six minutes to six seconds—or even less. Over the same time, derivatives have increased in value traded from zero to even greater than the "cash" market.

As tough as it now is to identify predictably superior investment managers, Vanguard's Daniel W. Newhall[6] and his manager search and oversight team have been striving to do exactly that for a long time, and overall they have been successful. Low fees to managers are a big reason.[7]

For any active management firm chosen by Dan Newhall's team and approved by Vanguard's global investment committee and the board of directors, being one of Vanguard's active managers can have important business benefits. The basic attractions are Vanguard's ability to deliver those enormous sums for a manager to invest, and to take care of all investor servicing and all operational tasks, including shareholder record-keeping, legal and compliance, and shareholder communications. The selected investment managers can focus entirely on managing portfolios with the help of a skilled group of analysts, portfolio managers and traders, *and* all the advanced information technology that active managers use to compete in today's demanding market. Investment managers also enjoy the low account turnover of working with Vanguard.

Vanguard knows all this too, so it is a disciplined negotiator of managers' compensation. The result is that Vanguard's client-owners get "only for Vanguard" low manager fees.

As Newhall proudly reports, over 60 percent of Vanguard's actively managed funds have outperformed their peer group, *after* fees, by an average of 25 basis points per annum. (See the chart below for results over four recent periods.) The selection and monitoring of investment process by Newhall and his teams also benefit investors by protecting them from "flame out" managers, and perhaps from themselves. Studies show that individual investors' actions wipe out up to one-third of the returns they would have enjoyed if only they had stayed with their managers longer. Vanguard investors stay longer.

Relative to competitors, it helps that Vanguard has enjoyed a substantial expense advantage of 0.59 percent annualized for the past 15 years. If Vanguard funds had had the headwind of its peers' higher average cost, excess returns would, of course, be less by that amount. Vanguard's focus on keeping costs low, finding skilled managers, being patient when great managers inevitably go through difficult performance periods and removing managers when confidence is lost has driven performance superior to competitors' active equity funds.

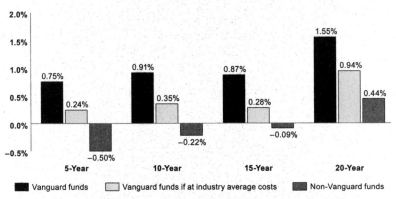

Vanguard's active equity funds have outperformed peers

Vanguard's actively managed equity funds have outperformed their competitors net of fees on an asset-weighted basis over various time horizons. While part of this outperformance has stemmed from a considerable cost advantage of 50–60 basis points compared to competitors, Vanguard funds would still have outperformed if their costs were as high as the industry average (center bars). The right-hand bars represent the asset-weighted excess returns over benchmarks (alpha) of non-Vanguard active equity funds. The data show that the active mutual fund industry in general usually has not generated enough alpha to cover its costs.

Source: Vanguard calculations, using data from Morningstar. All data as of December 31, 2015.

Another way of evaluating Vanguard's experience with its active managers is to compare each fund to its benchmark index, which includes no fees. (See the graphic below.) As expected, the results are not as favorable. Still, over 10 years, 43 percent outperform their no-fee benchmarks. And over 15 years, 42 percent outperform. The average superiority is only nine basis points over 10 years and only three basis points over 15 years. The median is a modest negative 18 basis points over 10 years and 21 basis points over 15 years. Ten out of 28 funds have outperformed in each period by more than their negotiated fees. As the table shows, Vanguard's success in selecting and managing external managers has been good—better than most other managers of managers.

Name	Benchmark	10-YR vs. benchmark	15-YR vs. benchmark	Merged / liquidated
Health Care	Spliced Health Care	2.04	2.87	
PRIMECAP	S&P 500	2.04	2.71	
International Growth	Spliced International	3.99	2.71	
Capital Opportunity	Russell Mid Cap Growth	0.83	1.65	
Dividend Growth	Spliced Dividend Growth	−0.18	1.32	
Energy	Spliced Energy	1.89	1.20	
International Value	Spliced International	0.50	0.92	
Wellington™	Wellington Composite	−0.47	0.75	
Global Equity	MSCI ACWI	1.23	0.73	
Wellesley® Income	Wellesley Income Composite	0.40	0.46	
Windsor™ II	Russell 1000 Value	−0.07	0.01	
International Explorer	S&P EPAC Small-Cap	−0.31	−0.15	
Equity-Income	Spliced Equity Income	−0.17	−0.18	
Morgan™ Growth	Russell 3000 Growth	−0.83	−0.29	
Growth & Income	S&P 500	−0.32	−0.52	
US Value	Russell 3000 Value	0.01	−0.54	
US Growth	Russell 1000 Growth	−0.81	−0.60	
Mid Cap Growth	Russell Mid Cap Growth	−1.72	−0.61	
Explorer	Russell 2500 Growth	−0.54	−0.66	
Selected Value	Russell Mid Cap Value	−1.17	−0.72	
Windsor™	Russell 1000 Value	0.78	−0.73	
Strategic Equity	MSCI US Small&Mid Cap 2200	−0.25	−0.96	
Capital Value	Russell 3000 Value	1.93	−1.31	
Growth Equity	Russell 1000 Growth	−1.06	−1.40	1/31/14
Global Capital Cycles	Spliced Global Capital Cycles	−4.30	−2.48	
Asset Allocation	Asset Allocation Composite	−1.68	−3.39	1/31/12
PRIMECAP Core	MSCI US Prime Market 750	1.47		
Strategic Small-Cap Equity	MSCI US Small Cap 1750	−0.60		
	% Outperforming benchmark	43%	42%	
	Average excess return	0.09	0.03	
	Median excess return	−0.18	−0.23	

Benchmarks are a sterner test

Source: Vanguard

Vanguard actively manages its active managers, sometimes moving assets away from a management firm in whole or in part. When James Barrow of Barrow, Hanley, Mewhinney & Strauss retired in 2015 after years of successfully managing Vanguard's Windsor II Fund, Vanguard evaluated others at his firm and found none comparable. The assets Barrow had been managing were brought back to Vanguard to be managed internally.[8]

Vanguard goes further. If a fund or type of fund seems to be attracting too much money to be invested effectively, or attracting too many new investors, quite possibly for speculative rather than long-term investment reasons, it will either close that fund entirely to new investors or restrict purchases. Acadian Asset Management had a long, successful record with Vanguard, particularly investing in emerging markets, and had multiplied its assets under management to about $500 million, a size that Vanguard thought might challenge Acadian's investing. So Vanguard took $100 million back to headquarters where it would be managed quantitatively. Tim Buckley led a Vanguard delegation to Boston to explain the decision and thank the Acadian team for their good work.[9]

During the tech bubble of 1999–2002, the cross-functional team overseeing Vanguard's investment product development met weekly to discuss funds in the pipeline and new offerings to consider. Every week the sales representatives from each of the client-facing divisions asked Jeff Molitor, then the head of the Portfolio Review Department, when Vanguard would offer a tech fund. Clients were clamoring for one and the retail division complained that large sums were moving out of Vanguard to tech-heavy fund groups. Each week Molitor said no. The pressure built as tech-sector returns flew skyward, but Molitor was steadfast: "I will not bring out a tech fund at the height of the market. It's not good for our clients." When the tech bubble burst, Molitor was vindicated and investor assets that had gone rushing out to competitors came rolling back into Vanguard.

Total active equity investment assets are now more than $460 billion, making Vanguard one of the largest and most experienced manager-selection organizations in the world. Newhall and his team of 23 manager analysts have currently selected 26 firms (25 independent of Vanguard and 1 internal quantitative group) employing 45 separate teams of active managers of all types to oversee a line-up of

34 stock and balanced mutual funds. In a typical year, they screen as many as a thousand investment firms, meet with up to 200 of them and conduct in-depth evaluation of 50 managers. Of these finalists, they select as many as 5 managers for Vanguard clients. One benefit of their extensive outreach is that the group is continuously accumulating insights into contemporary best practice in active investing.

Jack Bogle initiated "active quant" investing at Vanguard in the late 1980s. This investment strategy uses computer models to attempt to identify stocks that are undervalued and therefore likely to outperform. The strategy then employs another computer model designed to combine the attractive stocks into a portfolio in such a way that the risk of the fund is reasonable for the type of investment. Bogle hired Franklin Portfolio Associates, run by John Nagorniak, for the first foray into active quantitative investing. Bogle wanted to develop the capability to manage active quant funds within Vanguard, believing that was a natural complement to the indexing capability Vanguard had already built. Gus Sauter had the necessary capabilities and entrepreneurial drive to make it happen.

"By 1991," Sauter said, "we were managing our first active portfolio, as part of Windsor II. A year later, we took over portfolio management for a portion of the W. L. Morgan Growth Fund, and in 1995, we launched Strategic Equity." More active quant replication would follow, including small cap blend investing (investing in stocks of small companies where neither growth nor value characteristics predominate).[10]

As Sauter explained,

> In traditional investment management, industry and company analysts recommend individual stocks based on perceived upside potential. Then the portfolio manager, with a focus on risk, decides how much of each stock to buy. We do pretty much the same in quant investing, but it's all computer and database driven rather than people based. On a daily basis we rank-order the stocks in each industry based on valuations relative to growth prospects. While many money managers do not want to be referred to as a GARP manager—growth at a reasonable price—it really is pretty descriptive of our quant process.

The key to a good or bad investment is the initial price you pay. To simplify the description of our process, we generally looked for stocks that are reasonably priced for their growth prospects. So, in the energy industry, for example, we would compare various valuations of a stock, say Chevron Texaco, using its current price relative to company fundamentals such as earnings or sales and various measures of expected earnings, to find probable pricing errors. Then we use a computer program called an optimizer to determine the appropriate position size or weight that will maximize the return, subject to not taking more risk relative to the market than we want. We want to provide excess return, or alpha, by old fashioned stock picking, not by placing factor bets, such as over-weighting an industry or buying the FAANG stocks* of the day.[11]

Sauter recognizes the theoretical opportunity of exploiting various "factors" such as momentum or value in investing. But for most investors, factor investing requires far too much patience. Like deer hunting, most of the time nothing is going on. Then the factor pays off for a while—and then there is another long time with nothing going on. Most investors take too long to believe it when a particular factor is working, so by the time they decide to invest, that particular "factor game" may already be over. Sauter cautioned, "You should always be careful to separate a factor's effect from true alpha."

In 1983, an article in *Pensions & Investment Age* caught Jack Brennan's attention: two superb investors he had gotten to know and respect, Howard Schow and Mitch Milias, had just left one of the most admired firms in the investment world—Capital Group, manager of the American Funds group of mutual funds—to launch a new firm called Primecap Management Company. Brennan called and asked, "Do you ever come to New York City?" He knew that would be much easier for them than meeting in Philadelphia.

---

* Facebook, now called Meta Platforms (FB), Amazon (AMZN), Apple (AAPL), Netflix (NFLX), and Google, now called Alphabet (GOOG).

Soon Brennan was sitting down in a wood-paneled private dining room at Christ Cella, then Manhattan's premier steakhouse. A fortunate ice breaker came when Milias and the waiter serving the table began talking and joking in Croatian, but at first the discussions, while friendly, did not go well. Schow and Milias showed no interest in Vanguard. "We are not interested in the mutual funds business: too much administrative detail, too many regulations that require too many noninvestment people," they told Brennan. "We intend to focus entirely on investing and intend to build our business based solely on having very large institutional clients so we can do just that, focus on investing."

Capital was known for outstanding research on companies and industries, and for its exemplary culture and business practices. It was recognized for success in recruiting and developing investment professionals and greatly admired for keeping its people "forever." Everyone agreed Capital was a great place to work if you were very good. Almost nobody ever left Capital. But now, two of the firm's seniors *were* leaving and taking a few stellar young analysts with them to establish a new firm. Primecap's business strategy was simple: attract 20 jumbo accounts—later increased to 25—from the best and biggest institutions around the country and around the world, maintain top-level communications with clients, and establish a deep shared understanding of Primecap's way of investing. With this combination, clients would stay with Primecap a long, long time. Instead of having lots of out-of-town, away-from-home travel seeking new business, Schow and Milias could concentrate their skills and energy on what they most wanted to do: provide superior investment results.

Brennan had just the right response: "Great! Vanguard will be *one* of your clients—and hopefully, in time, your single *largest* client. Meanwhile, we will do all the admin and shareholder servicing. You'll have none of the traditional mutual fund responsibilities." Both sides came quickly to agreement and a splendid partnership was initiated.[12] Over many years, it would work out even better than Brennan had hoped.

His concept was to combine Vanguard's capabilities in retail distribution with Primecap's capabilities as investment managers, not far from Bogle's dream for Wellington's old merger with the Bostonians but better thought out. The strategic fit was compelling.

Vanguard sought attractive investment alternatives to offer clients while Primecap had no retail distribution and no interest in the retail market of serving individual investors via mutual funds. There would be no "opportunity cost" for this exciting new firm if it linked up with Vanguard. If Vanguard linked up with Primecap, it could offer retail investors a proven new investment team with a fire in the belly determination to achieve superior long-term investment results.

Schow had earned a reputation as a great long-term investor with ability to recognize fundamental change in companies and industries at an early stage. There were many examples. Anticipating the paperwork revolution of xerography, he had taken a major position in what was still called Haloid. With Joseph C. Wilson's inspiring leadership, it would become Xerox, the most profitable growth stock of the early 1960s. When Schow invested in Haloid, the company was still struggling to produce what would later become the fabulous 914 copier, the first successful plain-paper copier. In another example, when oil prices jumped to unheard-of record prices per barrel, Schow understood that price would discourage demand, so the high prices couldn't last. Producers would ramp up their exploration and most consumers would reduce their consumption and look for alternatives. While it would take many years, supply would inevitably surge and demand would be cut back, so oil prices would surely decline, which they did—for 18 long years. As a percentage of the S&P 500 index's market capitalization, oil stocks fell from 35 percent to 3 percent. Schow sold off all oil stocks early, giving his investment record a major boost.

The journey from Capital Group to Primecap and Vanguard started in a car. Schow and Milias lived near each other in Pasadena, California, so they agreed to take turns driving to work at their office in Los Angeles. Both were early risers and, inherently competitive, both liked to be in their offices and ready to work each morning before 7 a.m.—the 10 a.m. Eastern time opening bell at the New York Stock Exchange.* This meant leaving their homes by 6:15. When Capital's office building began to open at 6:30 a.m., they left home a half hour earlier. Both men instinctively liked being on time, so both liked it that the other also cared about being punctual. More important,

---

* The NYSE moved the market open to 9:30 a.m. in 1985.

they had an uninterrupted half-hour each way every day to exchange information and ideas about investing and investments. They soon developed both a strong friendship and a great respect for each other's expertise and judgment.

Schow surprised Milias one morning: "I may be leaving Capital. If I do, I'll want you to come with me."[13]

Milias was stunned. Schow was clearly one of Capital's strongest investors and a much-admired leader. Capital was growing rapidly in assets and even more rapidly in earnings. The growth was almost certain to continue and probably accelerate. Milias's first thought was that Schow, as the second largest shareholder in Capital, would be making a substantial financial sacrifice. Capital's leader, Jon Lovelace, had worked out a stock ownership program that required any shareholder leaving the private firm to sell back all shares at a substantially and deliberately understated book value. A few months later, after much soul-searching and several long talks with Lovelace, Schow had made his decision. "I'm leaving, Mitch. Let's go!" Given the professional, personal, and economic attractions of staying with Capital, it took Milias several weeks to decide he would indeed join Schow.

Over the 35 years since that first agreement, Primecap's capabilities have resulted in such strong retail demand that the three different stock funds it managed for Vanguard were eventually closed to new investors. Primecap now manages over $145 billion for Vanguard. As a lean, small organization, it is superbly profitable.

In today's world of investing, a large institutional account might total $50 million. By comparison, Vanguard investors' total investments with Primecap are nearly 3,000 times larger. Vanguard Primecap Fund has a long-term performance premium over its peers of more than 3 percentage points. And Primecap's concentrated Vanguard Capital Opportunity Fund, with a boost from the FAANG technology stocks, has grown at 12.1 percent versus 5.8 percent for the S&P 500—more than twice the annual return. Of course, the obvious irony of performance records is that while investors make their investment decisions on past results, what they get are the future results.

CHAPTER 8

INDEX INVESTING

While Vanguard is famous for index investing, it is officially agnostic on active management versus indexing, so long as both feature low costs and low fees. It offers both approaches and is increasingly a global leader in both.

Vanguard manages more than 200 index funds and index-based ETFs, offering them individually to clients and as components of its increasingly popular Target Retirement and LifeStrategy funds (see Chapter 17). What began as Gus Sauter and one assistant has grown into an organization of 80, including several PhDs, who work with Rodney Comegys in the Equity Index Group.[1] The group analyzes the many indexes they replicate both to anticipate small changes and to develop trading strategies to moderate any market impact the funds' trading might have in the 40 different stock markets in which Vanguard now operates. "Continuous improvement, ideally every day, is part of the Vanguard culture," said Comegys. "Indexing is a precision business."[2]

One consistent objective is to minimize transaction costs, often by using futures to manage portfolio changes rather than suddenly buying or selling huge blocks of shares, or by spreading over several days or even

> "Continuous improvement, ideally every day, is part of the Vanguard culture," said Comegys. "Indexing is a precision business."

weeks the full execution of a portfolio change made in response to a change in the index being tracked. Another objective is to reduce and even offset entirely the index funds' small expenses with income earned from Vanguard's conservative securities lending program (see Chapter 6).

Index fund investors often focus on tracking error; they usually expect a fund or ETF to stay within one or two basis points of the target index. Vanguard's portfolio managers monitor their trading to avoid being either early or late on index-matching or too quick in effecting portfolio changes. Extra care is taken when managing index funds that represent small market segments or volatile foreign markets—especially those few markets that may tolerate "unusual" trading practices at or near their daily close.

Comegys and his senior staff travel the world to work with dozens of stock exchanges and their regulators, advising on ways to improve market efficiency and integrity. Since Vanguard is a large investor with extensive global experience and long-term focus, he and his colleagues are welcomed and listened to all over the world. Total index funds assets at Vanguard were $5.3 trillion in 2021.

Index funds are, by nature, buy-and-hold investors. Average portfolio turnover of the indexes Vanguard tracks runs only 3 to 4 percent a year. The average investment holding period for index investors is about 10 years. The holding period is understandably somewhat shorter for 401(k) investors who are older and near to or in retirement.

Indexing has become more and more highly sophisticated, particularly over the past decade. Trading is an all-day, global endeavor, so in every 24-hour period Vanguard passes control of its trading book around the world from Australia to Europe and then the United States. The firm's trading partners in various stock markets are expected to provide "best execution" and consistently fair treatment. As broker-dealers have developed innovative algorithms to accumulate or distribute shares, a central question is which firms have the best trading tools. The volume of its business and the expertise of its index fund managers are so appealing that all major securities dealers want to be major service providers to Vanguard, even with its exacting requirements for excellent support by broker-dealers and its minimal per-trade commissions. The amount Vanguard pays in commissions is so low that it is proprietary information.

Vanguard's experienced traders knew well in advance that a "mother of all trades" was coming their way on December 18, 2020, when Standard & Poor's would make Tesla's stock part of the S&P 500. It would put index funds' expertise in trading to a severe test. Tesla was no ordinary stock. Prone to price gyrations, it had shot up nearly *sevenfold* during the past year—and over 40 percent just since S&P announced its intention to add it to the index. Tesla had not been added sooner because S&P required each newly included company to have at least four consecutive profitable quarters, a requirement aimed at keeping small, volatile stocks from fluttering in and out of the index. Tesla would be, on day one, the fifth largest stock in the index. The day it joined the S&P 500 would be the largest single day's trading in the history of replicating the largest index. The index funds would need to make enormous purchases of Tesla. In addition, all the actively managed funds that were benchmarked to the S&P 500 might be active, too. Of course, an equally large dollar volume of the other stocks in the index would have to be sold to make room for Tesla and have sufficient funds to simultaneously pay for the purchase.

All the other companies managing index funds would have the same mandate to sell 500 other stocks and buy Tesla. Total required buying and selling: $57 billion of Tesla buying *plus* $57 billion of selling. In addition, non-index traders would be looking for opportunities to take advantage of the necessary trading spree. As Comegys said, "It was a game of cat and mouse."[3] The scale of the trading could not have been even imagined 20 or 30 years ago. The obvious question for managers: Could all that trading be done without throwing the markets into turmoil? Fortunately, December 18 would be what traders call a "quadruple witching day" when futures and options expire simultaneously, so market liquidity would be extra high.

For the traders, it was game theory—anticipation of anticipations of other traders' anticipations of other traders. "Well in advance of that day, and particularly during the day, we had great information coming our way from sources on the Street," Comegys said. Never a trader himself, he would be relying on his team, some with

25 years of trading experience, to plan their strategies, anticipate all potential difficulties, and prepare appropriate responses. Vanguard would not, of course, have any contact with the other major index fund managers.

The real test came at the NYSE closing bell. While Tesla shares were up 6 percent, the capacity of the market to provide liquidity was certainly proven. In the end, the Tesla trade was like Y2K in the computer world: lots of alarmist anticipation followed by a nonevent—another triumph for well-informed experts operating in a free market.

Gus Sauter had worked for five other employers before he arrived at Vanguard. In his first week, he realized that Vanguard had a uniquely strong culture: "I knew in my first week at Vanguard that this was the firm I wanted to retire from at the end of my career. Everyone worked hard and there was a singular focus on doing what was right for the investors in the funds. Most investment firms, whether public or private, want to maximize profits for the owners of the *firm.* That can create a conflict of interests with the investors in the funds, as higher fees are better for the owners of the management company but worse for the investors in the funds. Vanguard is unique in the mutual fund industry in that it is owned by the funds themselves, which are, in turn, owned by the investors in the funds. So there is no profit to be generated for some other ownership group. This structure is part of the reason Vanguard had such a strong culture and such dedication to the investors in the funds."[4]

> **Vanguard is unique in the mutual fund industry in that it is owned by the funds themselves, which are, in turn, owned by the investors in the funds.**

When Sauter joined in October 1987, Vanguard had one internally managed equity index fund, the Vanguard 500 Index Fund, which had $1.2 billion in assets. Two weeks later, when the S&P 500 index plunged more than 22 percent in a single day, the fund's assets fell to $850 million. With his delight in ironic humor, he told the Vanguard board with a straight face, "Honestly, this is *not* my fault."

Persuading brokers to sell the first index fund had been hard (see Chapter 3). In the fall of 1987, before the Crash, Vanguard had planned to launch a second equity index fund in December, and now it certainly did not want another launch failure or even a major struggle. So in addition to dealing with the Crash and its aftermath, Sauter spent his first two months at Vanguard developing the needed software. The index chosen was the Wilshire 4500 Extended Market Index, covering not 500 but approximately 4,500 stocks. Academic research had shown that the "small firm effect" implied that a widely diversified portfolio would earn a higher rate of return, but with more volatile pricing. The computer algorithm to manage an S&P 500 index fund is not complicated. In fact, for a mathematician it's rather trivial. However, a different management technique is needed to manage an index fund tracking 4,500-plus stocks. A sampling process is used instead of the complete replication strategy used to manage an S&P 500 fund. Complete replication is simple, but sampling is far more complicated, requiring a much more complex computer model with a lot more math, and Vanguard did not have that model. "Looking back," Sauter now wryly says, "you learn a lot under those baptism-by-fire conditions. We worked *all* the time: late nights and weekends."

Sauter is modest about the surging growth in indexing: "Efficiency in pricing is what markets are supposed to do. And over time, that's what they *do*. Over time, markets become more and more efficient as they grow, attract more and different participants who obtain more and better information, and develop increasing skill, acquire better tools—particularly computers—and develop better and cheaper market clearing processes. Investment management is Darwinian: always deleting the weaker competitors so the continuing crowd gets better and better."

At the same time the equity group (then called Core Management, now the Quantitative Equity Group, or QEG) was developing the active quant lineup of funds, Vanguard ramped up its index offerings, launching Vanguard Small Cap Index Fund (1989), European Stock Index (1990), Pacific Stock Index (1990), Growth Index (1992), Value Index (1992), Balanced Index (1992), Emerging Markets Stock Index (1994) and Total International Stock Index (1996). In the middle of this proliferation, Jack Brennan approached Sauter and said, "Gus, we've decided to stop messing around. We're going to launch the true one-stop-shopping index fund." That was the Total Stock Market Index Fund, consisting of essentially all listed US stocks and launched on April 27, 1992.

In the month leading up to the launch, members of Jeremy Duffield's Planning and Development Group, of which Sauter's Core Management Group was a part, took guesses as to what the size of the assets would be at launch. For some perspective, the original S&P 500 Index Fund, launched in 1976, collected only $11.4 million, and 11 years later the second offering, the Extended Market Index Fund, gathered only $3.5 million. (For more perspective, the 500 Index Fund was launched on the heels of the significant 1973–74 bear market and the Total Stock Market Index Fund got off the ground shortly after the soft market of 1991.) To everyone's surprise, the Total Stock Market Index Fund gathered more than $100 million on its first day. Today, the Total Stock Market Index Fund is the largest mutual fund in the world. Assets topped $1 trillion in November 2020.

In the 1990s, local newspapers liked to organize "investor weekends" for individual investors. They were typically held in a convention center with exhibitors offering all kinds of investments or investment services. There would also be multiple large rooms for concurrent sessions on various investment topics and typically a large convention hall for a couple of keynote speeches. These investor conferences were open to anyone who wanted to hear interesting speakers, explore the exhibits, and generally learn more about investing. Sauter was a regular participant: "One year I spoke at about 25 of them, usually as a member of a three-person panel paired with two active managers who had recently had great performance—otherwise, of course, they would not be invited to speak. I was asked to present and defend the case for indexing, which was still in its infancy, not well understood and definitely not widely accepted."

He added: "The irony was that even though I had built and managed Vanguard's equity index group, the two funds that I personally managed were both active quant funds. That fact never came up, but over time many people have asked how Vanguard could justifiably offer both active and index funds. And that's because Vanguard's true 'religion' is low-cost investing, *not* active or passive. Both active and passive can have a place in an investor's portfolio, but only if they're low cost."[5]

Slowly but surely, indexing started to grow. In Sauter's view, three major catalysts ultimately propelled it to equal billing with active investing:

> **Both active and passive can have a place in an investor's portfolio, but only if they're low cost.**

- During the tech bubble in the last several years of the nineties, large-cap growth stocks, led by GE, Microsoft, Cisco, Intel, and others, helped the S&P 500, which is a large-cap index, outperform more than 90 percent of active mutual funds. At the time, the S&P 500 was synonymous with indexing, even though a total market index is a better representation of the market. Nothing attracts articles in the press—and cash flow—like major outperformance. That was the first huge spike up in indexed assets.

- When the tech, or dot-com, bubble burst at the beginning of the millennium, many investors were overweight in the once high-flying growth stocks. Many financial advisers had large positions of these stocks in their clients' portfolios. What goes up must come down; those stocks crashed as the bubble burst. This painful lesson reinforced perhaps the largest proposition of Modern Portfolio Theory—investors can reduce risk without reducing expected returns by diversifying their portfolios. Advisers and investors realized the need to diversify. No fund is more diversified than a total market index fund, so another huge wave of cash flowed into index funds, and in particular, total market index funds.

- The global financial crisis of 2008 had a profound impact on how people viewed the future of investing. Many, arguably most, people believed that economic growth would, for years and years, be much slower than historic rates of growth. In that case, it was presumed that investor returns would also be much lower than historic norms. The expectation of lower returns meant that fees were increasingly recognized as important to investor profit, so investors sought low-cost funds. Since index fund fees are only a fraction of the cost of an average active fund, this made them especially attractive, and a third wave of cash flow—a veritable tidal wave—rolled into index funds.

Underlying these major events has been index funds' outperforming most active funds for decades. Another is the increasing recognition, particularly at major corporations, that their fiduciary responsibilities under ERISA, the federal law that sets minimum standards for pension plans, were best met by using low-cost, widely diversified index funds.

When Vanguard's total equity-indexed assets surpassed $3 billion—up from $1 billion when Sauter started in 1987—Bogle appeared in the doorway of Sauter's office and said, "Gus, you wait, someday indexing will be really big. It will cross $10 billion in assets." At that time Sauter wondered if it would happen in his working career. When he retired in 2012, Vanguard had more than 100 times Bogle's hopeful estimate: $1 trillion in indexed assets. And indexing has since multiplied, to more than $5 trillion in 2022.

CHAPTER 9

EXCHANGE-TRADED FUNDS

"**G**us!" came a familiar booming, gravelly voice from the top of the stairs above the crowded grand foyer to the company cafeteria. "Gus! What the heck is going on around here?" Fresh back from his annual month-long vacation at Lake Placid, Jack Bogle was clearly upset.

Why? Because Gus Sauter had found a way to "destroy" Vanguard's indexing with an ETF! Or so Bogle seemed to think; he had opposed ETFs from "before the beginning."

Ever since the day he rejected Nathan Most's innovative idea of launching the first ETF,* Bogle had been opposed to ETFs and in favor of the conventional offering of index mutual funds. ETFs, he believed, were the mortal enemy of true investors because they would tempt investors to trade, and short-term trading almost always hurt returns. Index funds were the ally and friend of the long-term, buy-and-hold investor. Yes, they were boring, but that was their big advantage: Boring made it easier to stay invested, and staying invested was the key to long-term success.[1]

To explain "what the heck was going on?" you'd need to go back almost two years, to the beginning of 1998 when Sauter was concerned that the Asian financial crisis of 1997, known as the "Asian

---

* Most was head of new product development at the American Stock Exchange.

Contagion," could spread throughout the world. His fear was rein-forced later that year by the Russian debt crisis. Sauter had joined Vanguard exactly two weeks before the Crash of 1987, when the mar-ket melted down 22.61 percent in just one day. As he said, "We're shaped by our experiences, and that event definitely left a mark on me."

In reality, the redemptions from Vanguard's sole index fund dur-ing the Crash of '87 had been much less than those experienced by most equity funds. Still, Sauter feared that a similar event would have a far greater impact on Vanguard's funds because by 1998 the assets were so much bigger. If many investors redeemed their fund invest-ments, the funds would have to sell stock into a weak market to cover the redemptions.

Sauter had majored in math and economics at Dartmouth and enjoyed solving quantitative puzzles.[2] He saw the problem as a quan-titative challenge and decided to try to solve the dilemma. His first step was to recognize that conventional index funds and ETFs had one attribute in common: basic indexing. What distinguished them was the investors' primary purpose and the related decision criteria. Those investing in index funds expected to stay there for years. They had zero interest in hour-to-hour liquidity.* Those investing in ETFs *might* stay invested for many years, but they liked having the *option* to sell whenever they *might* decide to sell. Registered Investment Advisers, or RIAs, and their clients were an important part of this second group.

Historically, Vanguard had refused to offer sales support pay-ments to brokers and advisers for distribution, which most fund managers gladly did, so Vanguard got little help from RIAs and others. But ETFs were different. Traded on an exchange, ETFs gen-erated commissions. The challenge for Vanguard would be to win a share of the ETF volume going through that channel of distribution.

Sauter considered: Why not create an ETF "sleeve"—or index fund access vehicle—to the conventional index fund? That way, ETF investors could have both indexing and liquidity without causing disruption to the host index fund. Reversing the question, Sauter

---

* Unlike mutual funds, which are valued once daily, ETFs can be traded any time the markets are open. (For a more detailed discussion, see Appendix 1: "ETFs 101.")

devoted nine long months to exploring all the possible negatives he might have somehow missed. He kept asking colleagues in quantitative investing what could go wrong. He spent hours with colleagues in the legal department "looking for trouble." He challenged marketing people: Would this really meet the needs of RIAs and other financial intermediaries? Would they flock to Vanguard, and if so, why? Would demand be large enough to make it all worthwhile? By asking question after question, and then asking even more questions, Sauter became sufficiently confident that he had invented something of real value, and that, with some trepidation, he should finally take it up with Jack Brennan.

Brennan's initial reaction was skepticism, but the very next day—in the way college friends relate to each other—he admitted to Sauter that this might not be Sauter's worst idea. In truth, Brennan was enthusiastic, and said, "Gus, let's bring it up with the board right away."[3]

The board of directors approved moving ahead quickly. Then the pace returned to s-l-o-w while Vanguard sought SEC approval for this product: the first ETF based on an existing mutual fund. As a regulator of a notoriously creative industry, the SEC knows from experience to evaluate complex innovations with caution. All other ETFs were self-contained, so if investors rushed to sell, the ETF would simply wind down. If the ETF were directly linked to a large, existing mutual fund, what collateral damage might be forced onto the investors in the conventional shares of the fund that had nothing to do with the ETF shares? What unforeseen problem could the addition of ETF shares lead to for markets or for the regulators? A non-negative ruling—meaning regulators neither ban nor endorse the action—takes time; in this case, it took two full years for the SEC to agree that the amount of share selling would be the same, whether originating in the ETF shares or the index funds.[4]

One indicator of the "invention's" significance: Sauter's six patents related to ETFs. Vanguard launched its first ETFs in 2001 under the collective name Vipers. By structuring each ETF as a share class of one of its large, established index funds, Vanguard was able to use the scale advantage of the large fund and charge an expense ratio of only 0.15 percent—less than half the 0.35 percent expense ratio of market leader Barclays Global Investors (BGI). In 2006, it dropped the name Vipers and renamed its various ETFs simply Vanguard ETF. A full roster of Vanguard ETFs was soon produced; by March of 2007, it offered 32. ETFs were marketed as providing instant liquidity, and several sponsors disparaged traditional mutual funds for only allowing purchases and redemptions at the end of the day. What if investors wanted to get into a market that was soaring? ETFs provided the opportunity to get *in* at any time of the day. And if the market was collapsing, an investor could get *out* in the middle of the day, instead of having to wait until the end of the day. With that marketing theme, most people presumed that ETF clients were traders or speculators, not long-term investors. That was certainly Jack Bogle's view. His view *seemed* to be supported by the tremendous trading volume of the SPDR 500, the first ETF designed to track the S&P 500 Index.

Bogle believed ETF trading volume meant individuals must be doing the trading. He was making a big mistake. Most of the trading volume actually came from institutions, particularly hedge funds that frequently traded ETFs as a way to offset risk in their portfolios. ETF arbitrageurs also generated a lot of activity as they traded to keep ETFs close to their underlying portfolio values.

Short-term trading is not always speculation. To be obvious, a one-second in-and-out trade is not speculation. Nobody bets or speculates on what will happen in one second—or a tenth of a second. Even habitually long-term investors can have non-investment reasons for a short-term position. For example, when a pension fund or endowment terminates a manager, where does it "park" its money for one to three months while it searches for a new long-term manager?

Furthermore, a large and growing percentage of ETF trades are made by financial advisers for their clients. There was a presumption that advisers wanted the flexibility to be able to make a shorter-term call on the market if they chose to. But most financial advisers have a long-term view, and it didn't ring true to Sauter that they liked ETFs just for short-term investments.

Early in the millennium, many market participants, including financial advisers, began to talk about the possibility of offering actively managed ETFs. The advisers' interest in this wasn't clear to Sauter. In 2003, Vanguard hosted a conference for advisers in Chicago. He was a presenter and the night before the event,

Vanguard held a dinner for some of its larger adviser clients and prospects. Sauter was seated with five Registered Investment Advisers, and naturally all six were talking shop. The conversation had been friendly and candid, so Sauter decided it would be okay to ask the question that had been bothering him. "I understand why you would want the flexibility of trading that indexed ETFs provide, but I don't understand why you want *active* ETFs. Certainly no one believes they can time a manager's alpha."

The response was unanimous. It was *not* about timing managers. It was all about advisers' record-keeping platforms. They use a brokerage platform to keep the records for their clients, and buying an ETF fits nicely into the platform, just like a stock. You place an order at 11:03 a.m. and by 11:04 the execution is already recorded. The adviser knows instantly how many shares were bought and at what price. Traditional mutual funds don't fit so nicely into this system, since you place your order during the day but it's not executed until the market close. Then the mutual fund company has to calculate the price for the fund and process the trade. It could be 5 or 5:30 p.m. before the adviser and the client could know exactly how much they bought and at what price. It was all about ease of administration.

From the start, marketers have declared that ETFs were a great new product. Sauter contended that ETFs were *not* a new product. They were simply a way to distribute an old product—an index fund—through a new distribution channel. The advisers' response to his questions confirmed his belief.

They were simply a way to distribute an old product—an index fund—through a new distribution channel.

Before Vanguard offered ETFs, its business volume with advisers was a fairly small portion of Vanguard's assets. With this whole new way to distribute now open to advisers, that business has grown to more than $2.4 trillion.

PART THREE

Organization Builders

CHAPTER 10

CHANGEOVER

Jack Bogle and Jack Brennan were for many years a rewardingly balanced team—Mr. Outside and Mr. Inside, CEO and COO, working father and son. Both believed deeply in the Vanguard mission of serving investors with solid investments and good service at low cost with high integrity. During their first 15 years, they found many ways to enjoy working together. Both were frugal: simple offices, mid-range cars, off-the-rack suits. (Bogle's well-worn suits looked old, Brennan's were well pressed and replaced sooner.) As they worked together, they were increasingly impressed with each other.

Both put in long hours. Both were facile with numbers. Each was finding the other wonderfully complementary in skills and interests, and they knew they were making great progress in developing Vanguard toward its potential. The two soon developed a familial relationship: they were in and out of each other's offices multiple times a day to share information or ideas, and usually had lunch together. Friends believed Bogle had an even closer and stronger relationship with Brennan than he had with his own children. (He did make Brennan trustee for the children's trusts.) Both believed in long hours at work and, in what may have been an early red-light signal, both were highly competitive. Bogle's brother told of Bogle's saying, "I used to get to work at 7:30, but then Brennan came at 7, so I started to come at 7. Then Brennan started to get there at 6:30, so I started being there at 6:30." He could never let Brennan be first.

As Brennan settled into his new job as Bogle's assistant, he became increasingly aware of several key factors: he liked his position and its prospects even more than he had expected; his managerial skills and interests were more in demand than he had expected; and the long-term opportunities at Vanguard were wider and deeper than he had realized. People warned Brennan that Bogle had impossibly high standards. Brennan saw that as a great learning opportunity.

Brennan had no trouble deferring to Bogle in the early years and no trouble being designated as Bogle's assistant, as so many others had been before going on to great careers. Promotions came swiftly. Both knew they were on an interesting and exciting adventure, and had many reasons to believe they were on their way to a major success. Brennan couldn't say enough good things to express his admiration of Bogle.

In the 1990s, by then president, Brennan was a quietly bold user of computers despite knowing Bogle's resistance to the technology's dismaying upfront costs. Bogle, still enamored with his slide rule, had not objected so long as computers were confined to back-office operations, where he had little interest. Still, he persistently dismissed computers as too expensive, waving away talk of the operational savings that would make those investments pay off. Brennan moved quietly to install computers and search for opportunities to use technology as an alternative to labor both to reduce costs and to increase value, particularly in services to clients. Because so many operational aspects of financial services are relatively routine, this strategy proved highly productive. Rivals such as Fidelity and T. Rowe Price were so far ahead in automation that catching up—or at least not being left even further behind—had become a competitive imperative.

In the long arc of their time together, the two Jacks might have been seen as surefire exemplars of an ideal transition in leadership. But that would eventually prove impossible. Years before, the personal forces driving Bogle had led Jim Riepe to realize that Bogle could not and so would not relinquish or even share control as CEO. The board of directors pleaded with Riepe to stay and assured him of eventually becoming CEO, but once he had come to understand Bogle, he realized that he would need to leave Vanguard to have the career he wanted.

Brennan and Bogle had fundamentally different concepts of organizational leadership. These differences became more visible with time and Brennan's rapidly expanding responsibilities. One difference hadn't mattered in the early stages of the relationship. Brennan was not offended by Bogle's habitual use of the possessive "my"—as in "my company" or "my leadership"—when discussing Vanguard in public. After all, it had been exactly that in the beginning. Yes, Vanguard had a board of directors, but Bogle saw it as his board. He had recruited each of them and believed they joined because they wanted to be part of the wonderful work he was doing with Vanguard.

It never seemed to bother Brennan when Bogle took credit for advancements that had been conceived and developed by Brennan, such as the Partnership Plan, the Swiss Army, and connecting with Primecap. If Bogle cared so much about being celebrated publicly, so be it.

Always pragmatic, Brennan cared about the progress of the whole Vanguard organization. As a veteran team player in lacrosse, hockey, and soccer, he cared little about personal recognition but greatly about the team winning. Brennan was and is modest: "Being famous was never part of my agenda."

These personal differences may be tolerated in the short or even medium term, but as time passes and examples accumulate, they can go from tolerable, to troublesome, to difficult, to annoying, to unacceptable. Brennan had a thick skin and a deep appreciation for Bogle's capabilities, so he was able to take the long view. Near-term tolerance and patience made great sense for anyone with a long-term perspective and ample time for transition. After all, Vanguard's policy requiring retirement at 70 had been set by Bogle and Riepe many years before, and Bogle's health was clearly compromised and declining.

> "Being famous was never part of my agenda."

Bogle was the classic entrepreneurial founder: tough, creative, decisive, unrelenting; driven to succeed and self-confident; skeptical of the capabilities or commitments of others, though sure that he sought others' best ideas; and, on all sorts of decisions, controlling. A small indication of his need for control was his compulsion to restructure, reorganize, and edit almost every sentence of every memo or report he had insisted others prepare. Bogle was proudly a fighter and liked battles. He not only enjoyed winning, but also enjoyed defeating his adversary. In contrast, Brennan saw fights and battles as a waste of energy and time.

As military history has shown again and again, while success on the attack usually produces the most exciting adventure stories, the absolute imperative for sustained success is good governance long after the sound and fury of combat have passed. Bright and quick and right so often, Bogle had learned to trust his own instincts and judgment. But astute as he was, the odds of being always right on every matter were obviously stacked against him. Defining himself as *the* leader and dismissing all those who were "mere managers," he did not recognize, as Vanguard grew, the accelerating need for skillful, collegial managers and sustained, systematic processes throughout the organization. As the business grew and grew, Bogle's perceptions understandably tended to be retrospective rather than prospective. He knew and took justified pride in how far Vanguard had come. But it was hard to see as clearly how much Vanguard needed to change how it operated to continue achieving what it had promised, explicitly and implicitly, to each of its rapidly increasing number of investors.

> The absolute imperative for sustained success is good governance long after the sound and fury of combat have passed.

Brennan progressed rapidly in responsibilities and in titles. He became CFO in 1985, executive vice president and a member of the board of directors a year later, and president in 1989. He was just 34. At the directors' urging, Bogle began to encourage Brennan to give public speeches, meet with large investors, and discuss major strategy decisions with the board of directors. Brennan recognized the need for strong managers in one part of Vanguard after another, so he went looking for the experienced business managers now needed.

Brennan was a professional manager—a "servant leader," always striving to find ways for Vanguard to improve at every level. Modest, deliberate, and steady, he liked building teams and developing a strong organization centered on systems and process. He looked for ways to upgrade the capabilities of middle and senior managers, and their teamwork. Managers gained confidence and strength by joining Brennan to set realistic objectives that were matched with rigorous performance reviews. Promising managers rotated every few years from one managerial responsibility to another, gaining in-depth understanding of other parts of the Vanguard organization.

In his 1992 sacred-cows speech, Bogle declared that Vanguard would strive to be the industry's technology leader. Brennan spread responsibility for technology throughout the company and warned senior managers that their jobs depended on their mastering technology, saying, "If [then head of institutional business Jim] Gately lacks the technology ability to be successful, then Gately gets fired, not [technology chief Robert] DiStefano."

Bogle was still clearly CEO, the inspirational leader of the enterprise and the principal decision maker who managed the board of directors and made all public announcements and spoke with the media. But directors knew that Brennan was the agent of change—advocating investments in information technology to increase the speed and convenience of shareholder services and expand capacity to ensure growth in number of accounts, transactions, and dollars; bringing down costs so Vanguard could keep reducing the funds' expense ratios; and developing a stronger and larger team of experienced, able managers.

Brennan recognized that Vanguard's management was stretched in several areas. In ETFs, a major innovation that Bogle had dismissed years before, State Street and others were establishing a commanding market share in a rapidly growing sector. Indexing was attracting stronger competition, so Vanguard needed to be even more innovative and aggressive. The institutional business, while a major opportunity, particularly with the surging growth of 401(k) plans, was indifferently managed and losing market share and money. More broadly, Vanguard's many units were increasingly siloed and separated. Vanguard was missing the bottom-up, close-to-the-market awareness needed for an effective business development strategy.

Jim Gately, a mid-career financial services executive with senior managerial promise, had been recruited from the pension division of Prudential in 1989 by Jack Brennan to solve a problem. Because

Vanguard focused on retail, whatever institutional business that "came in over the transom" was taken catch as catch can. In the fast-growing institutional market, Vanguard had no defined objectives, no clear strategy, no defined target market, no clarity on what the firm wanted salespeople to sell, no consistent pricing policies, little leadership or management, and no support from headquarters. Salespeople in the institutional division were on their own and were expected to improvise. So they did. Beyond selling Vanguard's mutual funds and record-keeping capabilities, all decisions on what was offered to corporate prospects—even what fees and service standards were promised—were controlled by individual sales representatives, whose main focus was getting a new account and getting their incentive compensation.

This guaranteed trouble for the people in the Operations Group back at Vanguard. They were expected to deliver on the sales commitments and promises, but had no say in what was being promised. "As might be anticipated in such a set-up," recalled Gately, Vanguard was winning only small 401(k) plans by making big commitments for special services. To make matters worse, the sales promises differed a lot from customer to customer. "It was a grab bag of clients and a grab bag of commitments," the direct opposite of how a business should operate.

The salespeople were effectively working for themselves, not for Vanguard. They scrambled to close sales, any sales, and pocket their bonuses. Few looked back to see how things had worked out. So, Gately found, "Vanguard was not learning from experience and was not improving in any way: not in product design, not in service capabilities, not in pricing and not even in sales process. And nobody knew which accounts or which lines of business might be made profitable or which were serious losers."[1]

Brennan had been candid with Gately: "The unit needs focus. We've already decided it should come out of Retail and become a stand-alone Institutional business unit. We have a consultant's study of the opportunities in the corporate market that shows that the 401(k) retirement plan business is destined to boom." Plan sponsors had no great love for traditional "defined benefit" pensions because of increased regulations, charges for Pension Benefit Guaranty Corporation insurance, and the uncertain impact on earnings from

CHANGEOVER

be factored into current earnings reports. Employees did not all like
the traditional defined benefit plans either. If workers left within five
years of starting, they got zero benefits. There was usually no protection from inflation, and that worried workers a lot, since the 1970s
Not only was the 401(k) business sure to be fast growing,
there were only three major providers: Fidelity, T. Rowe Price, and
Vanguard. Fidelity was by far the largest and, with a clear strategy
Gately was getting really interested. "Jack, is there a job description?" "Yeah," Brennan replied with a smile, "and it comes in two
parts: First, figure out what to do. Second, get it done!" That sold
Gately.[2]
All he knew for certain was that the business unit he was taking over was saddled with a very high expense ratio, not growing as it
should, and not headed in any particular strategic direction. He saw
major changes were needed. He also soon decided that most of the
salespeople would have to be replaced. Of 15, he kept 3.
New salespeople without bad habits were recruited. Many were
Vanguard saw an ideal opportunity to join Gately in a promising new
ing them experts on Vanguard and on the needs of carefully selected
prospects. By starting afresh with a new sales team, Gately could
change the entire direction of the unit. Known for calm optimism,
Gately learned that, surrounded with challenges, he was "free to
Next came a typically savvy move by Brennan. He assigned a cluster of rising stars from various areas of Vanguard to work with Gately: Paul Heller, Martha King, Greg Barton, and Bill McNabb. Gately and his new team quickly developed a "strategic tripod" to build the 401(k) business:

> Gately learned that, surrounded with challenges, he was "free to attack in all directions."

- Vanguard would focus on its major competitive strength: low-cost investing in stocks, bonds, and money market funds.

- Each new corporate prospect would be qualified, using a simple checklist of what Vanguard was really looking for in new clients. To ensure consistency, qualifying was centralized in a small steering committee of people from Operations and Legal. Sales reps were strongly encouraged to concentrate their time and effort on the most attractive prospects— 401(k) plans that Vanguard really wanted for the long term and prospects that would really want what Vanguard was best able to deliver. Gately explained, "We were looking to build a strong portfolio of clients that we knew we could serve really well and that Vanguard would want to keep forever. We developed special educational programs for our crew and were able to demonstrate to our clients and prospects that if their key people developed a solid understanding of why best practices were important in designing their 401(k) plans, they would actually save money by adopting those practices."

- Salespeople would be trained to understand and take advantage of an important reality of selling 401(k) plans in the corporate market. Almost always, success depended on two separate sales successes: one in finance to the treasurer or a deputy specializing in pensions, and another with the head of human resources. Often, particularly in larger corporations, these executives would not know each other well and might even be jealous, turf-protecting rivals. Special sales skills were often needed to complete a successful two-level sale.

Geographically, Gately and his new team began with the companies near the Vanguard headquarters outside Philadelphia. As sales and service resources grew, they expanded to the mid-Atlantic region and then, by stages, nationwide. Gately recalled, "Every time we were able to get included in a competition, we offered prospects two great choices: index funds or Windsor Fund with John Neff. Later we also offered Primecap with a great growth stock record or Batterymarch, then a remarkable investment innovator. Fidelity would counter by putting up Peter Lynch during the era when his Magellan Fund was having great performance. Fidelity had a big advantage in pricing. Because most mutual funds had wide profit margins, particularly on incremental business, Fidelity could offset any losses on record keeping with high mutual fund fee income. Since our funds already operated at cost, we couldn't do that. But once we got properly organized, we went about 50-50 overall in competitions against Fidelity. Low cost was the key to our success."

Asked for one tip he always gave his salespeople, Gately smiled and said, "Make your client look smart to his boss."

Developing a strong service culture, according to Gately, depends on "knowing how to keep your best people." Vanguard was able to keep Gately for 27 years. To signal how important they were to Vanguard, he gave the best relationship managers a special title: relationship executive. They gathered together for an annual dinner and got an extra share in the Partnership Plan.

> "Make your client look smart to his boss."

Years later, when he was heading the 401(k) business, Bill McNabb met monthly with a group of relationship executives, each giving a 10-minute "highlights" presentation of what they were seeing and hearing in the field. This sort of commitment from senior managers to understand marketplace realities was meaningful to the front-line salespeople, underlining how valuable their work was to the firm and that their challenges were recognized.

In 1994, Jack Brennan asked Gately to move over to the Individual Investor group. "My first reaction was to say, 'Jack, this comes as a real surprise, and I have to admit I don't quite get it. Why are you asking me? Retail would be entirely new for me. I don't know anything about retail except that it's very different from the institutional business where I've spent my whole career.' Several days later, I found myself thinking, if your boss knows you and respects your capabilities, and thinks a particular spot would be good for you and good for the organization, you might be wise to give it some serious consideration." Brennan believed that regular rotations kept leader-managers from complacency, that they reenergized themselves, learned to think about "whole Vanguard" and brought fresh thinking, different experiences, objectivity, and energy to their new units. Soon

Gately was heading up the Individual Investors Group and achieving another success.

"After a year or so, just as Jack had predicted when he surprised me with my new assignment, I was loving retail. We segmented the individual investor market and introduced Admiral Share pricing: 'even lower than low fees' for large accounts. In addition, we developed several types of specialists to focus on different groups of individual investors: IRA specialists, 403(b) specialists, large 'Flagship' investor specialists, etc."[3]

> Brennan believed that regular rotations kept leader-managers from complacency, that they reenergized themselves, learned to think about "whole Vanguard" and brought fresh thinking, different experiences, objectivity, and energy to their new units.

For Bogle and Brennan, the coming change in command over several years looked only moderately more difficult than other similar changes. They were each "age appropriate," comparably committed to Vanguard and, thanks to Brennan's having no need for the limelight, their priorities did not visibly conflict. Both were devoted to Vanguard's being the best Vanguard that Vanguard could be. But they differed in personality and style, in their interest in recognition, and in their emphasis on distributed management strength versus centralized command leadership, among other things.

Leadership transitions may appear natural and easy from the outside, but seldom are. Even if management style, corporate strategy, and personalities are all closely aligned, change is usually hard for the individuals most directly involved. Taking control, power, stature, and significance away from a driven leader is no gentle act.

Brennan—private, modest, and humorously self-effacing—would later be comfortable quietly easing out of the CEO position at only age 55, chuckling at how anonymous he had always been. Bogle, 30 years his senior, was still described by friends as a "complete media hound"[4] who couldn't stop citing his "never-ending examples of rhetorical brilliance or citing passages from his own speeches verbatim off the top of his head."[5] And then Bogle would carefully project humility with self-deprecations such as "I'm an extremely ordinary human being" or "my brothers were both smarter" or "the fact that I'm not brilliant is Vanguard's greatest asset."

Brennan had an unusual ability to lead a collaborative team of senior managers to its highest performance. His general counsel, Heidi Stam, recalled, "Basically, we were brothers and sisters who looked out for one another and didn't mind calling each other out when we disagreed. It was never personal. We persuaded each other with reasoning and kept open minds, and when we reached a conclusion we were all in with our support for the decision. We were expected to and genuinely wanted to help our colleagues by giving them people of talent and funding out of our own division's budget if it was for the overall good of Vanguard. There was no tolerance for anyone who was not a team player, and Jack never put anyone on the senior team who wasn't a team player."

Brennan increasingly demonstrated his capabilities as a leader and his versatility: integrating technology with organizational units, transforming business units, identifying and engaging future leaders, and moving the whole organization forward in new directions and upward in standards of performance. The board of directors, and particularly chairman J. Lawrence Wilson, recognized that Brennan was demonstrating how effective a leader he would be. The timing seemed right. Brennan was coming up just as Bogle, who had been increasingly seriously ill, would be going into retirement. Some felt his retirement was coming somewhat later than optimal for Vanguard, but Bogle had achieved so much in the past that many felt it would have been unfair to push him out sooner.

Directors knew it was their responsibility to provide balanced judgment on the timing of the transition. They knew Bogle's focus on costs made him too reluctant to invest substantially in computer power and automation as key competitors were doing. As Vanguard grew in scale and complexity, it would need a different organizational structure to serve many more investors in more markets with more and better services.

Directors understood the need to switch from a pioneering entrepreneur founder to an organization builder-manager and knew making that change was their responsibility. By early 1995, it was clear that it was time for Brennan to become CEO and for Bogle to enjoy well-earned retirement. At a distance, the transition from

Bogle to Brennan seemed a perfect illustration of the classic sequence from entrepreneurial founder-proprietor to professional manager and organization developer.

Brennan was the only colleague Bogle told in advance of his May 24, 1995, announcement to the board of directors that he would step aside as CEO on January 31, 1996—but would, if approved by the board, continue as senior chairman. The press release announcing his retirement quoted Bogle as saying, "I will still be around," and explained that Brennan would not become CEO for seven months.

Bogle's cardiologist declared that his condition was "progressing"— getting worse—and that his chances of living even one more year were in jeopardy. His hands and feet were badly swollen, and he had difficulty breathing or walking. Bogle needed a heart transplant— soon. Then, because his condition was so terrible, he was upgraded on the waiting list for a transplant.

On October 18, 1995, he went into Philadelphia's Hahnemann University Hospital to wait for his new heart. Bogle being Bogle, he organized his hospital room into an office with a computer, telephone, and files. He continued writing articles, memos, and letters, and made frequent phone calls to the Vanguard crew, to clients, and of course to his many friends in the media. Brennan visited with Bogle in his hospital "office" at least two or three times a week, and on Christmas Eve was there with his wife and kids to cheer the patient.

During the four months of waiting for the transplant and the subsequent months of Bogle's recuperation, Brennan was pouring it on at Vanguard to forge ahead on automation and computerization. He organized a rigorous evaluation of every major aspect of the organization and developed a complete reconceptualization of the management structure and staffing. He pressed a transformation of Vanguard operations, which had fallen behind the competition. Organizational capacity expanded and productivity increased to accommodate the burgeoning volume of transactions.

For all those months, the nurses had been treating Bogle with the deference accorded senators, corporate CEOs, movie stars, and major hospital donors. Finally, on February 21, 1996, a nurse confirmed: "Well, Mr. Bogle, today is certainly your big day. After all your patient waiting, it proves the proverb: All things come to he who waits."

"Yes and no, nurse."

"Meaning what, Mr. Bogle?"

"Yes, it's a big day for me on a personal level. After waiting 128 days in this hospital, never being sure of ever getting one in time, we now know that before the day is over, I'll have a new heart, thank the Lord. But no. No, it wasn't patience, nurse; it's never patience. It's always personal commitment: deciding what you want to accomplish, figuring out how to make it happen and then having the courage to press on regardless with great commitment, the commitment of the individual in the ring, in the action."[6]

The heart transplant was a great success. Bogle's luck provided him with a 28-year-old's heart which, combined with Bogle's drive and determination, made his recovery—in both speed and degree—simply phenomenal. He was home from the hospital in just nine days. Six weeks later, he was back in his office. Day after day, he felt stronger. On May 8, his sixty-seventh birthday, he gave a rousing speech on the benefits of indexing. A few days later, he was hitting balls in a squash court. Said an admiring friend, "It was absolutely amazing to see him playing squash again. And it's very clear that if he'd known that he'd come out of the surgery and feel the way he did, he would never have given up the CEO position in the first place."

Some directors worried that Brennan might have already lost his edge—the will to lead—after 14 years of serving under Bogle. Others believed the opposite: that those years of experience had compressed Brennan's energy and drive, like a coiled spring, into an even stronger and more determined sense of purpose. As directors discussed the leadership transition, they became increasingly clear about how much Brennan had already been effectively the real CEO responsible for several strategic decisions he had carried out.

While Bogle had epitomized Vanguard and its beliefs externally, Brennan, as chief operating officer, had been crucial to its internal success. Brennan designed the Partnership Plan after recognizing a need, borrowing the idea from his prior employer and adapting it for Vanguard (see Chapter 6). Sending Jim Gately in to diagnose and then revamp the floundering institutional business into a major success exemplified Brennan's talent for delegating strategic initiatives to other leader-managers instead of insisting on being the locus of control like Bogle. He supported leaders like Gately or Bill McNabb with a cluster of talented, young, ambitious teammates so they would have many hands and eyes to figure out major managerial problems. Rotating able people at all levels from one assignment to another challenged them to develop different skills and see themselves not in a job, but in a career. They learned about Vanguard as a whole and how each of the major parts connects with and can best relate with other parts.

"Brennan sought people who are different: different in skills and experiences, different in the way they think about big issues, whether problems or opportunities," managing director Michael Miller said. "He believed that the search for people with real differences is the key to true diversity, the best protection against groupthink, the best way to assure creativity. Each senior manager had a different perspective, a different previous history or a different experience. We knew each of us had been selected for that reason, so we became great believers in airing different views. But once a decision had been agreed, Jack always expected all of us to line up in support of and make a 100 percent commitment to the success of that collective decision. When he committed to Six Sigma as a disciplined approach to problem solving, Jack would not let go. He changed the program from GE's model to Vanguard's Unmatchable Excellence and he was determined to make it work for Vanguard."[7]

Brennan was confident of his ability to identify and develop future leaders. He'd been doing just that at Vanguard since he had first arrived. At one of the first management offsites he attended, Bogle had noticed. After the meeting, he turned to Brennan: "I know what you were doing. Evaluating everyone. So give me your report."

Looking for favorable surprises but also quick to see mistakes, Brennan took notes on people and their responsibilities so he would always have them at hand. He was always looking for leaders and managers with strong growth potential such as Gus Sauter, Mike Miller, Heidi Stam, Bob DiStefano, Glenn Reed, Jim Gately, Tim Buckley, and Bill McNabb. He thought productively about how and why candidates might become well matched to the responsibilities of each new position. What will she add? What will he be able to learn? How will this particular assignment help develop this particular manager's career at Vanguard?

Mistakes have been few but can be painful. "What really bothers us now," Brennan said, "is when we decide, after three years of experience at Vanguard, that a man or woman is not working out, and we go back and look and see our assessments had identified the key problem the person had—three years ago!" Then, with his eyebrows rising, Brennan shares the lesson: "You can't teach brains and you can't teach character."[8]

Naturally, every time anyone is advanced to a new role, at least several others will wonder, "Why not me?" So, instead of thinking just about who will be best for this role, Brennan thought about the "not chosen" and figured out beforehand what to say and when to say it to them, because they too are important to the organization.

Every year Brennan averaged nearly 200 of his skip-level meetings with those who reported to his direct reports, usually at a quiet lunch table off to the side in the Galley. (Do the math: these meetings were clearly a top priority.) The participants were guaranteed that their comments would be held in confidence. Brennan was completely open with these colleagues. Some were intimidated at first, or worried that they were being "taken to the woodshed." But he was so low key, and so obviously interested in learning, that virtually everyone soon relaxed and opened up—to everyone's benefit, particularly Vanguard's. Brennan observed: "Top-level people are always 'selling' their policies and strategies to folks on the firing line and need to know what the people on the firing line are hearing and accepting . . . and what they are not 'buying' and why not. Meanwhile, those on the firing line want to know what top-level executives don't fully understand or appreciate."

> Instead of thinking just about who will be best for this role, Brennan thought about the "not chosen" and figured out beforehand what to say and when to say it to them, because they too are important to the organization.

Operating in the highly regulated securities industry, Brennan made special efforts to know and be known by government regulators. He invited them to meet with senior staff and directors so key people at Vanguard would understand how the regulators were thinking about the industry, about Vanguard and about the major issues in front of them and coming up. And the regulators got to know and appreciate Vanguard.

Readers will recognize how important each of these practices was in developing the collaborative culture at Vanguard and to its remarkable transformation from a small proprietorship to a large organization capable of growing into an investment industry leader that serves tens of millions of investors unusually well. Today Vanguard is entrusted with more retail investor assets than the combined assets of the three next largest competitors and has compelled its competitors to adopt two of its main strategic thrusts: lower fees and offering investors more advice. As Brennan observed, "The long-term thinking and behavior required for successful investing is different from the transactional focus of traditional investment services that dominated the investment industry in the past. Vanguard is moving out to intercept and succeed with this profound transformation just when investors are recognizing their need for a different kind of investment service that is centered on sound, customized advice."

In 1999, Bogle turned 70, the age of mandatory retirement at Vanguard. He assumed the retirement-at-70 policy he and Riepe had established many years before would not apply to him; after all, he was the founder. When the directors realized how upset Bogle was about holding to his own policy, they were amenable to his staying on a year longer as senior chairman. Bogle saw this as a token gesture and refused.

Bogle was upset by a quote from a source in the *Philadelphia Enquirer*, "If you have been happy with Vanguard during the past three years you have Jack Brennan to thank for that," and reacted typically: "There was a bull market, and I think the company's success might have something to do with index funds and managers I chose, the structure of the company—all of which I take responsibility for. To credit that to someone else is extraordinary, unbelievable, and irresponsible."

Some fund shareholders, not knowing the nature of the board of directors' extensive discussions, reacted to the retirement news on the Vanguard Investors' Forum maintained by Morningstar, suggesting that as a mutual fund organization, Vanguard should put such critical policy matters to a vote by the shareholders. One shareholder caught the thinking of the dissidents: "No matter how difficult it is to live with The Saint, management should realize that it is counterproductive—if not self-destructive—to make him a martyr in the house he founded, especially now that he has become a symbol of Integrity and Honesty in a world almost synonymous with fraudulence and back-stabbing."

"Memo to Vanguard: Have you lost your *minds*?" Jim Cramer, cofounder of thestreet.com, an investing website, said. "You can't kick John Bogle off the board like he's just some sort of old guy that needs to be sent to the mutual fund pasture. . . . He is the only person willing to speak freely about how mutual funds routinely overcharge people and don't give you value versus the index funds."

Although most who commented online wanted Bogle to stay, some were not upset. "I'll hate to see the day when the old, contentious warhorse Mr. Bogle is gone from the scene, but I see no evidence that Vanguard will suffer much for it," a writer named "Mohuck" posted on Morningstar's site. "Bogle isn't the sum total of Vanguard, and I think Mr. Brennan, the current directorship and management are positioning the company correctly in order for it to maintain its leadership position in the rapidly changing financial services industry."

As Jack Bogle saw it, the obvious move was for him to return as chairman of the board and take up the leadership of Vanguard again, right where he had been obliged to leave off. He felt great and was increasingly focused on the future—his future at Vanguard, which he always described as "my company." But by then, Jack Brennan was established as CEO and making great progress in developing a strong leadership team and catching up in technology.

When Bogle later learned about the accelerated investment in computers (and a modest increase in advertising), he expressed his objections clearly: "My company is going to hell!" But the board of directors did not agree. The change in leadership was working well, even better than expected, and the directors were determined to do all they could to help the new leadership succeed. They were relieved and delighted to see Brennan performing so effectively as CEO. They were most certainly not going to displace him now—particularly since Bogle was so close to the mandatory retirement age of 70 he himself had set long ago.[9]

Bogle rejected that thinking. Surely an exception could and should be made for Vanguard's founder! But the directors stood firm. When asked by a TV reporter, "Are you happy with Brennan as your successor?" Bogle replied, "Happy? Not really. I'm not really so sure he's ready for all that responsibility just yet." Brennan was stunned and confronted Bogle directly: "After all I did for you all those times, you go public with a statement doubting I can do the job as CEO? You are not *so sure* of me?" The cord of trust and confidence had been broken.

Informed observers, then and now, agree unanimously that without Bogle, Vanguard could never have come into being or developed into an early success. Bogle established Vanguard as a low-cost, low-fee provider with a high-integrity culture focused on investors' long-term success. Bogle was present at the creation. He made it happen. Through force of will, persistence, impassioned persuasion, clever legal maneuvers, and crucial lucky breaks, he lifted Vanguard from a narrowly limited, small entity into a new kind of investment company. As Burt Malkiel, Bogle's close friend and a long-serving Vanguard director, put it, "Vanguard could never have been conceived, launched, or made successful in its early years without the unrelenting drive, determination, and creativity of Jack Bogle *and* Vanguard could never have become the great success it so clearly has become without Jack Brennan taking over as CEO."

The directors had great affection for Bogle, and they tried time and again to find ways for him to leave graciously. But it was taking an unusually long time to negotiate the final terms of his separation agreement. Finally, Bogle understood that the board would not go any further, and that he would be wise to accept the final offer or risk seeing it start to unwind. Vanguard agreed to provide Bogle with a three-person staff, generous annual expenses, an office suite in the main Vanguard building in Malvern, Pennsylvania, access to Vanguard's computers and its extensive database, plus a car and driver—and an unusually large one-time payout. Bogle accepted.[10]

When Brennan learned the magnitude of that settlement, he went for a long, long run.

Taking the long view of the history of Vanguard thus far, both Brennan and Bogle "won." Jack Bogle was driven to win recognition and fame that would save him from his fear of being forgotten and make his many great contributions worth remembering and admiring. As the next chapter will show, those hopes have been more than fulfilled.

Jack Brennan, not interested in whether or how the world would perceive him, quietly concentrated on converting Vanguard into an effective, self-sustaining, large-scale, persistently innovative, continuous-process organization 10 times the size of the outfit he took over. He left it fully capable of self-financing bold strategic moves to create its own future, and to change the global investment management industry again—and again.

CHAPTER 11

BOGLE'S LEGACY

When Bogle left his office as senior chairman in 1999 to go to a small suite of offices on a second floor in the same building, ironically named Victory, he did not go alone nor empty-handed. Besides the staff of three, ample time on Vanguard's computers, full access to its huge data resources, and the car and driver—all at no cost to him—Bogle had his superb network of relationships with editors and reporters, built up over many years.

Jack Bogle was easy to admire for his remarkable creative talents, his undeniable charm (unless you dared to oppose him), his exceptional facility with numbers, the years he continued working long hours, the strength of his convictions, and the range of his command of facts and figures in support of his decisions and beliefs. He was admirable for his capacity to endure fortune's outrages as a child and as a young man, and for his success in school and college. He survived a long series of heart attacks that nearly took his life, ascended to the top of one of the first mutual fund organizations, overcame dismissal by the company he had tried to transform with an innovative merger, experienced an unwelcome retirement from the company he had organized and built up from nearly nothing, and, in retirement, burnished a superb public reputation for integrity and truth-telling through his work at the Bogle Financial Markets Research Center.

He projected almost a religious moral authority. "It's fair to say I'm a missionary. Give me a cause and I'll run with it as far as it will go." Commenting on Bogle's moral rectitude, an admirer said, "No question, he had a holier-than-thou attitude." He exuded conviction. Most people with direct contact with Bogle were intimidated by him. He was demanding, particularly concerning the sanctity of his reputation and his carefully curated personal story.

One of Bogle's charms as he set out on his long crusade for everyday investors was his disarming self-deprecation: "I was plain stupid." "How could anyone have made the mistakes I made?" He never complained about the hardships of his childhood. He always revered his mother. Reporters would see him tear up with recollections of her suffering as he allowed them into his private memories, but they might not know that he was always "on script," in perfect control—down to the right moment to shed tears. He had a personal story to tell and made sure that story would always be reported exactly as he told it every time.

Friends who knew him well recognized his deeply felt insecurity and his fear of being forgotten. His books were one way of being remembered. That may be why he revised his writing so many times. Striving for perfection may be why two or three times a year he would meet with his fellow Princetonian, the exemplary writer and teacher John McPhee, to seek advice on particular aspects of his writing.

Nothing helps a lone advocate gain attention and credibility quite so much as having apostles take up his message and carry it on to others. For Jack Bogle, such a pleasing development began with the founding of a group of individual investors that began as posters on a Morningstar online forum in March 1998 and would soon call themselves the "Bogleheads."

When Taylor Larimore, an investor and former paratrooper, posted, "I thank Jack Bogle and Vanguard—first for their unsurpassed educational tools, second for providing an investment service that is unsurpassed," Bogle promptly sent a handwritten letter saying he was inspired by Taylor's post and asking if "there would be any interest in a conference of like-minded people for a day at a convenient (non-resort, I think) location?" Larimore and Mel Lindauer organized the first meeting of what would become the Bogleheads around Bogle's scheduled speech at the *Miami Herald*'s

> **Nothing helps a lone advocate gain attention and credibility quite so much as having apostles take up his message and carry it on to others.**

"Meeting Money" seminar in March 2000. Twenty-two gathered for dinner with Bogle at Larimore's Miami condo. Obviously encouraged by Larimore, the *Herald* described the event in that Sunday's business section. The next annual event was in Philadelphia; Bogleheads heard a talk by Jason Zweig, who then wrote a five-page story for *Money*, where he was then a senior writer. Its title: "Here Come the Bogleheads."[1]

In 2007 the Bogleheads launched their independent website, bogleheads.org. By 2009, it had over 20,000 registered members with an average of over 9,000 visits each day. Adding face-to-face meetings, 38 local chapters now gather periodically to discuss investments and investing. Momentum and press coverage continued to build. Holding meetings where Bogle was speaking made logistics almost easy.

Through the website, the group makes this set of Bogle-centric rules for successful investing widely available:

- Develop a workable financial and investment plan that you put in writing and keep revising as you learn more about yourself, your finances, and investing.

- Invest early in life and often. Having your chosen amount of saving automatically transferred from your checking account at the same time your pay goes in is strongly recommended.

- Never bear too much or too little risk.

- Never try to time the market.

- Use index funds when possible.

- Keep costs low.

- Diversify.

- Minimize taxes.

- Keep it simple.

- Stay the course.

Anyone experienced in investing will know that these principles are sound. For each principle, the website provides a short video.

Anyone can ask virtually any question on finance or investing on the Bogleheads forum, but investors are encouraged to start with a review of the basics.

In *The Bogleheads' Guide to Investing,*[2] the familiar precepts are expanded in clear, direct language and can be summarized as follows:

- Live below your means or income.

- Start saving early.

- Costs matter: keep them low.

- Invest in the most tax-efficient way.

- Rebalance to control risk.

- Insurance is for protection, not investment.

- Master your emotions.

- Make your investment plan as simple as possible.

- Avoid market timing and chasing performance.

The authors conclude: "We feel there's beauty in simplicity. Be forewarned that there will undoubtedly be numerous distractions along the way that will cause you to think about straying from your chosen course."

At nearly 90, Jack Bogle was still working hard out of his suite of offices at Vanguard championing sensible, long-term investing centered on low-cost index funds and still following his mantra: "Press on regardless!" In concert with low costs, Bogle insisted on candor with investors. After all, Vanguard was not *selling* anything other than its availability; it was simply working hard for the investors.

Bogle held himself accountable for living out the image of himself that he wanted to project, the image he wanted all others to hold of who he was and what he'd done. When he died in early 2019 at age 89, the many appreciative farewells—more than for any other businessman or investor in that year—would have delighted him. He had earned the plaudits through his

> Save, plan for the long term, index at low cost, and stay the course.

persistent work on behalf of the millions of "everyday investors" who got his message about sensible investing: save, plan for the long term, index at low cost, and stay the course. By one estimate, Jack Bogle had saved individual investors $1 billion in fees *not* paid. For those who followed the rules for long-term investment success, the total benefits were surely many times larger.

CHAPTER 12

PARTNERS AGAIN

U nlikely as it would have seemed at the fraught time of Bogle's war with Wellington nearly 25 years before, Wellington, led by Bob Doran, and Vanguard, led by Jack Brennan, began to develop a strong symbiotic relationship. Today their relationship is dynamic, collegial, and extraordinarily beneficial to both. In one of the most successful large-scale working relationships in the investment world, Vanguard is again Wellington's largest business relationship and Wellington is Vanguard's largest too.

Back at the nadir of their relationship, when Bogle was determined to hurt Wellington while building up Vanguard, the situation facing Doran and his colleagues at Wellington was grim. At Vanguard board meetings, Bogle always had a documented argument for reducing the fees paid to Wellington or for switching from Wellington to another manager, and his directors almost always felt obliged to go along. Bogle was at war, determined to "press on regardless" to spur Vanguard's growth and prominence—particularly at the expense of Wellington (see Chapter 4). He took the profitable business away, but there was never a complete break. Wellington continued to have many teams managing many Vanguard mutual funds.

It would have been a great time for Wellington to make a major acquisition to offset those Bogle-driven losses of assets and earnings. A potential home run deal suddenly presented itself in 1976. The SEC, concerned about conflicts of interest when brokers controlled captive asset managers, gave securities firms with investment management subsidiaries just two years to divest those units. This meant that stockbroker Donaldson, Lufkin & Jenrette had to divest its highly profitable subsidiary Alliance Capital Management. That presented an ideal opportunity for Peter Vermilye, who was both CEO and chief investment officer of Alliance Capital.[1] While Alliance and its owner, DLJ, were headquartered in New York City, Vermilye had established his own office in Boston. He resided in nearby Manchester-by-the-Sea and did not enjoy commuting to New York City. The perfect solution for Vermilye was clear: Alliance Capital could merge with Wellington and he would lead the buildup of Wellington's pension business from a base in Boston.

Negotiations quickly began with Doran and Vermilye playing the key roles. They got along well. Vermilye had a slightly intimidating way of going silent for long moments during a discussion. Doran soon found himself doing the same.

Suddenly, what had appeared to be an easy win-win combination hit a serious pothole when the SEC began an investigation of the commission rates charged to Alliance Capital by its broker-owner, DLJ. The risk of a major fine, potential lawsuits, or both—and the loss of big accounts that might be expected to follow—could have caused a serious loss of business and even thrown Alliance Capital into the red.

Had the SEC inquiry quietly evaporated, as it eventually did, the combination would have been a formidable solution to the profitability problems then facing Wellington. However, some of Wellington's partners were concerned because, in a private partnership, any loss would get charged against the personal accounts of the partners. Key partners saw no reason to embrace a possible large loss. So they insisted DLJ indemnify Wellington against any such loss. DLJ refused.[2]

At Wellington, the recollection is that the Wellington partners, led by John Neff, the risk-focused investor, were prepared to vote against the merger, so Doran called Dick Jenrette with the news. At DLJ, the recollection was that partner Harold Newman went to Jenrette, pleading that he not sell DLJ's "crown jewel" to Wellington, so Jenrette decided not to sell. Either way, the *New York Times* reported the impasse the next day, and the Wellington-Alliance merger was, at the last minute, called off. There was to be no quick, easy solution for Wellington to Bogle's continuing siege against its assets and revenues. Meanwhile, Vanguard was losing assets as investors redeemed shares of the old, out-of-fashion and underper-forming Wellington Fund.

About then, the Massachusetts Institute of Technology's endowment, long managed by the Colonial mutual fund group, decided to establish a new investment-manager relationship. After screening many firms, MIT invited Wellington to compete to become the new investment manager. The plan was to link MIT with a strong investment research and portfolio management team at one of Boston's major firms. At the time, both Harvard and Yale had sole-manager relationships with Boston-based investment firms: State Street Research & Management and Endowment Management & Research.

MIT invited two other firms to compete. Wellington knew Fidelity would be its toughest challenge.[3] "We *are* in the finals," said Doran to the small team he had carefully chosen, "but being in the finals is not our objective. Our goal is to *win*! So every day each of us must make winning the MIT mandate our first priority. We're going to meet every Monday to bring our best ideas together into action plans until we *win* this competition." He added: "MIT wants no mistakes or any doubts or questions about their process. Our goal is to come through with more and better reasons for MIT to select Wellington than can be found to select anyone else. And remember, with all the turbulence caused by the Bogle difficulties, we are starting this race well behind our competition. So we have to catch up first, but we *must* win—or we could be on our way to going out of business. It's that serious."[4]

The length of the search process—over a year—became a major advantage for Wellington. A short process would probably have led to an easy win for one of the other competitors. But the long search gave Wellington ample time to demonstrate its research strengths by parading its many expert analysts; to show the strength of its collegial professional culture; and to give Doran, by nature low key and soft spoken, the time to show how strong he would be as a leader of a professional organization. After a long year of top-priority focus on winning MIT, Wellington won in 1977.

Years later, Doran was told, "Wellington was the firm we thought we could go through tough times with." In other words, as Doran had hoped, the key factor was Wellington's culture. One of the major benefits for Wellington was that in competing for MIT, it had hammered out exactly what kind of firm it wanted to be over the long term, and this self-definition became the core of its proposition when competing for other business.

After the dark days, an extraordinary cluster of favorable business developments strengthened Wellington Management Company. A new kind of business came its way at just the right time. First, the directors of the OTC Fund went looking for a new investment manager and called on Wellington. Would it be willing to serve as a subadviser, responsible for investing a portion of OTC's assets? An investment firm serving a subadviser was a new concept and would need the SEC's approval, but after some discussion the appropriate answer became clear: this was a new kind of business and a great opportunity for Wellington.

Other organizations turned to Wellington for help. The Ohio State Teachers' Retirement Fund made a flat-fee arrangement with Wellington. The Hartford Insurance Company came next. The Hartford wanted to build a major investment business. Strong in sales and client service and responsible for substantial mutual fund assets as well as its own portfolio, the company had concluded that it was not competitive in investing and would be wiser to contract with a strong investment specialist than to try to build competitive in-house capabilities. Would Wellington be interested in becoming a subadviser? A major business relationship soon developed.

Wellington was encouraged to develop a variety of new capabilities. These new services combined with a realization that subadvisory relationships—ironically, so comparable to its relationship with Vanguard—presented a major growth opportunity. Over the next several years, Wellington, the only investment manager pursuing this rapidly growing, long-term relationship business, turned investment subadvisory work into a major growth business.

As the world's fastest-growing investment services organization, Vanguard has an expanding need for first-rate active investment management capacity and relies for much of that capacity on exceptional external managers. Wellington Management Company has developed a strong professional culture and is one of the world's largest and most diversified organizations serving institutional investors worldwide. It serves as subadviser for several mutual fund groups but offers no retail mutual funds directly to consumers, so it's glad to access the enormous individual investor market indirectly through Vanguard.

The table below lists many of the mutual funds the two organizations manage together and the assets of each fund. The scale of the relationship between the two organizations is huge and growing. In 2021 Wellington managed $450 billion for Vanguard—$158 billion in bonds and $292 billion in equities.

Fund	Assets (millions)
Capital Value Fund	$683
Dividend Growth Fund	$40,271
Emerging Mkts Select Stock - Wellington Sub-Portfolio	$143
Energy - Wellington Sub-Portfolio	$4,391
Equity Income - Wellington Sub-Portfolio	$21,600
Explorer - Wellington Sub-Portfolio	$5,406
Global ESG Select Stock Fund	$131
Global Wellesley Income Fund (Equity)	$164
Global Wellesley Income Fund (Fixed Income)	$290
Global Wellington Fund (Equity)	$773
Global Wellington Fund (Fixed Income)	$445
GNMA Fund	$26,499
Health Care Fund	$47,516
High-Yield Corp Fund	$25,554
International Explorer - Wellington Sub-Portfolio	$703
International Core Stock Fund	$175
Long-Term Investment-Grade - Wellington Sub-Portfolio	$17,245
Mid-Cap Growth - Wellington Sub-Portfolio	$348
Global Capital Cycles Fund	$1,005
U.S. Growth - Wellington Sub-Portfolio	$8,508
VVIF-Balanced Portfolio (Equity)	$1,948
VVIF-Balanced Portfolio (Fixed Income)	$1,100
VVIF-Equity Income - Wellington Sub-Portfolio	$1,052
VVIF-Growth - Wellington Sub-Portfolio	$489
VVIF-High-Yield Bond	$811
Wellesley Income Fund (Equity)	$21,534
Wellesley Income Fund (Fixed Income)	$37,062
Wellington Fund (Equity)	$66,958
Wellington Fund (Fixed Income)	$36,612
Windsor - Wellington Sub-Portfolio	$11,854

All's well that ends well. But just how did two organizations go from a messy, painful divorce to a mutually beneficial working partnership? The story can be briefly told in personal terms. After Bogle was no longer working to take business away from Wellington, and specifically after the more collaborative Brennan became CEO, the leaders on both sides recognized that working out a joint solution was clearly in the best interests of both. Another part, as will be seen, was luck, good and bad.

The key players were Brennan for Vanguard and Bob Doran and Duncan McFarland for Wellington, but there was leadership on every level, from long-term policy to day-to-day operations, involving many others. Brennan and Doran were convinced that they could make it work and were determined to be patient and persistent. They first put their emphasis on understanding the goals and interests of both firms, and the personal objectives of the other firm's leaders.

McFarland, one of Bogle's assistants several years before and now a leader at Wellington, took on the vital role of representing Wellington in managing its still-complex relationship with Vanguard. This involved two- and three-day meetings at Vanguard every few weeks plus preparation and follow-up. The purpose of all these meetings? Making sure each of the Wellington fund managers made a successful presentation to Vanguard's senior staff, who were responsible for evaluating managers for Vanguard funds, and to the Vanguard directors, who took a serious role in selecting and terminating external investment managers. McFarland looked for potential obstacles so he could surmount them quickly and made sure that all communications between Vanguard and Wellington were complete, open, and objective; he knew that it would take time to build a reservoir of trust and understanding.

Jack Brennan performed the most important role: peacemaker. As CEO, he knew far more than anyone else that Vanguard faced an array of daunting challenges. Of these, the one most visible to the world would be investment performance, particularly if ever it fell seriously short. While many other firms were in the investment management business, only a few could meet three vital criteria for a Vanguard partner: a strong professional culture that would continuously attract and keep top investment talent; the ability to achieve superior long-term returns for investors in many investment categories; and willingness to accept low fees in exchange for the opportunity to work with Vanguard to serve millions of investors. Brennan saw that unusual "strategic troika" in Doran's Wellington.

The supply of high-capability long-term managers was limited. As Vanguard grew, that limit could constrain Vanguard's own growth. Wellington had many types of investment capabilities *and* the culture to keep its professional leaders for their whole careers. With his pragmatism, Brennan made building a win-win relationship between the two organizations his top priority.

Bob Doran specialized in developing and preserving the professional culture that attracted the most accomplished investment professionals to Wellington. He believed that in every professional organization, the dominating factor is always the same: culture. The best people in every field each have special talent. Those people look for comparably special qualities in the organization in which they will spend their careers. Doran may have learned the lessons of teamwork playing fullback on the Andover football team and the importance of combining talent, discipline, and a sense of humor as a member of Yale's fun-loving a capella group, the Whiffenpoofs.

Each superior professional firm has developed its own distinctive, almost "tribal" culture, or set of values and ways of working together, with well-understood standards of behavior and achievement. In the very best firms, the pursuit of excellence is central to the values and expectations that each professional holds for himself or herself and expects of every other member of the organization. Symbols of culture include such things as dress code, how early or late people work, where lunch is eaten, attendance at one another's weddings and funerals—and always, at the best firms, exceptionally high standards of partnership collegiality and persistent commitment to excellent work for clients.*

Some of the symbols are generic. Some are unique, like Wellington's fabled Morning Meeting, inherited more than half a century ago from TDP&L. The Meeting, before the stock markets open, is precise on its start and end time and open to all—a daily forum for the swift exchange of views, information, and ideas among

---

* Readers interested in how the best firms in each major profession have all excelled at the same seven vital success factors—particularly firm culture—may enjoy my book *What It Takes*, published by Wiley in 2012.

the firm's analysts and portfolio managers. The open sharing of each professional's most valuable resource, winning investment ideas, was central to the partnership character that Thorndike, Doran, Paine & Lewis had developed before the merger with Wellington. It had been shunted aside during Bogle's headstrong tenure as CEO and then brought back to preeminence by Doran and other "culture carriers."

TDP&L was committed to a basic "structural" principle: no branch offices. But when partner Phil Gwynn expressed determination to locate in Atlanta, the firm agreed and set up a telecommunication so the "one firm" Morning Meeting could be continued, with one innovation: a meeting manager to ensure participation and pacing. Later, John Neff would participate from his office in Valley Forge. In the 1990s, to accommodate Wellington's international growth, offices were opened in London, Singapore, Sydney, Tokyo, Hong Kong, and Beijing.

Neff, with his hard-earned expertise on companies and industries, thought the Morning Meeting was a waste of his precious time, so he decided not to go. Doran went to Neff and gently shared his hopes: "John, we all know you are an expert and creative investor and hope you know it would mean a lot to all of us if you would be an active participant in our Morning Meetings. Could you do that for us, John?" Neff knew he could only say, "Yes, Bob, I'll come."[5]

Many other examples of accommodation to individuals' special situations were part of the Wellington culture of caring. Hazel Sanger, after delivering her first child a year before, had joined TDP&L in 1977 as a manager. Finding herself short of money, she requested permission to borrow a modest amount from her account in the profit-sharing plan. When Nick Thorndike told her, "It has been decided that you cannot borrow from your account," Sanger was naturally disappointed. But quickly she was relieved to hear, "But the firm will gladly lend whatever amount you want in anticipation of your year-end bonus."[6]

When a leading analyst, Bill Hicks, wanted to learn German, a group of learners were organized, and an instructor was brought in.

When partner John Gooch was having a "down" period he could not shake off, he went to Doran to ask, "Bob, do you think I should leave the firm?" Doran shook his head and suggested they share his office for at least a few weeks.

Julian Robertson, who was developing an exciting hedge fund organization in New York City, was courting one of Wellington's young portfolio managers with higher and higher pay packages. Finally, Doran asked the manager what exactly about the offer was so compelling. "It's not the money, Bob. It's the core *idea*. I really want to run a hedge fund!"

"OK, fine. Why not do it here?"

"Can I?"

"We've never done it before, but I'm sure we can work it out with the firm. Let's work together to build the case for Wellington managing hedge funds."[7]

As a result of that willingness to try something new, hedge funds became a significant part of Wellington, and their need for both long and short investment ideas provided a stimulating new challenge for the firm's analysts.

Exceptional investors are individualistic because "eagles do not flock." To develop a major investment organization, there are two ways to go. By far the most common way is to find a few talented professionals who agree on one particular category of investing such as growth, value, small cap, or large cap; develop around them a team of like-minded practitioners; and seek out prospective clients who want the specialty this group has defined as their one best way of investing. The strength of this approach is its clear focus; the weakness is that high incremental profitability tempts the managers to accept more and more accounts, and more assets. Success over time can attract more clients with more assets than the firm has the capacity to manage well.

The other way to develop a major organization is profoundly different: create an accommodating "umbrella" culture that attracts, and can accommodate, investors with *different* styles, each based on a set of strong investment beliefs, and facilitate their working unusually well in a "big tent" with strong central research resources, while differences in disciplined application are expected and appreciated.

Wellington chose the second, and that has made all the difference in its success. It developed a diversified portfolio of different investment capabilities, an important protection against the whole firm's being dangerously out of step with the market for two or three years and losing a lot of business by being "true to its convictions." Moreover, Wellington's several different business units' large *aggregate* capacity avoids the common problem of performance success leading to growth in asset size, which often makes it harder and hard to continue achieving superior performance.

Wellington could accommodate substantial asset growth *and* achieve superior performance because, even if particular portfolio managers decided to stop accepting additional assets, the organization could keep growing. Distributed responsibility empowered those with strong ideas to develop different modes of investment management, to a high standard. They created a diverse portfolio of investment units that could be custom-blended to suit each major client and, most particularly, Wellington's largest client: Vanguard.

Wellington's open organization and its investment-product complexity might have confused some clients and prospective clients, but Wellington managed that by developing an unusually skillful group of professional relationship managers. Most investment firms have great difficulty understanding the value of superb relationship managers, perhaps because they see them as much like the stock-brokerage salespeople they see every day, and not as professional equals. Wellington's relationship managers work closely with each client, ensuring the client and Wellington understand each other, and then jointly select the most suitable group of investment managers. That's what McFarland did with Vanguard for its many different Wellington mandates.

A key strength of Wellington is the large, experienced, skillful research organization built initially by Bill Hicks, who had joined the old Wellington in Philadelphia and then moved to Boston. Then Gene Tremblay made it clear that an industry or company analyst could make a great career as an analyst without managing investments; he introduced industry-specific "sector teams" that contributed importantly to the firm's success managing hedge funds. Another success factor was the openness to internal entrepreneurial experimentation and the personal nurturing provided by Doran and others. Later, they established a group of two or three managing partners who concentrated on operating the Wellington partnership as an organization, giving systematic attention to career development and compensation, which many investment management firms treat as only a sideline.

By the late 1970s, Wellington was gaining, not losing, assets under management, and profits were going up, not down. The spiritual impact of shifting from fear of losing to surging confidence in winning was as important as the turnaround in the firm's economics. The client base was diversified, and revenues were growing. The stock market soon entered the longest, strongest bull market in history. Wellington gathered enormous assets through Vanguard and its other clients.

The company's stock price, however, still wallowed in the mid-single digits, down almost 90 percent from its years-ago high (see Chapter 2). Wellington tried to lift the price with a share repurchase program, and then considered but decided against an Employee Stock Ownership Plan (ESOP), a popular concept at the time. Then one day in 1978, Nick Thorndike—noting that the "Bogle Wars" seemed over, and that revenues from diverse clients were growing—posed an intriguing notion: "I wonder if we could go private." A few smaller companies had done just that, but one, Hartz Mountain, had recently been challenged by the SEC and several lawsuits. The leaders of Wellington decided to consult with their adviser on financial matters, Noah Hurndon at Brown Brothers Harriman. After a feasibility study, his conclusion was that the window had closed on any such transactions.

Fortunately, Jim Walters, Wellington's general counsel, did his own additional research and found the perfect solution. Under ERISA, "fiduciary responsibility" had been defined in 1977 by the Department of Labor with two distinct requirements: the duty of loyalty, and the standard of care. Under the duty of loyalty, a fiduciary's sole responsibility is to act always in the best interests of the client. But in corporate law, a company always has a fiduciary duty to act in the best interests of its shareholders. As Walters pointed out, these two rules meant that a publicly owned corporate fiduciary like Wellington was in the contradictory position of having to serve two different masters at once.

As Walters explained, the elimination of public shareholders would provide Wellington with the "legitimate business purpose" required to go private under the laws of Delaware where it was incorporated—the need to focus 100 percent on always putting client interests first. This logic would hold up in court during two subsequent lawsuits.[8]

With Walters's solution, going private went from impossible to achievable—almost imperative. Still, a major issue was the form of organization that would be the surviving entity. Should Wellington Management be a corporation or a partnership? Other firms were moving away from general partnerships, because partners had unlimited liability. Was there a way that a prospective Wellington partnership could offer limited liability?

There was. Wellington's advisers determined that the firm's rigorous process in research and security selection, and its unusual openness with clients, met the tests of prudence under ERISA. This concept had been established as a solid defense against liability almost two centuries earlier by Judge Samuel Putnam, in the case of Harvard College v. Amory, and became famous as "the prudent man rule." This meant that Wellington could form a partnership to buy up the publicly owned shares, and then carry on the Wellington business as a private partnership. Wellington had not yet proven it could fully rebuild its business, and it might have to struggle with another bear market, but Bob Doran said, "I think we can make this work." He recommended buying in the publicly owned shares and becoming a private partnership.

Doran was making the most important financial decision of his life and urged his colleagues to take the plunge with him. Part of the purchase money would come from liquid assets inside Wellington and the rest from a loan from Brown Brothers Harriman, where Doran's brother-in-law worked. Doran and his partners all knew the private partnership would be open to lawsuits. In fact, Wellington's long internal deliberations were vital to its defense against a subsequent shareholder suit.

Dillon Read was retained to make an independent valuation of the shares, working jointly with three independent directors of Wellington, Professor Samuel Hayes of Harvard Business School, accountant Richard A. Eisner, and William P. Crozier, CEO of Bay Banks. They settled at first on $11 a share, but after declaring a large special dividend, changed that to $11.50, for a total valuation of about $11 million.[9]

It was not clear that most mutual fund investors and the newly established major institutional accounts would stay with Wellington—but they did. And no one could be sure that the stock market would head north soon enough—but it most certainly did.

An important decision yet to be made would be the terms on which a partner could retire and withdraw capital. Some partnerships had a book value balance-sheet policy based on each partner's exact date of departure. Some based withdrawals on a multiple of current earnings. Wellington decided on a 10-year formula based on declining percentages of future earnings. This dependency on the future would encourage retiring partners to focus on the continuing strength of the firm and its culture. The internal mantra, "Client/Firm/Self," made explicit the commitment to put the interests of the firm ahead of the partners'—and the clients' interests always first above all.

The process of going private, begun in May 1978, took 17 months, and was finally completed on October 31, 1979.[10]

For Vanguard, having Wellington prosper, grow, and continue increasing its professional skills in various specialties was clearly important. For Wellington, having Vanguard grow so dramatically was at least as important. The deliberately revived partnership and the organization-to-organization synergies, which had once come so close to hostile termination, have now been exemplary for over 40 years.

CHAPTER 13

BRENNAN'S WAYS

Jack Brennan had a morale problem, wrote Hal Lux in a 1999 feature article for *Institutional Investor*:

> It's early April, an important season is fast approaching, and the Vanguard chairman is stuck with a team that won't get to work. "They are all coming to me and saying, 'I've got to go on vacation,'" mutters Brennan. "Give me a break."
>
> Most people would cut Brennan's team some slack. They average, after all, just 14 years of age and are members of a youth lacrosse team. Spring break will soon be here. But Brennan, who runs the world's [then] second-largest mutual fund purveyor when he isn't demonstrating the finer points of stick handling in a Radnor, Pennsylvania youth league, doesn't want to hear about it. He wants to go undefeated. "I told them the first day: There's a big difference between being state champs and undefeated state champs," says Brennan, matter-of-factly.
>
> "Jack's no piece of cake," allows Philadelphia lawyer Peter Samson, who coaches the team's defense. "I think at first some kids don't think he's a nice guy. He plays to win. There's no question about it." . . . One of the problems of coaching kids, notes Brennan pal Samson, is that you will sometimes upset their parents, and they will come

complaining or screaming. "It can bother me for days."
Not Brennan. "It means nothing to him. It goes in one ear
and out the other. He has no memory of it. If Jack thinks
he's doing the right thing, he doesn't care what someone
thinks of him."[1]

The article included a citation from Brennan's booklet on leadership: "The facts of life in a dynamic, highly competitive and rapidly
growing business like ours, are that democracy has no place here
(another politically incorrect statement, I suppose!). Decisiveness,
particularly when tempered with great judgment, is an asset that you
won't find on our balance sheet but has helped us conquer many
obstacles and lead the way in this industry for
years and years."

The article concluded by noting that
Brennan's youth lacrosse team won the state
championship—undefeated.

> "Decisiveness,
> particularly when
> tempered with great
> judgment, is an
> asset that you won't
> find on our balance
> sheet but has helped
> us conquer many
> obstacles and lead
> the way in this
> industry for years
> and years."

John J. "Jack" Brennan grew up in a Boston
Irish Catholic family that stressed hard work
and achievement. Jack, his two sisters, and
one brother were raised in the Boston suburb of Winchester by their parents, Frank and
Mary. The Brennan family story was nearly as
upwardly mobile as the Bogle family's story
had been a slide. Jack Brennan graduated
from Harvard Business School in 1980; his
grandparents, Irish immigrants, had worked
as janitors at that same university. Jack's parents were the first in
their family to complete elementary school. His father, Frank, went
on to rank first in his high school class and planned to go to the
Wentworth Institute and become an electrician, but his guidance
counselor would have none of that. He tore up the Wentworth application and insisted Frank go to Boston College and "make something
of yourself—something important." Frank Brennan advanced to
achieve the classic American dream. He excelled as CEO of the midsize Union Warren Savings Bank, increasing its scale tenfold, and as
a leader of the Massachusetts Business Development Corporation,

president of the Massachusetts Bankers Association and a director of other financial institutions. In his seventies, he was named chairman of Boston Company's mutual fund division.

Frank Brennan was a great role model for his son Jack. In his nineties, he read and worked out a critique of the long, complex Dodd-Frank Act of 2010 and wanted to go over the key points about which he thought his son, as CEO of Vanguard, should do or say something. Frank mixed easily in the club world of Boston business and politics while always keeping the common touch. "All the important people in Massachusetts knew Frank Brennan," recalled William Bulger, former president of the Massachusetts State Senate and former president of the University of Massachusetts. "If there was an Irish music festival, you would look up and there would be the Brennans. It was always good to run into him and hear the latest gossip, the latest stories." Family friend Robert Sheridan, president of Savings Bank Life Insurance Co., said, "The father and mother were like the first couple of downtown Boston banking. Theirs was a high-quality, full-of-values family. All the children are successful." Success aside, the Brennans were frugal: one car in the driveway and summer jobs, mostly manual labor, for the children.

As Peter Samson told *Institutional Investor* about Jack, "If you followed him around all day, you would think he was broke. He mows his own lawn. His kids do chores around the house. The only luxury I know of is that he drives an Audi. A devoted family man with two sons and a daughter, Brennan shuns social engagements, preferring to stay home and coach sports. On summer weekends he flies to Cape Cod to spend time with his extended family." Even today, after a successful career with a seven-figure salary, Brennan lives a relatively modest life.

Quietly religious, Brennan is extremely close to his wife, Catherine. "It sounds corny," said Samson, "but he's really one of those rare American types who lives for God and family." Brennan chairs the board of trustees of the University of Notre Dame, where his children studied. A good student and a star high school athlete, Jack played for his father, a demanding youth hockey coach. "We were a '5 o'clock at the hockey rink' type family," he said. Brennan entered Dartmouth in 1972, studying economics and playing varsity hockey and lacrosse. Though he wasn't the most talented in these

Division 1 sports, he was fiercely determined. "Selfless always wins in my view," he said. "I taught my sons that in lacrosse, it's always about the number of assists scored, never about the goals." To prove the point, Brennan showed them an article from the Dartmouth student newspaper: Brennan 8 goals, 28 assists. "In lacrosse, as in other sports, and in life, it's never *your* goals, but always the *team's* score."[2]

Brennan got a lot of his assertive style from his sports experience. He proposed putting together a Vanguard hockey team. "I have played golf with him," said Vanguard's then technology chief Robert DiStefano. "I'm not sure I would want to play hockey."

After Dartmouth, Brennan worked for New York Bank for Savings in Manhattan before attending Harvard Business School. He moved to Racine, Wisconsin, after graduating to join S.C. Johnson & Son to work for a company that actually produced something— Windex and Pledge, among other products. "Coming out of HBS, I was going to go to Prudential, but then Mr. Johnson called with a chance to work with him and his leadership team for two or three years, so I took it instead. I couldn't turn down that opportunity." A few years later, Brennan was looking for a job in financial services.

Jeremy Duffield, then Bogle's assistant at Vanguard, was looking for someone to take his position and contacted Brennan, whose résumé he had found in a Harvard Business School recruiting database. Brennan knew little about the company that then had $5 billion in assets. "I had my money in Fidelity Cash Reserves," he says. "I had heard of Windsor. That was about it." A first round of interviews by phone, including one with Bogle, was arranged because Vanguard wouldn't spend the money to fly him to Philadelphia.

At Bogle's insistence, a psychologist gave Brennan an inkblot test. Asked for an evaluation, Brennan was blunt: "That test is lousy."

"How can you say that?" the psychologist asked. "You've just scored 100 percent *and* set a speed-to-completion record— outstanding compared to many, many others."

"That's not the point. It's absolute, not relative, results I care about. It's me versus my expectations. Besides, I could do better without you staring at me the whole time."[3]

Fast-growing Vanguard needed management and administrative skills, and Brennan was a natural. His practical approach complemented Bogle's visionary bent. "Jack Brennan is a very good manager," said Bogle. "His big accomplishment wasn't one thing. It was more continuous accomplishments as a manager.'"

When Brennan decided to join Vanguard, he told his wife it would only be a two-year diversion from their cherished dream-plan of living in New England. So, it came as a surprise to her when he announced one evening a few months later, "I've found the right organization to make my career."

While most financial service organizations were boldly adding new services, hoping to gain elusive scale advantages or to diversify by product, market, or both, Vanguard maintained its singular focus on mutual funds. It only cautiously expanded into international markets, always with the same focus on low cost. Citing the writings of Harvard Business School professor Michael Porter, Brennan argued that most financial services firms were racing to arrive first at the same destination and would necessarily fight each other forever, while Vanguard sought a unique position that would be unusually defendable strategically.

On ethics, Brennan is absolute and made that clear to everyone: *nobody ever gets a free pass.* One senior executive was fired immediately when he did not respond well when confronted with a corner-cutting issue. As Mike Miller, a proud University of Virginia graduate, put it: "It's like the UVA Honors Committee: no second chance! Early on, Brennan saw Legal and Compliance as expensive because he *knew* we always put our clients' interests first, so who needs lots of lawyers and compliance people?"

As Miller knows well, that didn't mean compliance would be neglected. "Our group began with about 100 crew members and four or five managers as my direct reports," he recalled. "Now, after 20 years, there are 1,500 crew members and 14 different working groups covering government relations, compliance, enterprise risk, corporate strategy and portfolio review of all internal and external investment managers. Corporate Compliance alone has 80 crew members. With Brennan, we were always a team. I never worked *for* Brennan, it was always working *with* him. So it's little wonder that after all those years of working together, I love him like a brother."[4]

Brennan is quietly self-disciplined. At Vanguard, he ran five or six miles daily, was at his desk by six in the morning, never raised his voice, and moved quickly from item to item on his calendar. If he had agreed to discuss something for 20 minutes, the discussion might run only 18 minutes but would almost never extend to 21 minutes. Some would say, "He gets to the key points quickly"; others found him brusque.

But he changed gears when it came time to clarify his views on how to advance as a Vanguard leader. Here, Brennan was almost long-winded, because he had a lot to share and wanted everyone to take it in. He had many people he wanted to know his views. With 15,000 working at Vanguard, even 1 percent, let alone 5 percent, would be too many to tell individually which principles guide senior management in its perpetual search for leaders. Instead, he put together a handsomely printed 53-page guide for wide distribution within Vanguard.[5] The guide is illustrated with nautical photos of halyards, cleats and lines, and adorned with short quotes from admired world leaders, authors, athletes, and historical figures. It centers on two insights:

- We have no patents or proprietary processes that protect us from competition.

- Our reputation and the trust that clients have in us represent Vanguard's true net worth.

The table of contents shows by itself how much Brennan had to say. For each of the charges, he had a page or more of thought development on how and why the particular item mattered to him and to the people of Vanguard, particularly those who wanted to become leaders.

Brennan cited 26 items, all of which you can view in Appendix 2. Here's a representative sampling, beginning with the one that summarizes all the others for Vanguard leaders:

Do the right thing: Vanguard people are allowed to make mistakes, but they are never allowed to make ethical mistakes. Violate the confidentiality of client information, and you're out. Accept a gift of material value from a client or a vendor, and you're out. Make investments that are forbidden because of your job responsibilities, and you're out. Ours is a "no ifs, ands, or buts" policy. There are no gray areas. We make no apologies for that black and white view.

Lead by example: Our great leaders must:

- Be the hardest workers.

- Be the most client-focused.

- Be the most driven to succeed.

- Be the most caring and compassionate.

- Be the most flexible.

- Be the best role models with unquestioned integrity.

- Be the most committed to excellence. . . .

Foster teamwork: In embracing this premise, the successful Vanguard leader "puts her ego in her pocket." Effective leaders exhibit personal humility, a trait that is vital in the investment management business considering that we ply our trade in the financial markets, an unpredictable environment in which we have very little control over the results. . . . The dustbin of history is littered with examples of financial firms that failed to stay humble.

Accept paradox: To accomplish our mission, we must be both the highest-quality provider of services in our business and the lowest-cost producer in our business. It is difficult to name a second organization, in any business, that is accomplishing both of these goals. This is why a focus on continual improvement is so important to our current and future competitive success. . . .

Compete tenaciously: The drive to succeed has been a critical element in our success at both the personal and corporate levels. One of my coworkers said it profoundly some years back on the day after the stock market's worst single-day setback in a decade. At the end of that day, when it was clear that our client service had been splendid and that all client transactions and requests had been handled, I asked, "How does this happen? How do we, alone in the industry, treat a day of surging volumes and great stress as a normal day, even an enjoyable one?" She responded, "Jack, you know as well as anyone, we're the most competitive firm in the world; we simply won't let someone be better than us on a day like today."

Be decisive and accept responsibility: A great leader accepts all the blame and distributes all the credit. Being the leader is credit enough. Decisiveness—particularly when tempered with sound judgment—is an asset that you won't find on our balance sheet but that has helped us conquer many obstacles and lead the way in this industry for years and years.

Value diversity: This is a people business, and we must have the best people working for us in all positions, at all locations, and at all times. It would be foolish for any of us to think that all of those people should look "just like me." . . .

Embrace change: For years, I've heard people outside the company say Vanguard hasn't changed much through the years. "Still dominated by mutual funds . . . still owned by the clients . . . still focused on low cost . . . still not too glitzy." On the surface, it's true. We haven't changed much. Actually, this organization has changed frequently and the people who have embraced change are the ones who have led us to success and have thrived. Those who have resisted change have slowed our development and—not coincidentally—have hurt their own careers.

Be personal: One tremendous difference between good leaders and great leaders is this: The great ones are personal. By "personal," I mean they work at being more than a boss, more than someone who guides a team. Vanguard's great leaders open themselves up, letting their people in on their personal lives, their hobbies, their families, their likes and dislikes. In turn, our most effective leaders want to be let in on their team's lives, too, so they can know the crew as people, not just employees.* The personal can never get in the way of the professional, but it sure can enhance it. We want everyone on the crew to have both a professional relationship and care about you as a person and know about your children—or your partner if you're gay.

Be positive: Face it. Work is work. Most people don't choose to work; they must. . . .
   That said, a leader's job is to make work challenging, enjoyable, and rewarding. You cannot do that except in a positive environment. The need for a positive environment places a big burden on our leaders. The great ones recognize one simple fact: they can never have a bad day. Because if they have a bad day, their work unit has a bad day. And if that happens, the client will know it.

Brennan added one of his own most important beliefs: "A momentary lapse from the straight and narrow could be enough to ruin Vanguard's reputation for many years to come, perhaps forever." And that takes him back to Vanguard's centrality: Do the right thing.

According to Brennan, "One of the big cultural improvements at Vanguard in this century was the notion of DAWAW: Don't Ask *Who*—Ask *Why*! It forced us to approach problem solving in a new way, to search for root causes." It also fit with his "no office politics" admonition. Brennan focused on making Vanguard a learning or continuous improvement organization by making both learning and teaching a focus for all leaders. "One of the greatest thrills that you

---

* "Do we *have* to go—*again*—to the company Christmas party?" When they were children, the young Brennans were hoping for an option. For their father, there was no option. "Of course! We *all* go. It's important for everyone to see us and know us as normal, real people—as a husband and father, a wife and mother, *and* kids."

can experience as a leader of an organization—especially at Vanguard—is to be told by a colleague that you are his or her mentor. A big part of attaining that exalted status is teaching. Teaching matches learning—as two hands clapping."

Brennan had an effective way of clarifying decisions about people, particularly promotion decisions. He urged everyone to ask, "Would I want this person to be my child's first boss?" With a quick smile of apparent surprise, he reflected briefly, "It's remarkable how people react when I ask them that simple question."[6]

> "Don't Ask *Who*— Ask *Why!* It forced us to approach problem solving in a new way, to search for root causes."

His policy of rotating the most promising performers every few years into "stretch" jobs in different parts of the organization not only gave managers a greater understanding of the whole organization, but also greater respect for the achievements of predecessor leaders. Their management skills had room to improve, and Vanguard could see whether and to what extent each manager was able to continue growing. People decisions also challenged Brennan and other senior leaders to evaluate their own skills of assessing both people chosen and people *not* chosen, and of the difficulties or opportunities faced by newly assigned managers.

"Filling the pipeline with exceptional people is the biggest contribution any Vanguard leader can make to this organization," Brennan emphasized. "First, hiring and developing great people will, without a doubt, make a leader look good in the eyes of other leaders at Vanguard. Second, having able successors in place frees the leader to move on to new challenges and assignments when opportunities arise."

Brennan liked to bring the rigor of quantification to decisions, particularly when dealing with troubles. When he was still Bogle's COO, he recalled, "We decided to survey the crew, asking about their experiences and attitudes. We were stunned by the results. Put simply, the strong conviction across the company was that, while senior management was fine, the line supervisors were not. This was a classic wake-up call. So we did two major things. First, we made clear that we accepted the findings as accurate, disturbing as they were, and declared that we in management now owned the problem. We did this by publishing the findings in our Crew's News newsletter to the crew. Second, as you can well imagine, we went right after that reality to make major changes. Repeating the same survey one year later, the improvement was dramatic: turnover was cut in half."[7]

Years later, with turnover again higher than expected, Brennan asked Kathy Gubanich, head of HR, to look into it. She conducted a bunch of exit interviews and soon knew what the key problem was: Vanguard's dress code. To symbolize the professional work of the crew, Brennan insisted on professional attire: neckties and suits. But in IT, jeans and tees were a tribal uniform—what the best tech folks always wore. Brennan was adamant: "If they really feel a need to dress like they work in the mailroom, they can come to work . . . in the *mail room*." But after further thought, through six long months and lots of advice, Brennan relented and allowed casual dress on Fridays. (Bill McNabb later made casual dress the norm. In 2019, Tim Buckley decided that Vanguard crew were allowed to wear jeans.)

Brennan saw hundreds of individual performance reviews of Vanguard leaders every year. Each review was rigorous, some might say almost neurotically so, because even with the organization's huge, repeated expenditures on computers and communications technology, Vanguard is centered on and dependent on the crew. Both efficiency and effectiveness depend on the full integration of professional people and advanced technology.

One of Brennan's most unusual practices was one of the most effective: do it yourself *first*. When an important managerial position was to be filled, Brennan took that job himself for a few months of rolling up his sleeves and getting his hands dirty—or as long as six months in areas like technology, where change was clearly needed so it would take longer to figure out the priorities. "While Vanguard's core values and principles have never changed, the *way* we do business must continue to change. When changing a major unit's leader, I like to take that job for a period of time, to learn what sort of leadership is needed, clean up some of the problems and then decide who will be best as that unit's leader and who will grow the most as a result of taking that job."[8]

Do it yourself *first*.

Brennan's lieutenants knew that he understood the realities they were facing and had chosen them to deal effectively with those realities. So did all the other unit heads the lieutenants would be working with. And so did others who were *not* chosen for this particular responsibility. The result was a remarkable kind of trust that permeated the senior staff.

Office politics at Vanguard is, and is clearly expected to be, very low—ideally, zero. As Brennan explained, "At Vanguard, it is never about you or me as individuals. It's always about *us* and how we can better serve clients. We strive to get the right people on the bus with no assigned seats. We want great athletes who want to learn how to become the best players they can be."[9] Vanguard wants to continue having institutional humility.

Certain "No" decisions were also important during Brennan's years as CEO:

- No local sales offices

- No "me too" decisions following others

- No offering home mortgages

- No paying for distribution

- No major commitment to international distribution

Nobody's perfect, and Jack Brennan's record had strategic weaknesses. Vanguard was not a major factor in most international markets, in part because national governments notoriously protect their financial markets, and it had not yet figured out how to deliver investment advice or make advice a strategic priority (see Chapter 17). Operationally, the balance between cost-effectiveness and prompt response to clients' calls sometimes wobbled. But when he retired in 2008 and Bill McNabb became CEO, Vanguard was incomparably stronger than when he took over from Jack Bogle. Nobody would ever describe Brennan as emotional, but he showed in his every behavior how much he cared about person-to-person connection. He set the example and has been clearly central to the development and maturation of today's Vanguard culture.

CHAPTER 14

CAPITAL POWER

N othing begins at the beginning. The before, and the before the before, and the before the before the before—all are part of the "beginning." And so it was in 2009 when a major new direction for Vanguard took shape. Barclays Bank decided to sell all or part of its investment arm, Barclays Global Investors, and BlackRock decided to buy BGI for $13.5 billion. Vanguard astounded industry observers with a multibillion-dollar cash offer for just the ETF part of BGI, leaving BGI's index mutual funds with Barclays PLC.

Vanguard was not entirely new to acquisitions. A few years earlier, it had briefly considered acquiring TIAA-CREF, the enormous retirement fund for college and university faculty and staff. Both organizations had substantial assets dominated by long-term retirement accounts invested in index funds. That acquisition possibility was quickly dropped, for three major reasons, clarified through rigorous discussion: the cultures of the two organizations, while *generally* similar, were sufficiently different to raise doubts about the success of integration; achieving the savings advantages that would make the merger financially attractive would depend on terminating a large majority of the TIAA-CREF employees, clearly counter to the core "loyalty up, loyalty down" values of Vanguard; and, as became clear during the senior staff and board discussions, growth in assets was *not* a primary objective of Vanguard.[1] Vanguard's focus was singular: what was best for each of Vanguard's present investors over the long term.

What had become Barclays Global Investors had begun as an experimental unit of Wells Fargo Bank's investment department, led by James R. Vertin, an avid duck hunter who habitually took only enough shells to match the legal limit—and never missed. A serious student of pioneering work on efficient markets, Jim Vertin became convinced of the merits of indexing in the early 1970s and created Wells Fargo Investment Advisors, which later became part of a joint venture with Nikko Securities. The two units continued to operate as separate business units. In 1994, Merrill Lynch came close to acquiring Wells Fargo Investment Advisors but decided against it when, according to Jerry Kenney, then a top Merrill executive, two important investment managers pleaded with CEO Bill Schreyer: "If you acquire this index business, it will kill all we have done or can do to build up Merrill Lynch Asset Management as an active manager."[2] As a result, the way was left open for Barclays Bank to acquire Wells Fargo Nikko, which it did for $400 million as part of its nascent globalization strategy. Barclays merged this combination with the investment management division of Barclays DeZoete Wedd Investors to form BGI in 1995. By 2006, BGI had pre-tax profits of $1.3 billion and a profit margin of 43.9 percent.

In April 2009, a small article in the *Wall Street Journal* described an offer by the private equity firm CVC Capital to buy the iShares ETF business of Barclays Global Investors, a deal arranged by Lazard, the prior firm of Barclays' chairman. In the depths of the global recession, Barclays Bank was under pressure from British banking authorities to raise equity capital. Fortunately for Vanguard, the announced CVC deal included a so-called "go shop" provision allowing Barclays to consider other, higher bids for the iShares business, which, if accepted, would entitle CVC to a breakup fee. Brennan, by then Vanguard's chairman, saw the article and went to Glenn Reed, head of the Strategy and Finance division, and CEO Bill McNabb to ask, "Do you think we should take a look?"[3]

BGI's iShares business was large, approximately $350 billion in assets at the time. It was the leading global ETF business in an industry that most analysts felt had a long future growth runway. iShares dominated the American ETF market and had established small but growing market positions in the United Kingdom, Europe, and

Asia. Acquiring iShares would immediately establish Vanguard as the leading US provider of ETFs and could jump-start its then modest international business.

Reed soon concluded that Vanguard should engage an investment bank to advise and represent its interests in a possible bid for the iShares business. The obvious initial choice was Goldman Sachs, which had faithfully called on Vanguard for several years, even though Vanguard had always been an unlikely consumer of investment banking services. Here, at last, was an opportunity to reward that firm for its efforts—but Goldman had already been retained by a client interested in the same transaction, so it could not also work for Vanguard.

April 2009 was a low point in Wall Street transaction volume and, in the absence of other activity, the CVC–iShares announcement attracted considerable interest among financial services industry participants and the private equity community.[4] As a result, the same conflicted situation prevailed at every major New York investment bank. So Reed, raised in the Midwest himself, suggested that Vanguard hire William Blair, the leading Chicago securities and corporate finance firm. Brennan and McNabb readily agreed.

William Blair put together a stellar team to help Vanguard analyze and evaluate the iShares business. During the initial conversations, there was confusion as to how Vanguard, as a mutual organization—"not for profit" to outsiders—could obtain the enormous capital that would be required to outbid CVC. Reed explained that the Vanguard Group, Inc. could, by the terms of its relationship with the funds, call for capital from the Vanguard mutual funds, up to approximately $2 billion. With $2 billion in equity capital, Vanguard could readily borrow another two or three billion for a total of around $5 billion.

"Wow! How soon could you do that?"

"Virtually overnight."

The silence on the phone made clear that any confusion had been cleared up. Vanguard had significant capital commitment capabilities. They had just not been widely nor clearly understood.

Reed had known that William Blair had a first-rate relationship with Warren Buffett and Berkshire Hathaway, having introduced the Dairy Queen acquisition to Berkshire several years before. Reed asked Blair to contact Buffett on Vanguard's behalf, to see if he might have an interest in learning more about Vanguard's ambitions for iShares.

Buffett confirmed to William Blair's representative that he had always had a high regard for Vanguard and invited Brennan, McNabb, and Reed to visit Berkshire Hathaway's headquarters in the Kiewit Building in Omaha. The Vanguard team got there early and decided to wait for time to pass at the building's first floor coffee shop, where they ordered some food that none of them really wanted. At the appointed time, they took the elevator to the Berkshire Hathaway floor. Getting out of the elevator, however, the three men were unsure which door to enter from the elevator lobby, when Warren Buffett suddenly opened a door and invited them in, taking them down the hall to a modest room with a desk, a sofa, and a couple of high-backed chairs.

After introductions, Brennan, McNabb, and Reed described Vanguard's interest in iShares, after which Buffett asked, "How can we help?" Moving to his desk, he took out a yellow pad, made some notes with a pencil, and announced that "[we] can lend you $2½ billion," which was just what Vanguard needed to go with the $2 billion it could raise internally.

After a short tour of the modest Berkshire Hathaway offices, including Buffett's extensive array of University of Nebraska football memorabilia, Buffett gave the keys to his car to his assistant and asked her to give the three from Vanguard a ride to the Omaha airport. The entire visit took no more than 90 minutes.[5]

If Vanguard could win iShares, it would benefit from the high brand loyalty of ETF investors: they repeatedly use the one "family" of ETFs they have gotten used to. Vanguard would coordinate, but not combine and integrate, the BGI line of ETFs with its own. Similarly, avoiding layoffs, Vanguard would not try to combine the two organizations, one on the West Coast and one on the East Coast. This would limit the opportunity for "rightsizing" to enhance the economics.

BlackRock, an organization with unusually strong leadership, did have a focus on size and, as a public company, on increasing revenues and earnings to enhance the value of its common stock, a major part of the personal wealth of CEO Larry Fink and his executive team. Having recently completed the integration of a major investment management acquisition, Merrill Lynch Asset Management, some BlackRock executives were unsure their organization had the energy and bandwidth to succeed so soon with another major acquisition.

Barclays Bank needed a capital infusion of £15 billion when chairman Bob Diamond's Gulfstream landed late in 2008 in Doha, Qatar, as Philip Augar related in his splendid account of Barclays Bank's travails, *The Bank That Lived a Little.*[6] On October 13, Her Majesty's government announced that it had taken major stakes in three of the United Kingdom's largest banks for an enormous total of £37 billion. Barclays Bank announced that it would not need government funding but would be independently raising £4.5 billion, £1.5 billion through management actions and £2 billion by not paying out the year's final dividend, plus a new money commitment by Qatar of £1 billion; it would also raise around £10 billion in debt.

The idea of Barclays Bank selling BGI, driven by an acute need for equity capital, was originated in London by Hector Sants, the highly regarded head of the Financial Services Authority (FSA), then the City of London's powerful regulator. The first would-be buyer, CVC, was only interested in the iShares business. Barclays wanted to explore alternative moves and remembered that six years earlier, Bob Diamond, an American and newly named Barclays chairman, had discussed selling the whole BGI organization with BlackRock's Larry Fink, but discussions had not advanced very far.

Diamond noticed on his bankwide schedule of major meetings that the Barclays Capital team serving BlackRock was hosting its senior people at a Yankees baseball game, the first game in the new Yankee Stadium. While a devoted Red Sox fan himself, he decided this was an important opportunity. He went to Barclays' private lounge at the stadium and, near the end of the game, went for a walk with BlackRock's president, Robert Kapito, asking him to arrange a meeting with Fink a few days later.*

---

* In another telling, Kapito bought a scalper's ticket and went to Barclays' box to pull Diamond out and urge him to sell all of BGI to BlackRock.

At that meeting, Diamond offered an exclusive deal for the whole BGI business, and Fink said he would now buy all of BGI.[7] This bold move completely changed the competition. First, it would provide Barclays Bank with all the capital it needed to meet its regulators' requirements—and would do so in a single transaction. Second, it took Vanguard out of the competition: Vanguard could arrange a $5 billion transaction, but not one for $13 billion—and particularly not when Vanguard had no strategic reason to expand in index fund investing, where it was already the market leader.

BlackRock's deal was announced in June for $13.5 billion, composed of £4.2 billion in cash and 19.9 percent ownership of BlackRock. Fink was correctly convinced the financial crisis was over. When the deal closed on December 1, 2009, BlackRock's market capitalization soared by $6.3 billion to $15.2 billion. Barclays Bank's take was more than 30 times what it had paid to create BGI 14 years earlier, and the bank was in the clear financially.

Bob Diamond received $36 million for stock he had purchased for $10 million just seven years before. With costs cut and assets doubling, profits had risen rapidly—more than fivefold. BGI had decided in early 1999 that while ETFs were superior as a product, establishing a strong market demand would require a full spectrum product line, a major educational program, and a dedicated sales force. BGI hired over 100 salespeople, rebranded its ETFs as iShares, matched each major index with an iShare ETF, budgeted $12 million for print and TV ads, created its own award-winning website, and addressed retail investors. Its sales force focused on three kinds of advisers: Registered Investment Adviser (RIA) firms, national and regional securities firms, and small firms. As its retail business grew, BGI launched a major effort with institutional investors, hedge funds, mutual funds, and wealth managers. By 2006, BGI managed an array of 194 ETFs worldwide and had spent $100 million on market development. BGI was the largest ETF sponsor, with $284 billion in assets under management. State Street Global had $101 billion, Bank of New York had $27 billion, and Vanguard ranked fifth with $22 billion, having begun only in 2002.

Glenn Reed took comfort in his late father-in-law's sage advice to "never look back and worry about a deal not done." Many good things came to Vanguard from the iShares deal not done:

- To ensure that Vanguard would not find out later that it had simply been just a stalking horse for other bidders, Vanguard had required Barclays to cover Vanguard's due diligence costs in the event a deal was completed with someone else. Barclays honored the commitment, and reimbursed substantially all of Vanguard's nearly $1 million in out-of-pocket expenses. In Reed's view, "The Vanguard team got a great education in the ways of M&A . . . all on full scholarship."

- Vanguard reaffirmed its ability to raise large amounts of capital by drawing funds from the Vanguard mutual funds or borrowing from third parties. Vanguard confirmed it could also raise substantial capital by increasing its client fees by merely one basis point, or by *not reducing* fees by the same tiny amount. As assets under management rose beyond $8 trillion, this financial power became increasingly formidable. Reed said, "This was a defining time for Vanguard and its strategists."

- Most important, having lost its bid to acquire iShares, Vanguard and its board recommitted to building energetically on what it already had—a formidable ETF business in its own right—by expanding that product line and investing to expand its sales organization.

Vanguard had clarified its decision criteria: a keen interest in acquiring assets in ETFs but no interest in adding by acquisition to its business in index funds; interest only in actions that would benefit its current investors; and extreme caution about culture clash.

While publicly owned competitors like BlackRock would understandably focus on getting *bigger* in assets, revenues, and profits, Vanguard would not. Vanguard's focus would always be on getting *better*—better at serving each investor. Furthermore, the burgeoning financial power of Vanguard, while latent before, was now clear: for the right investment, Vanguard had become a financial powerhouse—and knew it.

As board chairman Alfred Rankin put it to Bill McNabb and Jack Brennan, "Now that you've proven you have the ability to raise and deploy $5 billion if the right opportunity comes your way, don't you have an implicit challenge to go *looking* for $5 billion opportunities?"[8]

CHAPTER 15

FLYWHEEL

U sing a personal experience, Bill McNabb makes his point on the value of teamwork and strong, shared commitment. "As a kid in Rochester, I delivered an evening newspaper, the *Times-Union*, with a friend. We split the route. When we worked together, it took us *each* 35 minutes. He complained that he didn't like to work as fast as I preferred. Once, when my friend went on a trip with his family, I had my two younger brothers help me. We developed a system. We'd put the papers in a wheelbarrow, which I'd push up the street as fast as I could. They'd grab the papers and run them to people's doorsteps. We could do the whole route in just 20 minutes!"

Six foot five inches tall, F. William McNabb III is modest, self-disciplined, and a rower. Crew is an ultimate team sport with no heroic individuals; it requires each person, through discipline and dedication, to perform anonymously yet superbly for the success of the team. McNabb grew up in Rochester, New York, and moved to Boston at 14. He graduated from Dartmouth with a BA in government in 1979.

Bill McNabb is comfortable with unemotional, evidence-based, incremental decisions. "I've asked myself three questions about each job I've taken: Is it interesting? Will I learn a lot? Who will I work for? Coming out of Dartmouth, I accepted a teaching position at Haverford School near Philadelphia. It turned out to be one of the best things that ever happened to me. At 22, I had to design my own program, from choosing the textbook to planning the course syllabus. I had to be comfortable talking in front of both the students and the parents who were paying a lot of money for the school. I remained at Haverford for two years and continued to coach crew at the school while attending Wharton for an MBA in finance."[1] After two years as a schoolteacher, McNabb worked at Chase Manhattan Bank, first as a credit analyst and then in a group working out deals that had been highly leveraged in the early 1980s. He joined Vanguard in 1986 to manage guaranteed investment contracts—similar to CDs—issued by insurance companies to 401(k) investors. By 2008, he had led each of Vanguard's business divisions that directly serve clients.

> "I've asked myself three questions about each job I've taken: Is it interesting? Will I learn a lot? Who will I work for?"

When Jack Brennan told the board in January 2008 that he planned to step down as CEO, he was only 54. All the directors thought it was far too soon: "Jack, you're too young to retire now!" "Everything is going so well! Why stop now?" "Jack, some of your best years are ahead of you. You won't want to miss the fun of achieving even more successes, so don't stop now!" But Brennan, as usual, had given a lot of quiet thought to his decision. He summarized his thorough self-examination this way: "My head says I should stay, but my heart says it's time to go. I'm seeing too much of the 'founder's dilemma' in my thoughts and I'm starting to be protective." As they realized Brennan had made his decision and would stick to it, the inevitable question was: Who would be the next CEO?

Tim Buckley was an easy choice: a deep believer in Vanguard's values and mission, with impressive talents and leadership skills, and modest, he radiated enjoyability as a person and competence as a professional. Still, Brennan said, "No—not yet. He'll be even better as our CEO after a few more years of experience and giving others more time to recognize his capabilities."

Brennan was confident that the new CEO should be Bill McNabb. He had demonstrated his broad leadership capabilities and was ready for the job. At the next regular board meeting, the schedule was to have Jim Norris, managing director of Vanguard International, conduct a soup-to-nuts review of Vanguard's international businesses. Then it would be McNabb's turn to make what he expected to be a routine presentation.

McNabb could tell something was off kilter. "The directors, for the first time in all my years of experience with them, did not seem engaged or even particularly well prepared for the discussion. This was highly unusual. Vanguard directors always took their responsibilities seriously and always came to meetings well prepared." McNabb knew with a sinking feeling that he had somehow lost their attention.

Then it got worse. Brennan stepped in—which had never happened before—and called for a pause in the meeting for an impromptu phone break. Brennan then turned to McNabb: "Let's go to the penalty box"—the small room next to the big boardroom where "next up" executives typically would wait to be called into the meeting. Flustered, McNabb didn't wait for Brennan to lower the boom. He began to apologize for somehow losing the directors' interest. Brennan cut him off with a surprise:

"Bill, you've just been elected president and CEO of Vanguard! Congratulations!"

As Brennan knew, the board was formalizing the appointment as he spoke. McNabb was stunned. Brennan was only three years older and was at the peak of his effectiveness. McNabb had expected to serve out his whole career working on Brennan's team and was known to say, "I'd follow the guy anywhere!"

Now he said: "Get serious!"

"Bill, it's time for me, time for you, and time for Vanguard."[2]

On his first day as CEO, McNabb made a point of going to Bogle's suite of offices on a different floor of the same building for a brief personal visit. Bogle said, "He was *very* nice. Very thoughtful. I will try to comport myself so as to not give him any problems. If I have issues—and there will be plenty of those—I will talk to him about them. Bill has been very gracious."[3] Of course, that did not curb Bogle's acerbic comments on industry pricing practices or ETFs. Bogle would forever insist on being "independent."

That courtesy meeting recalled a more portentous appointment. When first interviewing for a job at Vanguard, McNabb had met with Bogle. As McNabb recalled, "He looked at my résumé, and the first thing he said to me is, 'Why would you come here? You're working on Wall Street with a big firm. We've got only $20 billion under management. I can't imagine how we're ever getting to 25. I don't know why you would come here.' We spent the next hour and a half where he talked to me about all the things wrong on Wall Street, and when I got home, my wife said, "How'd it go?" I said, "I don't know. I didn't say much. But there's one thing I do know: I really, really want to go there because I heard this incredibly compelling vision of what this organization could be."[4]

Bogle provided the vision and founded the company. He provided the principle and the values and got everyone behind him. But it was really Jack Brennan—not just after he took over, but when he was understudying Bogle—who built the team, the processes, the modern thinking and the management capabilities to make it work. In that sense, they were complementary. McNabb worked with and learned from both men, and could see both sides, taking the best of both and blending them together.

When leading Vanguard's powerful 401(k) business to industry leadership, Bill McNabb had used a simple, low-tech way of building sales effectiveness and teamwork. He met frequently with the sales group and asked each member to take 10 or 15 minutes to share with him and with the others the nitty-gritty specifics of prospects and customers. This kept everyone focused on what would work, and why. They saw their own challenges in context, and took ideas and suggestions from other salespeople that they could use. They confirmed that McNabb, as their leader, was keeping up on market realities.

"Jack Brennan may go down in financial history as the greatest market timer in history," McNabb chuckled as he reflected on the grave situation he faced as he became Vanguard's CEO.[5] Brennan had enjoyed the longest, strongest, bull market ever as the background for his long tenure, and then passed the CEO's baton. McNabb officially took over as CEO on August 31, 2008. Almost immediately, McNabb would face the stresses of the sharpest market drop in decades.

"Navigating that crisis was important for Vanguard and of course for me as a leader coming after such a successful, beloved and admired teacher-leader as Jack Brennan. Going in, we fortunately had positioned ourselves and our investor-owners conservatively. Having absolutely no Lehman Brothers paper helped us come out of that challenging period even stronger. On Monday, September 15, I was in Washington, D.C., giving a talk to a group of 400 of our largest

401(k) client CEOs on the importance of investors always taking a sober, long-term perspective when Lehman Brothers hit. Someone said, 'The world is melting down as we speak.' At that same time, Gus Sauter was on the trading desk striving to deal with the staccato of ultra-short calls for specific decisions to protect our clients' savings."

To stay on top of the fast-developing situation and be sure they were in control to the extent possible, McNabb and all his senior staff met at the beginning of every morning, again at midday, and at the end of every afternoon for three straight months. "Of course that was a great internal bonding experience, but our focus was always on two groups. Number one: our clients. Number two: our crew. We took every opportunity to reach out to make contact with each of our investors as frequently as possible. Sometimes, to be honest, it was minute by minute. We were getting a record volume of internet hits. Clients were on the phones. We did webcasts for our clients—the first one had 50,000 hits. We did CNBC and Bloomberg. We stayed the course and came through it very well. And that commitment made an important difference to our clients and the crew because it reaffirmed our commitment to both groups: do the right thing."

McNabb later said, "During that period, when Wall Street banks were going under or being bailed out, Vanguard hunkered down internally while at the same time reaching out to jittery investors." As Wall Street firms fired thousands of employees, McNabb determined there would be no employee layoffs at Vanguard. "Of course, the number of transactions does not go down all that much when prices drop," he explained. "But assets and revenues do, so we had to increase the expense ratios of our mutual funds to make up the difference. Investors accepted this as a small price to pay, but the impact on crew morale and confidence in their new leadership was huge."

McNabb explained, "We thought if our crew were distracted by questions like, 'Do I have a job or do I *not* have a job?' there was no way they were going to serve clients well. The cost savings we would have gained were fairly modest, and we thought it was incredibly important to send a positive message to our people: focus on the client, focus *only* on the client. We're going to be fine as an organization."[6]

McNabb added, "We have a missionary zeal for our core purpose—to take a stand for all investors, to treat them fairly, and to give them the best chance of investment success. We've elevated that purpose into a belief that we can change the way the world invests."

After that crisis, he recalled, "we knew that things had fundamentally shifted in our industry. Given our corporate structure and our values, we knew we had an opportunity to take command of the industry. To do that, we needed people to appreciate what made us different. Internally, we needed to keep the focus on the client. I told our people, 'We are here for the investor. Nothing else matters.'"

Flying to the west coast, Bill McNabb realized that the man sitting next to him couldn't help noticing that he was persistently working on one Vanguard memo after another.

"I see how hard you're working," the man said. "Do you work at Vanguard?"

"Yes."

"What do you do there?"

"A little of everything. All depends."

"Makes me feel like one of the best investors in the world to be with Vanguard. Most of my friends are moving into cash. Any advice?"

"Stay in and diversify."

Telling that story, McNabb added, "I think one lesson that has been reinforced during the crisis is that 'boring' really works."[7]

In October 2008, 100,000 viewers came to that page on the website to see what Vanguard meant by its "working for you" commitment, unusually high numbers for Vanguard customers then. McNabb and Gus Sauter made the case for expecting a solid market recovery and the importance of staying focused on the long term. Less than six months later, in March, the crisis had passed and the stock market soared.

When Vanguard was experiencing a surge in clients several years ago, an increase in crew was needed but could not be filled through normal recruiting. Kathy Gubanich came up with a solution: a cash bonus to any crew member who brought someone to Vanguard who was hired. Good idea! Who but a crew member would better understand what a great place Vanguard was to work? And who would better understand the values that Vanguard sought in a candidate? Of course, a nice bonus would be a savvy incentive. The bonus plan was explained in an attractive booklet and a series of small group meetings. Anticipation was high, but nothing happened. The bonus was increased, with some fanfare. Still, nothing happened.

Gubanich decided to do some interviews. Was the increased bonus still too low? Were there doubts about the program? She soon discovered the real problem. A representative crew member explained: "I enjoy time with my friends, and I love my work at Vanguard. But my friends just wouldn't make the cut at Vanguard. If I introduce them here, they'll get turned down. So I'll lose my friends *and* I'll lose my good standing here. Why would I ever try to pick up a few hundred dollars and wind up losing both my friends and my reputation at Vanguard?"[8]

"Vanguarding" was an advertising concept developed out of a brainstorming session at an ad agency. Someone put "Vanguard your money" on the whiteboard. Converting Vanguard into "Vanguarding" made it a call to action. McNabb emphasized that the cost of the media campaign—reported to be $50 million, up from a previous year's $20 million—was dramatically lower as a proportion of assets managed than it had been 20 years ago. Bogle, of course, focused on the cash: "People should look at the absolute dollars, not the ratio." When Vanguard managed $1.4 trillion with an expense ratio of 0.20 percent—down from a 0.30 percent ratio when it had managed $900 million—Bogle had focused on operating expenses in dollars. He argued that the one-third decline did not seem like "significant economies of scale" to him.

McNabb stayed on guard. "When I became CEO," he recalled, "I started to worry that just the slightest bit of complacency might have crept into the organization. I'd hear, 'What are we worried about?' But in fact we were actually losing share on the retail indexing side. That's when I took my senior team on a retreat to aggressively map our future course." McNabb adopted a powerful strategic management concept from the writings of business author Jim Collins. It was an effective image to summarize Vanguard's business strategy: a flywheel, an axle-mounted disk that at first spins slowly due to inertia, but with effort gains speed and finally spins on its own momentum. McNabb elaborated: "The Vanguard flywheel starts with low-cost funds, which drive lower fees. Lower fees drive better returns for investors which result in more investors investing more money with Vanguard, which enables Vanguard, in a powerful virtuous cycle or flywheel, to reduce fees, which enables Vanguard to attract more assets, reduce fees, attract assets, reduce fees, etc."[9]

McNabb made the flywheel a common Vanguard term, facilitating understanding across the organization. After meeting with Collins in Colorado, senior staff identified 10 major goals based on the concept. The goals were then reduced from 10 to 5, known collectively as Flywheel 2.0. "First, we focused on next-generation products and services; second, we wanted to become a truly global company; third, we strove to continue to bend the cost curve; fourth, we needed to protect our flanks by managing risks including cybersecurity and regulatory changes; and fifth, we wanted to continue the emphasis on A-plus leadership. Flywheel 2.0 was a critical moment for us. We decided that we were not going to be all things to all people. We were not going to go into banking like Schwab. We were not going to invest in private equity deals like BlackRock."

Goals—stretch goals—were also set on four core dimensions: 90 percent of actively managed funds would outperform their peer groups after fees over 10 years; 80 percent of Vanguard client-investor-owners would give Vanguard high "net promoter" scores, reflecting likelihood of recommending it to others; the ratio of "engaged" crew versus "disengaged" crew would meet or beat 9 to 1; and the average Vanguard expense ratio would be taken down by 10 basis points, from 0.20 percent to 0.10 percent. The key focus would be automation to increase service values at lower and lower costs.

"Given the large scale at which Vanguard now operates, the investable dollars that are thrown off are enormous," McNabb said. On an average day, Vanguard receives over $1 billion of new assets to manage. "We can write several $100 million checks to finance exciting new developments in our pursuit of our corporate mission to give all investors a fair shake."

In sum, he said, "Our core values must continue to be our core values, but every generation must change the way those core values are realized. It's necessary to change the specifics of implementation in order to have a smooth transition. Vanguard investors increasingly compare their experience not with Fidelity or Schwab, but with technology leaders like Amazon and Google, and the means of contact is shifting from iPads to iPhones."

McNabb agrees with those who believe financial advice can be a major benefit to Vanguard's client-investors. As he puts it, "Given all the changes in the stock market that have made it so much more efficient, Vanguard may not be able to do much to help investors beat the market, but we can certainly do a lot to help investors develop sound long-term financial plans for each individual investor and help them stay on those plans and *not* make costly mistakes."[10]

An accelerating challenge during McNabb's years as CEO was cybersecurity. Security has long been a priority at Vanguard to protect both client-investors' assets and their home addresses, Social Security numbers, and other personal information. Unfortunately, our modern world harbors increasingly formidable bad guys scheming to break into computer systems at large financial service organizations. Vanguard averages 300,000 cyberattacks a *day*, often from foreign national organizations seeking to disrupt the firm as part of America's financial system. Some hits are by organized crime seeking to defraud or collect ransom money, and some by amateur "hack artists," explained John Marcante, global chief information officer.

> "Our core values must continue to be our core values, but every generation must change the way those core values are realized. It's necessary to change the specifics of implementation in order to have a smooth transition."

Vanguard has a complex, multilevel defense, and 83 percent of attacks bounce off the outer-outer perimeter barrier. With 95 percent of all applications segmented or separated from other parts of the system, the defenses are strong. In addition, it counterattacks. Vanguard knows the attackers can rebuild their capabilities and start attacking again—but always at a real cost to them. Over time, these "rebuild" costs add up. So one of the firm's best defenses is to be much more costly to attack than most alternative targets, and so convince attackers to go elsewhere and leave Vanguard alone.

To protect clients' accounts and information, Vanguard is always looking for unusual or "unpredicted" online behavior. When a client who habitually connects with Vanguard during business hours (or evenings or early morning) comes in at a different time, it might not actually be that client at all. If concerned, Vanguard will defer the transaction until it can be explicitly confirmed by checking with the real client, increasingly by texting a code to the client's cell phone.[11]

In 2015, Vanguard managed $244 billion, largely in index funds, for non-US investors, more than twice what it managed in 2007. "We had been overseas, but we weren't very serious in our commitment," commented McNabb. "Competitive restraints are numerous, particularly in Asia. Many nations' financial regulations are designed to favor local banks as fund distributors." But changes are coming— slowly and unevenly.

A strong proponent of Vanguard's expanding internationally, McNabb monitored evolving opportunities in China, the world's second largest economy where household savings reportedly topped $8 trillion. In 2014, a series of regulatory shifts opened access between Hong Kong and China. Regulators established mutual recognition of publicly offered funds between China and Hong Kong, which meant that funds domiciled in Hong Kong were eligible for cross-border sale in China and vice versa. McNabb said, "We are having conversations with all the right groups there. I believe we can be the largest asset manager of Chinese investments in the medium term." However, "It's not feasible for us to enter China as an asset management company unless the rules change. We do not want to be a minority in a joint venture." Recent Chinese aggressiveness toward Hong Kong has complicated prospects there, and in March 2021 Vanguard suspended plans to launch a mutual fund business in China, saying it would concentrate for now on a venture to provide financial advice.[12]

Other nations have been more receptive. In the United Kingdom, for example, McNabb noted that the government's 2006 Retail Distribution Review, or RDR, led to a 2012 ban on directing brokerage commissions as compensation for advice. "This caused advisers to change their focus from the hottest stocks to long-term financial planning, asset allocation and financial coaching. The focus on indexing really increased too, so RDR was a nice tailwind for us."[13]

"Ten years is enough for any CEO to do his best on the changes he thinks are most important, the changes he believes will do the most good in the long run," said McNabb in a philosophical reflection on his own years of service. "After 10 years, a CEO will have achieved, or failed to achieve, his top priorities, and will most likely have less energy and also face more organizational resistance. So it's better for the individual and for the organization to change the CEO. Also, it's good for the organization to know that changing the CEO is part of the dynamic of a vibrant, healthy organization."[14]

On July 14, 2017, in a clear move to show orderly succession after a seven-year surge of assets managed from $1 trillion to $4.4 trillion, Vanguard announced that the 60-year-old McNabb would be succeeded by 48-year-old Tim Buckley on January 1, 2018. As Landon Thomas Jr. observed in the *New York Times*, "Vanguard has one of the more tightly knit cultures in corporate America, with just about all the firm's senior leaders having worked at its corporate headquarters . . . for decades."[15] Or, as Bill McNabb put it, "It has never been about me personally—it's about the team."

CHAPTER 16

TIM BUCKLEY

"I don't know you, but my dad says I should work for Vanguard." That's how Tim Buckley started his letter to Jack Brennan while he was still an undergraduate at Harvard. Brennan, confident in his ability to size up people quickly, enjoyed the challenge of making accurate "people calls" early. In a celebrated example, after first meeting Buckley, he announced: "I just met a future CEO of Vanguard!"

At their second meeting, Buckley noted that he already had a great offer in his pocket from one of Philadelphia's leading investment firms. Both men were good negotiators, so their conversation, which both found increasingly interesting and even compelling, advanced rapidly. At just the right moment, Buckley said, "I have a firm offer from Cooke & Bieler for the summer." Brennan smiled and responded with an "exploding" offer of a summer job—good for just five minutes. After a short pause, Buckley smiled back: "I'll take it."

Mortimer J. Buckley, always known as Tim, was born in 1969, the son of Dr. Mortimer and Marilyn Buckley. His father was chief of the cardiac surgical unit at Massachusetts General Hospital. Tim earned his BA in economics and went on to Harvard Business School, returning to Vanguard for the summers between academic years. He was taking the school's iconic course on investment management when the case study of the day was on Vanguard. Since he had been working at Vanguard, Buckley kept quiet as the class of 80 students, guided by professor André Perold, identified one after another competitive strength of Vanguard: low operating costs and a unique mutual ownership that enabled lower and lower fees, which attracted larger and larger assets, enabling the firm to further reduce costs and fees while delivering good service and winning client loyalty—the virtuous cycle that had made Vanguard the industry leader in mutual fund assets and, year after year, in growth of assets. The organizational culture and opportunities for career growth, he explained, were unusually attractive. There was no risk of a disruptive acquisition upsetting careers and no risk of firm failure, an all too frequent reality in the industry.

"So," said professor Perold near the end of the 90-minute case discussion, "Vanguard is the ideal investment organization and the industry leader in America. Also, it has a good business in the small market we call Australia, which certainly indicates that its low costs, low fees, reliably great products, and good client service can be exported to other markets. So the opportunities for leadership are numerous and large. This must mean Vanguard has a great future and presents great opportunities for talented and motivated young professionals such as we have in this classroom today." Turning to one of the students, Perold asked, "What about you, Phil?"

"Actually, I've already accepted an offer from a major hedge fund."

"Congratulations, Phil. How about you, Nancy?"

"Committed last week to a private equity firm."

"Alison?"

"Already accepted an offer from a boutique investment bank."

The course had always been fast paced and full of lively discussion, often with a challenging ending question or dilemma that students would want to think about after class. But this time, the discussion was apparently coming to a dull close when professor Perold asked, "Will no one go to Vanguard?"

Buckley raised his hand. "As many of you know, I have worked at Vanguard the past two summers, and I'm going back—not for a job, but for a career. And I'd like to tell you why in the two minutes left in this session." Calmly, Buckley began to list his reasons and how they connected with the core values he saw at Vanguard, strongly attracting him to make and feel confident about his decision.

When he finished, there was a brief silence. Then his classmates burst into applause.[1]

Brennan understood the importance of a "guiding hand" in any future leader's development and had decided to perform that role for Buckley—including not rushing him; Buckley would have ample time to gain deep knowledge of the organization, and for the organization to appreciate Buckley as a leader. The first step: in 1991, Buckley served as Jack Bogle's assistant, to get immersed in the values important to Vanguard *and* to win Bogle's confidence. Buckley was made a principal in 1998 and chief information officer in 2001 with overall responsibility as managing director for the Information Technology Division. This division, central to Vanguard's future, was where Vanguard had been striving to catch up with its competitors. That same year, he joined the Global Investment Committee. In 2006, he rotated to managing director for the important Retail Investors Group, and in 2013 he became chief investment officer. As part of his planned leadership development, he also served as chairman of the board of Children's Hospital in Philadelphia from 2011 to 2017. Having had experience in major parts of Vanguard and outside, Buckley had shown his leadership capabilities to both the board of directors and to the overall Vanguard organization. He was the obvious choice to be president in 2017, and a year later he succeeded Bill McNabb as CEO.

In his first year, Buckley "did nothing"—on purpose. He took that year to devote time to meet individually and multiple times with all the senior and up-and-coming junior managers to assess their present and potential future capabilities, develop closer and deeper relationships, and give each of them unhurried opportunities to get to know him. Then he was ready to assert leadership.

After that first year, he made important changes in the board of directors, increasing diversity and adding strong capabilities to an already stellar group that included Emerson Fullwood, former vice president of Xerox; Amy Gutmann, president of the University of Pennsylvania; Joseph Loughrey, retired president of Cummins; professor Perold; and Peter Volanakis, former president of Corning. New directors are Scott Malpass, formerly the celebrated chief investment officer and vice president of Notre Dame; Deanna Mulligan, board chair and previous CEO of Guardian Life Insurance of America; Sarah Bloom Raskin, formerly deputy secretary of Treasury and a governor of the Federal Reserve Board; and Mark Loughridge, formerly CFO and senior vice president of IBM, who became Vanguard's lead independent director. Loughridge called regular meetings of the 10 independent directors, often with senior managers—some with and some without Buckley, who was the only Vanguard director not "independent."

He took that year to devote time to meet individually and multiple times with all the senior and up-and-coming junior managers to assess their present and potential future capabilities, develop closer and deeper relationships, and give each of them unhurried opportunities to get to know him.

An important change has been in the way directors and senior managers work together. In the past, the usual pattern was traditional, as it still is with most boards: management makes a carefully crafted presentation and directors ask a few questions, get sensible answers, and give approval. This has given way at Vanguard to no-holds-barred give-and-take discussion between directors and executives that all agree is more engaging and productive of great ideas and better decisions. Small groups of directors frequently undertake a "deep dive" on any question that interests them, such as possible strategic moves, new technology initiatives, or linkages with other organizations. As a result, even from an early, formative stage of development, directors have a major impact on Vanguard's forward strategy.

"Partnerships," Buckley explained, "can accelerate improvements for clients, and we have a long and successful history of drawing on world-class external expertise across our investment management, technology, and client service functions."[2] Under Buckley, Vanguard soon announced two major new partnerships.

Private equity was a burgeoning area of investments that Vanguard had stayed out of, for such good reasons as the lack of liquidity, the lack of daily pricing, long-term lock-ups of capital, and the difficulty of evaluating managers. That changed in 2020, when Vanguard selected the global private equity firm HarbourVest

Partners as its strategic partner for private equity and venture capital investments. Once again, low fees were an important differentiation. Initially, the new offering was limited to institutional investors ready to commit at least $20 million, though Vanguard said from the first announcement that it expected to expand the partnership's offerings to a wider array of investors over time. Not long afterward, individual investors and "family offices" were able to invest $2 million. Private equity was more successful than expected. The first Vanguard–HarbourVest fund was closed with nearly double the expected assets under management, and a new fund was launched.

Both Vanguard and HarbourVest are managed conservatively and see themselves as career employers, and both have grown substantially. Over 35 years, HarbourVest accumulated more than $70 billion in assets managed. It has 600 employees and 125 investment professionals located in Europe, Asia, and across the Americas. It has committed over $40 billion to newly organized funds, completed $24 billion in secondary purchases and invested $17 billion directly in operating companies. HarbourVest is a mature organization with broad capabilities, deep experience, a strong culture that already has gone through leadership succession, and extensive relationships with world-class operating managers in private equity and venture capital.

Realistically, HarbourVest is too big and too diversified to expect it to be a top-quartile performer. That's not its ambition, nor is it Vanguard's. HarbourVest aims to be a reliable above-average or second-quartile manager of a full spectrum of private equity investments, and to nurture superior long-term relationships with both a diversified group of institutional investors and diverse managers of private equity investments of various kinds, spread over the world.

This strategic partnership was both assertive and defensive. Institutional investors and wealthy individuals had been making larger commitments to private equity, and Vanguard's not having this major asset class in its lineup had become a drag on its ability to build business with larger investors. Adding private equity would also help retain existing large clients who might decide to leave if that asset class were unavailable. For HarbourVest, linking up with Vanguard provided access to a potentially substantial new source of investable capital: Vanguard clients.

With extensive diversification, in national markets around the world, in the "vintage" years in which funds are launched, in types of investment and in HarbourVest's many investment managers, this partnership expects to achieve above-average investment results over time. Private equity investing is always challenging; investment performance varies dramatically from one manager to another, and the strongest managers with the best results are usually closed to new investors. The competition for access to a superior new fund can be intense. Private equity investors have learned that identifying strong general partners is the key requirement for long-term success.

Another requirement is, of course, to acquire investments at favorable or low prices. The strong past returns of private equity managers have attracted enormous cash inflows. One result is that the money private equity funds had raised from investors but not yet invested reached an enormous $841 billion in early 2021.[3] The American Investment Council reported that for the prior 10 years, overall private equity returns were only half a percentage point ahead of the S&P 500, at 14.2 percent versus 13.7 percent.[4] This return premium was modest compensation for investors having to give up liquidity and control for a decade or longer, making all the more important Vanguard's success in selecting the manager and in ensuring that investors understand the terms, including the use of leverage in the funds to enhance returns.

> **Private equity investors have learned that identifying strong general partners is the key requirement for long-term success.**

Technology can change the cost of doing things, and Vanguard is always looking for opportunities to further reduce costs. In July of 2020, Vanguard announced another important partnership, with Infosys, to provide cloud-based record keeping for Vanguard's industry-leading business managing 1,500 defined contribution pension plans.[5]

Infosys, based in India and with extensive operations in the United States, has had nearly 40 years of experience helping organizations in 46 different countries navigate their digital transformation. The company combines competence in artificial intelligence with large-scale operations and unusually low costs of operation. As an indication of the importance of this partnership, some 1,300 members of the Vanguard crew, led by Martha King, formerly managing director of Vanguard's institutional investor group, moved to Infosys facilities close to Vanguard offices in Malvern, Charlotte, and Scottsdale.* In Buckley's words, "Our partnership with Infosys will help us transform the retirement industry for the benefit of all investors."

Mohit Joshi, president of Infosys, said, "Our cloud-based platform will create a new standard for the industry as we seek to drastically improve the retirement savings experience for plan participants and sponsors through the use of cutting-edge digital technologies. The partnership will use a cloud-based platform to keep records for almost five million plan participants and 1,500 plan sponsors."

Infosys works with many of the world's largest and most advanced financial service organizations, including more than half of the top 20 US retirement service providers. Visitors to its headquarters in Bangalore are always impressed by well-kept green lawns and modern buildings displaying the names of major firms that the sophisticated workers in each building serve: Goldman Sachs, Morgan Stanley, UBS, American Express, Visa, and others. Founded with a mere $250 in 1981, Infosys surged to $13.5 billion in revenues in 2020 and a market capitalization over $80 billion.

Vanguard's strategic reason for deciding to outsource the recordkeeping business came in two parts. Achieving the intended large-scale transformation would take a major commitment of its own management time and talent if Vanguard's leaders did the work; the judgment was that it would be better to devote this resource to other priorities. By embracing Infosys's established cloud expertise, Vanguard could leap to the frontier of this technology almost immediately.

In its continuing efforts to squeeze out costs, Vanguard made a mistake in October 2021. It got swift, negative feedback from members of the crew, and Tim Buckley quickly reversed the decision he had

---

* Not everyone was convinced. On the Bogleheads website, doubters raised questions about how many of the 1,300 would still be there after a year and worried about jobs migrating from America to India.

announced. The firm had said it would end a healthcare benefit that accrued a credit of $5,500 a year for each crew member after age 40, and half as much for a spouse. After retirement, crew members over 50 who had worked at Vanguard for at least 10 years could use that credit to reimburse 75 percent of a health insurance premium. In exchange for giving up this benefit, Vanguard would make a one-time payment of $40,000 to eligible crew members, though some longtime members had amassed more than $100,000 in credits.[6]

Buckley followed up four days later with an email and a video to active and retired crew members, admitting, "We know we missed the mark." The previous benefit would hold for all retired crew and for any who retired by year-end 2022. For all others, any accrued benefit would be frozen at the level attained.

The major change now in the works as part of Tim Buckley's leadership is rotating Vanguard's overarching proposition from low-cost do-it-yourself investment products toward adding value with custom-tailored financial *advice*—enabled by impressive advances in artificial intelligence and other technology, supported by impressive capital investments. As Buckley and his team put increasing focus on advice, Vanguard will be in a strategic transformation that will lead the investment industry into disruptive challenges. They could prove more beneficial to investors than even Vanguard's prior challenge to conventional practices in the investment industry: low fees.

PART FOUR

Leading and Innovating

CHAPTER 17

ADVICE

As CEO, providing investment advice is Tim Buckley's top innovation priority. Vanguard is devoting major resources, financial and creative, to developing new ways advanced technology can be used to deliver custom-tailored advice to its investors. And none too soon.

Realistically, Vanguard has been late, as have most other investment firms, to recognize the importance of good advice in the overall experience of investors. Part of this lateness is due to the firm's history. In its early "if you build it, they will come" years, Vanguard depended on do-it-yourself retail investors attracted by unusually low fees. Investment advice is personal to each individual, so it has traditionally been labor intensive, with high-cost labor, and did not scale. So advice as a service was understandably slow in developing.

While committed to good service, the majority of Vanguard's clients are of moderate means, and the type of service they expect to pay for can be noticeably simpler than the top-end, individualized services of some competitors. As an example, for family offices of wealthy clients, Fidelity may provide a direct 800 number to a dedicated contact person and, more important, has people skilled at solving adjacent problems like what can be done to get better or less costly coverage in health insurance. It can bundle together requests from like-minded family offices to get lower costs or better service.

As a first small step toward offering advice, in 1993 Vanguard offered a PC-based software package to assist investors with retirement planning. A year later it introduced LifeStrategy Funds, four funds-of-funds offering prepackaged asset allocation suitable for four general risk levels: income, conservative growth, moderate growth, and growth. However, these "one size fits all" funds necessarily ignored the many ways people differed in such factors as wealth, life expectancy, and specific attitudes toward market risk.

Neither Jack Bogle nor Jack Brennan could find a way to make personalized advice cost-effective for investors *or* for Vanguard. This has been changing with advancements in information technology, bringing increasing focus by Bill McNabb on providing advice and even greater emphasis by Tim Buckley. Looking back, Brennan wishes he had been bolder sooner.

Providing advice on what each investor should do is, as Warren Buffett once said about investing, "simple, but not easy." First, clarify each investor's realistic goals in order of priority. Even quantitative goals like "enough for retirement" are obviously hard to specify unambiguously. Qualitative objectives like "more risk" or "less risk" are enormously difficult to quantify, and hard numbers have wide plus-or-minus boundaries. Second, specify the time available to achieve each goal. The combination of these two steps helps clarify what actions—particularly saving—will be needed each year to achieve goals. That's the "simple" part. Then comes the "not easy" part: helping the investor actually do the saving and stay on plan, even as the market behaves in its curiously disconcerting, distractive, provocative ways.

> Providing advice on what each investor should do is, as Warren Buffett once said about investing, "simple, but not easy."

For most workers, the move from traditional defined benefit pension plans to 401(k) plans shifted decision responsibility from full-time experts at corporate headquarters to the individual, who usually doesn't have the time, expertise, or interest to master the complexities of investing. Many individuals also lack the detachment to make consistently rational decisions about long-term investments—usually "benign neglect" or "stay the course." And most of the "advice" offered by most major financial firms is actually aimed at getting investors to buy services and products that are rather high cost, low value, or both—which, of course, is why they are hidden behind an "advice" wrapper.

Vanguard's advice-embedded products, such as the LifeStrategy Funds and later Target Retirement Funds, helped clients choose a disciplined long-term investment program using low-cost, low-turnover, tax-efficient index funds and ETFs. Since most of us are not experts on investing, most of us would do better—usually much better—if we got *and* followed sensible advice from trustworthy investment professionals. (See "The Grim Realities of Investing.")

The Grim Realities of Investing

- Behavioral economists have shown that 80 percent of us believe we are above average as investors.

- Most of us do not have an investment plan in writing.

- While most of us know we can claim Social Security at 62, we do not know how much more we will get if we wait till 70. It's much more than the 25 to 30 percent that most financial folks guess. For most of us, this is the most important investment decision of a lifetime, but we seldom know how to best think about our decision. Waiting eight years increases benefits by 76 percent.[1]

- Most of us believe fees for investment management are low.

- Most of us forget to subtract the impact of inflation when estimating investment returns.

- Most of us have an itch to sell when stocks have fallen a lot, and an itch to buy when stocks have risen a lot—even if we know we should do the reverse. Stocks may be the only purchase we shun when marked down and put "on sale" and the only one we rush to buy when the price goes up.

- When deciding on our asset mix, we tend to overlook the reality that most of us are really, really long-term investors—often from our twenties to our late eighties. Our invested retirement savings will only be spent many long years after today's excitement is forgotten.

- Most of us make "unforced errors" that cost us 20 percent to 30 percent of the returns achieved by our mutual funds.

In the sixties and seventies, "beating the market" became the dominant investor objective. In that very different stock market, active investing—stock picking—seemed the smart way to increase returns. Advice on long-term investment policy got sidelined. Sadly, most investors accepted the widely advertised possibilities of "outperformance" instead of the increasingly bleak, statistically low probabilities of achieving it. Moreover, as investors increasingly sought the better "performance" managers, fees rose—over time, more than doubling.

With fees and assets escalating from both new business and a generally rising market, income to management firms and their professional employees rose again. These larger financial rewards—along with the nonfinancial rewards of the always interesting work of active investing—attracted crowds of skillful competitors. Performance mutual funds, hedge funds, and other institutional investors with sophisticated computers drove any "less than the best" participants out of the business. Stock market activity has been transformed from less than 10 percent institutional trading to over 90 percent of trading by institutions. Almost all the professionals know almost all the same information at almost the same time, and they must buy from and sell to other experts; market prices quickly reflect almost all that is known by the experts. Most active managers are unable, after deducting management fees and costs of operations, to keep up with their chosen segment of the overall market. Not only have 89 percent of actively managed US funds fallen short of their chosen benchmark over 15 years, but identifying the outperforming 11 percent in advance is virtually impossible. Even worse, most of the past decade's winners will become losers in the following decade.

Even optimists must recognize that what worked in the past is not working today. The change forces that brought about this adverse transformation are unlikely to reverse, and very unlikely to reverse by enough for long enough to make active investing a rewarding game again for clients.

> Almost all the professionals know almost all the same information at almost the same time, and they must buy from and sell to other experts; market prices quickly reflect almost all that is known by the experts.

As noted in Chapter 7, Vanguard's main value-added in active investing is more important than doing *better* than the market: it helps protect clients from doing much *worse*. While usually outperforming most other active managers, even Vanguard's experienced, skillful "manager of managers" group is not, on average, beating index benchmarks. The limited prospects for beat-the-market active management operations make sensible, personalized advice on investment planning stand out as the best way for investors to achieve investment success over the long run.

Vanguard has been increasingly successful with two different kinds of offerings:

- **Products** with embedded strategy, as pioneered by the LifeStrategy funds, with characteristics and purpose specified upfront. They are low cost and come in an array of easy-to-use forms so investors can confidently make reasonable selections for themselves.

- **Services** tailored to meet the particular objectives of each investor, given the investor's assets, age, income, and other considerations.

From the start, the LifeStrategy Funds had low fees—one-third those of competitors—and allocated their investments differently. Compared to others, the Vanguard funds typically had over 10 percent more in equities at each stage of life and nearly 5 percent more in international stocks. The consequence of allocating more to equities was that those choosing Vanguard's age-based product would likely find that they experienced slightly more fluctuations over the short term and more growth in value over the long term. Vanguard's strong acceptance in the marketplace enabled it to catch up with competitors in age-based funds. Three years later, in 1997, it ranked third in assets so managed.

In 2003, Vanguard introduced Target Retirement Funds. These funds take as their target the year in which the investor will turn 65. Over the years, as the investor ages, the asset mix gradually shifts from equity index funds into bond index funds and cash. For example, for a 40-year-old investor, a fund might offer a portfolio of 60 percent stocks and 40 percent bonds, but for those age 50, the recommendation would be 50 percent in both stocks and bonds, and at age 70, a 70–30 bond-stock mix. Adhering to traditional allocations at these ages, the changes help offset the declining net present value of predictable future earned income as a person ages. In addition, since equity returns are "mean-reverting" (increasingly average), their long-term returns are less volatile and uncertain than their short-term returns.

These calculations don't consider the impact of inflation on real returns nor the importance of other assets an individual might hold, such as a home or Social Security benefits or working past 65. (See Chapter 19.) Nor do they reflect the opportunity to educate plan participants about the nature of stock markets so they could be less nervous. Still, Target Retirement Funds make sense for most people and relieve participants of year-to-year managerial responsibilities they often do not want, such as rebalancing a portfolio's asset mix as stock and bond market prices gyrate or staying on plan despite major market moves.

Target date funds (as commonly referred to in the industry) were introduced originally as a "default" investment option for 401(k) plan participants who were unsure how to invest their annual contributions. All too many 401(k) plan participants had been defaulting into a money market fund—okay for simple saving, *not* okay for long-term investment of retirement funds. While a generic "everyman" solution might not be just right for each investor, a well-known standardized solution that adjusted asset mix with aging was far better for most people than no plan at all.

Efforts to share the lower costs of serving larger investors can go astray. Target date funds are designed for investors with 401(k) or other tax-deferred accounts, but some investors hold them in taxable accounts. In 2021, Vanguard lowered the minimum investment for its lowest-fee target-date funds to $15 million from $100 million, and many institutions immediately moved their money to get the lower fees. This required the Vanguard funds for investors with more modest holdings to sell a lot of securities, saddling some taxable investors with large, unexpected tax bills. Some angry shareholders sensibly argued that Vanguard should have warned more effectively against holding these funds in taxable accounts. In a July 2022 settlement with Massachusetts securities regulators, Vanguard agreed to pay about $6 million, most of which will be restitution to eligible investors in that state.[2]

Vanguard entered the personal investment advisory and financial planning business in 1996. As Jack Brennan then said, "We are now able to serve the individual investors, retirement plan participants, and independent financial planners who have long been asking for assistance in preparing key components of personal investment plans."

That offering, Vanguard Personal Advisory Service, featured a Vanguard investment counselor who would examine each client's overall financial picture, including investment goals, spending needs, and risk tolerance. The counselor then determined the client's asset allocation in up to 10 low-cost Vanguard funds. The ongoing investment advisory fee was set at a maximum of 0.50 percent annually, with tiered reductions for investors with more than $500,000 invested at Vanguard. Investment planning featured a one-time review of a client's portfolio, along with asset allocation and fund recommendations. Retirement planning provided a detailed analysis of a client's financial needs for retirement. Estate planning sought to maximize estate and gift tax deductions, among other strategies. Vanguard's Personal Trust Services unit served as a fiduciary and provided professional assistance in establishing various types of trusts.

Brennan emphasized the low cost—"We are setting a new benchmark in cost efficiency for such services." He emphasized that Vanguard did not intend to compete with full-service financial planners. "Our focus is on offering selected services conveniently—over the telephone—to our current shareholders in contrast with the face-to-face, full spectrum of services offered by traditional planners."[3]

Vanguard continued to add advice offerings. In 1998, it introduced interactive retirement planning software for participants in its burgeoning 401(k) business. Three years later, it worked with Nobel Prize winner William Sharpe's Financial Engines company, offering its online portfolio management service free to clients with assets of $100,000. Vanguard simplified its original advice offering in 2006 and called it Vanguard Financial Planning, or VFP. The service consisted of a 10- to 20-page plan developed by a Certified Financial Planner for investors with at least $100,000.

Subsequently the firm developed Vanguard Asset Management Services, which offered continuing wealth management and trust and estate planning. This service was designed for clients whose focus was shifting from building wealth to preserving it for the future. The adviser would help the client clarify goals and investment preferences. While this provided professional portfolio management with proven solutions and trustworthy, personalized service at low cost, it featured relatively high minimums and—by Vanguard's standards—high fees. The minimum investable assets were $500,000 for individuals and $1 million for institutions. Annual fees were based on assets under management, with a minimum fee of $4,500.

In April 2015, Vanguard launched an investment advisory service combining traditional human contact with web-based advice and investment modeling algorithms under Karen Risi's leadership.[4] The service, Vanguard Personal Advisor Services, was limited to offering Vanguard products and emphasizes index funds and ETFs. The fee, only 0.3 percent of assets, is further reduced for accounts over $5 million. Vanguard recently increased its number of on-staff investment advisers in PAS from 300 to 1,000—all paid salary and bonus, rather than the usual commissions, which encourage trading—and invested $100 million to create a dynamic web interface.

"We wanted to bring our mission to an even broader audience," Risi explained. "When we analyzed why we lost retail clients, we saw it was because they felt we did not provide enough advice. We decided it wasn't enough to make our current advice offering better. We wanted to totally reinvent advice and we wanted to be disruptive. Sometimes the media misunderstands our Personal Advisor service. Some think we developed it in response to the new robo-advisers.* But that's not true, not at all. PAS was on the drawing board years ago."

She continued: "Technology enables us to give more advice to more people at lower and lower cost. That's the flywheel effect. Some investors want to work with a coach on investing who can make them feel comfortable with what they're doing as investors during life's major transitions, such as getting married or buying a new

---

* Services that provide digital financial advice or management with minimal human intervention.

home. Our investors also worry about retirement savings and rates of drawdown. . . . We wanted our offering to be extremely low cost. In setting the fee, our bogey was the industry average fee of 100 basis points. We ran some focus groups and found a willingness to pay 25 to 40 basis points. So, we focused on 30 basis points, less than a third of 1 percent, believing that if we were rigorous about customer segmentation and ran an efficient virtual experience, with the flywheel effect, we could make the economics work at that low price. Scale is the key to technology—and vice versa."[5]

Competitors that offer the traditional method of advising and charge 100 to 120 basis points won't be able to compete if investors are well informed about cost versus value. The traditional high-cost "labor" model, based on charm, individual trust and lots of services other than investment management, does not scale. Technology is the key to scalability, removing costs and allowing lower fees. Already, fees for advice are coming down.

With 6,500 crew members, including 1,000 Certified Financial Planners, Risi's group potentially serves Vanguard's 8 million individual investors outside 401(k) plans—a giant potential market for value-adding advice services. She has her focus on services and components of services that lend themselves to automation and the scale to absorb the capital costs and benefit from accelerating advances in technology, including artificial intelligence. Automation has been particularly productive in routine functions like enrolling new clients or transferring accounts into Vanguard from other organizations.

About two-thirds of the CFPs transferred in from other areas of Vanguard. The others are former Registered Investment Advisers who did not enjoy selling just to open new accounts, but do like working with investors to help determine their real long-term priorities and developing programs that enable them to accomplish those objectives.

Determining appropriate individualized advice is complex but can, Vanguard believes, be incorporated into the process without involving the investor in every detail—as a Swiss watch has lots of complexity inside but the user tells the time by a glance at the face. Advisers can walk individual investors step-by-step through their decisions and help them pull the trigger to take appropriate action.

Relationships are built by being trustworthy over time, defining each client's problems or opportunities, and designing the best solutions.

The main force driving the increase in demand for ETFs and index funds is not coming from individual investors, but instead from financial advisers who direct investors to them because of their low cost and ease of administration. In addition to serving existing Vanguard clients, Risi's group works with outside advisers through three main channels: RIAs, regional securities firms like Edward Jones, and national organizations such as JPMorgan Chase.

> Relationships are built by being trustworthy over time, defining each client's problems or opportunities, and designing the best solutions.

Working with RIAs has grown into a major business channel for another Vanguard advice-oriented operation, Financial Advisor Services (FAS), headed by Vanguard veteran Tom Rampulla. FAS focuses on RIAs and other financial intermediaries with a national salesforce and helps them deliver cost-effective advice to individual investors with low-cost ETFs. The core of the concept is recognition that the old beat-the-market mission of an RIA has become increasingly difficult to achieve. The adviser is encouraged to focus less on actively managing portfolios—trying to outperform the markets—and more on relationship-oriented services such as financial planning, developing custom-tailored, long-term investment programs and "behavioral coaching"—coaching clients on best practices about how to stay with their customized investment plans.

The Advisor's Alpha process, as FAS describes its techniques to help advisers add to clients' returns, starts with developing an investment plan, with the obvious view that even a simple plan is better than no plan. "If you fail to plan, plan to fail" has become the kind of phrasing Vanguard uses to make its messaging easy to remember. In developing a plan with a client, the adviser gains vital information, making it easier for both to focus on the client's major objectives.

Understanding the emotional drivers behind decisions is usually the key to understanding each client and to effective behavioral coaching. Vanguard's focus is on "the headlines in clients' lives, not the headlines in the financial news." We all like coaches who focus on how we are getting better, and dislike being confronted with our mistakes. RIAs are encouraged to celebrate clients' gains and improvements as they achieve more of their most important personal objectives with the help of the adviser as their behavioral coach.

Service is crucial in the competition for financial advisers' business, because the products various firms offer are so similar. Vanguard has a dedicated website serving financial advisers, where it promotes the Advisor's Alpha, showing specific ways an adviser can help clients increase returns by staying on plan through market gyrations to achieve long-term objectives such as children's college tuition or retirement security. Vanguard research highlights business-getting opportunities, such as showing that 69 percent of investors with over $5 million do not have a financial plan.

Vanguard tries to quantify Advisor's Alpha—how much good advice may enhance returns. Though easy to debate in terms of exact amounts, which obviously vary by individual investor and from one market environment to another, the components and magnitudes of the Advisor's Alpha that Vanguard emphasizes in this calculation seem credible—especially if you know how costly investors' unadvised mistakes usually are. The estimated total added value of 3 percent a year is perhaps overly generous, but the assumptions generally fit investors' experiences and actual costs.

Asset mix advice	0–.75 percent
Rebalancing the asset mix	0.35 percent
Spending strategy after retiring	1.10 percent
Guidance by RIA	1.50 percent
Total Advisor's Alpha	About 3 percent

Vanguard salespeople travel all over the United States serving over 1,000 financial advisory firms, which, in turn, serve investors with over $3 trillion in investments. Three components combine: technology, client expertise, and investment expertise. Because Vanguard's ETFs and mutual funds are so low cost, that leaves more room for the financial advisers' fees. As Vanguard continues to gain recognition among consumers, more advisers' clients know about and feel comfortable with Vanguard, particularly when using its ETFs. Vanguard makes its technology tools readily available to financial advisers to label with their own firms' names and use with their clients in new ways that increase their earnings.

Vanguard's commitment to advice led in July 2021 to its first-ever acquisition. Just Invest, a small, new firm, helps RIAs design customized, "direct" index portfolios for individuals who want to tailor specific aspects of their portfolios, such as excluding gun manufacturers or oil stocks or emphasizing specific ESG (environmental, social, and governance) stocks. With fractional shares now available, and new technologies making it possible to automate customization at low or even no cost, managers can offer customization economically. In another application, tax loss harvesting, investors can offset taxable gains with sales of stocks that have taken losses. Demand for direct indexing is expected to boom; BlackRock acquired Aperio, a direct indexer, in late 2020 for $1.05 billion. While Vanguard made no commitment, the technology could be used to serve individual investors too.

The value-adding work of an RIA lies partly in developing a trust-based relationship with each investor and partly in figuring out the best solution to a complex personal problem. Solving the life-time "money puzzle" of each investor is a labyrinthine, multivariate problem full of uncertain factors that influence each other in varying degrees, including the time available, the income and savings available, various future investment returns and various dates of retirement, the uncertain need for expensive health care or assisted living, the investor's philanthropic hopes, the complexities of estimating future returns during retirement and determining an appropriate drawdown in retirement—and a variety of other needs or wishes that many investors have. Difficult for humans to process, such problems are simple for advanced algorithms to solve swiftly at low cost *and* with no human reluctance to rework the whole solution almost instantaneously at any time.

Given the size of this opportunity, Vanguard intends to be a leader in the development of algorithmic investment advice for the millions of individual investors and the many financial advisers with whom it has established trust-based relationships. Making advice the leading edge of its strategy epitomizes Vanguard's drive to remain the investment management industry's leader in serving individual investors under Tim Buckley as chief executive.

CHAPTER 18

SETTING BOUNDARIES

As long-serving general counsel for Vanguard, Heidi Stam had a peculiar issue with the Securities and Exchange Commission. It was persistent, and there was not much she could do about it; she would have to learn to live with it. Her problem was simple, though ironic. While the SEC staff and commissioners often agreed with Vanguard's drive to give the ordinary investor a fair break, to be candid in shareholder communications, and to reduce fees, they couldn't always allow client-owned Vanguard to go forward with new initiatives because of the precedent it might set for other, traditionally organized fund companies. "Because Vanguard is so investor focused," explained Stam, "its approach aligns very well with the investor protection mission of the SEC. On a series of issues, we've been way out ahead of the industry."

As general counsel, Stam was responsible for giving "see the future" advice to protect Vanguard from future changes in regulations or possible lawsuits. The only sure way was a combination of keeping it simple and always doing the right thing. At a values-based organization like Vanguard, that comes naturally. In working with the SEC or any other regulator, Stam advised, "there is no need to be adversarial. We both want the same thing—what's best for investors."[1]

Over time, Vanguard found several ways to support regulators in their drive to make steady improvements:

- SEC chairman Arthur Levitt, concerned that investors were not well informed by the required prospectuses of mutual funds, invited the industry in 1997 to study the matter and make recommendations. The main recommendation was obvious; the long, detailed prospectuses crafted by pre-defensive lawyers were impenetrable. The commission recommended a simplified, informative four-page document with all the really important information clearly presented.

- In keeping with its plain-speaking practices, Vanguard has supported disclosure improvements with clear fee tables and "call out" boxes to focus readers' attention on matters of particular importance. Legalese is avoided. Some competitors seem to use it to obfuscate.

- The regulators pushed governance rules for mutual funds, particularly having a supermajority of independent directors on fund boards. Vanguard has always had only one or two employees on its board. When Bill McNabb became president, he joined the board. Later, when McNabb also took on the title of chairman of the board, Jack Brennan resigned from the board. All the other directors, now nine in number, are independent.

- Vanguard lowers costs. The so-called Vanguard Effect comes into play: when Vanguard enters a new market with its low fees, competitors promptly reduce their fees. In recent years, increasing numbers of investment managers have done so. Vanguard's price leadership has saved investors billions.

"If the commission is conducting an examination in preparation for a new rule, it will often go to Vanguard to be sure it makes sense, knowing that Vanguard always does the right thing," Stam said. "Let me correct that statement slightly. In my 19 years at Vanguard, we had only two small $15,000 FINRA (Financial Industry Regulatory Authority) fines—on minor technical matters of no real consequence. Other firms will budget large sums *every year* for fines and will see fines for rule violation as just another cost of doing business. The real difference is in attitude, with Vanguard always striving to do the right thing. When Vanguard got those small fines, you should have seen all the long, sad faces! Management took it all so seriously. The major comment was powerful: 'That's just *not* who we are!'"

Vanguard is proactive about compliance. For example, the legal and compliance team weighs in early in the development of a new offering to be sure that, from a compliance perspective, Vanguard has the best design. The firm was an early adopter of the web to distribute useful information in interactive formats to its millions of investors.

One of Heidi Stam's special moments as general counsel came in 2009, when regulators were examining all money market funds for investments in high-risk securities during the financial crisis. At issue were the use of CDOs (collateralized debt obligations) and subprime mortgage-backed securities in what were supposed to be relatively safe, stable-asset funds. Money market funds were a major part of Vanguard's business, and none of Vanguard's money market funds contained CDOs or questionable mortgage-backed securities. When the head of the Fixed Income Group, Robert Auwaerter, was called before the Vanguard board for an update on the money market crisis, a director asked, "Bob, can you explain why no Vanguard fund holds any of these securities?" Auwaerter replied, "I didn't buy them because I didn't understand them. I don't buy anything I don't understand."

One evening in September 2003, Stam received an email after a day-long training session with the legal team. The news wasn't good. New York Attorney General Eliot Spitzer had called a press conference to announce a mass investigation of mutual fund companies. "I ran to see the TV in our PR office," she remembers, "only to see Spitzer claiming that his investigation would unveil widespread predatory trading practices at the largest mutual fund firms, *including* Vanguard. That was impossible, so counter to Vanguard values. We were always out ahead when it came to protecting our investors. For years, Vanguard would always do the right thing—close 'hot' funds, turn away short-term money that would impair returns, and impose redemption fees to protect long-term investors."

> "I didn't buy them because I didn't understand them. I don't buy anything I don't understand."

The two practices Spitzer was investigating were illegal market timing (allowing a hedge fund to time fund trades in exchange for other business) and late trading (allowing the hedge fund to trade after 4 p.m. but receive the 4 p.m. price).

That day in September was the beginning of several very tense months. As Spitzer, and quickly on his heels the SEC, began issuing subpoenas, Stam knew Vanguard had to get out ahead of it—whatever it was. Every fund company was a target. That Vanguard had been mentioned by name in the press conference really rattled Stam. Spitzer had to have some reason to name Vanguard.

Frank Satterthwaite, the head of Internal Audit; Pauline Scalvino, the head of Corporate and Litigation in Legal; and Stam as head of Securities Regulation knew they had to find whatever it was before Spitzer or the SEC did—that way they could at least fix whatever it was before the regulators arrived. "We huddled every day, multiple times a day," Stam recalled. "We basically turned the entire organization upside down and shook it to see what if anything fell to the floor. Frank and his internal audit team began targeted searches to root out any evidence of wrongdoing. Pauline and her team played point on responding to the subpoenas that had requested hundreds of pages of documents—one from New York and the other from the SEC. The Securities Regulation team was looking at compliance with all the trading rules and speaking with our portfolio managers and front-line crew serving clients." Every Vanguard attorney and paralegal worked well into the nights reviewing emails that might reveal a connection to the Spitzer allegations.

And then, someone identified an email from a representative in the Retail Division bringing an unusual question to the division head. A potential client, a hedge fund, wanted to put a lot of money into Vanguard funds and was asking whether it might be able to trade more frequently than is normally permitted under Vanguard policies in exchange for committing further investments over time. Upon receiving the email, the head of Retail, clearly suspicious, shot off an email to Gus Sauter, then chief investment officer: "Gus, what do you think of this?" His answer, "Absolutely not, we would never agree to this. This practice would be terrible for the other shareholders in the funds."

As lawyers, Scalvino and Stam could not have been happier. They had the reverse of a smoking gun! Vanguard put together its subpoena response with this email chain prominently in evidence. Vanguard never heard another thing from the New York attorney general or the SEC on these issues and never got an apology from Spitzer's office. Apparently, the source on the trading scandals had mentioned Vanguard as "one of the firms." Yes, the hedge fund had *tried* to get into Vanguard, but Vanguard shut it out.

As Stam reflected happily years later, "It really was a great day for us. The rep knew the request was questionable, and was not so sales oriented that he would just agree to it. The head of Retail knew immediately it was problematic. And our chief investment officer was more interested in his fiduciary responsibilities to investors than gaining more assets to manage."[2]

While many people still call indexing "passive," for those doing the sophisticated work of continuously replicating the many market indexes that Vanguard matches, indexing is most definitely *active*. In addition to this operationally active work, as a shareholder Vanguard also takes an active role in good governance.

Half an hour before the end of one proxy voting period, Vanguard got an urgent call from the CEO of a major corporation: "I can't believe you voted *against* our directors! What difference can it possibly make to you? You *index*!" His company had fallen short on a long series of good governance criteria, prompting Vanguard to vote against reelecting its directors. Vanguard was taking seriously its role as a major, virtually perpetual shareowner on behalf of its investor-owners.

The proxy voting process and Vanguard's open advocacy are designed primarily to encourage corporate directors and managers to pay attention to their actual behavior versus best practices. While Vanguard makes its voting record public, to foster candor it does not disclose the specifics of engagements with individual companies. The focus is on laggards, striving to raise the overall average of corporate practice.

Jack Brennan wrote an early letter on corporate governance and on Vanguard as a corporate steward that went to the CEOs of all companies with shares held by Vanguard, saying the firm believes good governance contributes significantly to favorable long-term returns for shareholders. Vanguard seeks to raise the accepted standards of good governance by focusing on basic principles, making its views known, engaging with interested companies and publicly reporting its policies and its voting record.

Vanguard explains that it divides proxy voting into four categories or pillars of good governance:

> **The firm believes good governance contributes significantly to favorable long-term returns for shareholders.**

- **"Board composition:** good governance begins with a great board of directors. Our primary interest is to ensure that the individuals who represent the interests of all shareholders are independent, capable, and appropriately experienced. We also believe that diversity of thought, background, and experience, as well as of personal characteristics (such as gender, race, and age), meaningfully contribute to a board's ability to serve as effective, engaged stewards of shareholders' interests.*

- **"Governance structures:** we believe in the importance of governance structures that empower shareholders and ensure accountability of the board and management. We believe that shareholders should be able to hold directors accountable as needed through certain governance and bylaw provisions. Among these preferred provisions are that directors must stand for election by shareholders annually and must secure a majority of the votes in order to join or remain on the board.

- **"Oversight of risk & strategy:** boards are responsible for effective oversight and governance of the risks most relevant and material to each company and for governance of the company's long-term strategy. We believe that boards should take a thorough, integrated, and thoughtful approach to identifying, quantifying, mitigating, and disclosing risks

---

* For an organization truly committed to diversity, a large proportion of the top people 10 years ago came from one college, Dartmouth—Brennan, McNabb, Sauter— and rather few were people of color. On the other hand, many women now hold important positions and, due to Brennan's and McNabb's efforts, people of color are clearly visible on the board and in senior leadership positions.

that have the potential to affect shareholder value over the long term. Boards are also responsible for consulting on and overseeing a company's strategic direction and progress toward its objectives.

• **"Executive compensation:** we believe that performance-linked compensation policies and practices are fundamental drivers of sustainable, long-term value. The board plays a central role in determining appropriate executive pay that incentivizes performance relative to peers and competitors and disclosure of these practices and their alignment with company performance."

As Vanguard explains on its website, "We advocate for executive pay arrangements that are constructed to incentivize relative outperformance over the long term. When shareholders do well, so should executives, and when shareholders don't do well, executives' pay should move in the same direction. Performance-linked policies should motivate management to focus on long-term value creation instead of short-term goals. The board should ensure that the company's policies are appropriate compared with those of peers and the company's industry, and the details of any pay plan should be clearly disclosed to shareholders."

Taking the important example of stock-based compensation, Vanguard went deeper to share the 10 factors it would use in evaluating such proposals:

Factors *for* approval:

• Company requires senior executives to hold a minimum amount of company stock (frequently expressed as a multiple of salary).

• Company requires stock acquired through equity awards to be held for a certain period.

• Compensation program includes performance-vesting awards, indexed options, or other performance-linked grants.

• Concentration of equity grants to senior executives is limited (indicating that the plan is broad-based).

- Stock-based compensation is clearly used as a substitute for cash in delivering market-competitive total pay.

Factors *against* approval:

- Total potential dilution (including all stock-based plans) exceeds 15 percent of shares outstanding.

- Annual equity grants have exceeded 2 percent of shares outstanding.

- Plan permits repricing or replacement of options without shareholder approval.

- Plan provides for the issuance of "reload" options (that grant executives new options when they exercise the original ones).

- Plan contains automatic share replenishment (evergreen) feature.

Each of Vanguard's pillars of good governance can be complex, most are industry and company specific, and few are easy for outsiders to understand fully. But all can be monitored by experienced, diligent, capable board members, particularly if they have the requisite information and the interested cooperation of senior executives who understand and honor the important responsibilities of a governing board. Evidence shows progress: women are now about 30 percent of S&P 500 board members, up from 19 percent in 2014;[3] performance-based pay for CEOs has increased significantly; and majority voting for directors has more than doubled.[4]

Since it cannot simply sell a stock when concerned about the long-term policies of a corporation that its index funds invest in, Vanguard is necessarily a perpetual owner of shares so long as they remain in the index, and it seeks to be a constructive shareholder. Glenn Booraem leads a team of over 35 analysts working on good governance and proxy voting, an increase from just six in 2000. They formulate policies and communicate them to senior executives and directors of the companies whose shares are owned in the index funds. Responsibility for proxy voting by Vanguard's numerous active managers is delegated to those managers since they have more granular information.

Sunlight *is* the best disinfectant, and "we want to be transparent and proactive," said Booraem.[5] The volume and the quality of communication with companies have both risen since the Sarbanes-Oxley Act of 2002, designed to protect investors from fraudulent financial reporting by corporations. Since 2018, Vanguard has had direct contact with 1,500 companies that represent 75 percent of its assets under management. During the 2020 proxy season, it discussed executive compensation in about half its engagements. Engagement has increased, particularly internationally. While nations differ (and the United States is not always the most advanced), corporate practices are converging on global standards of best practice. Vanguard encourages this convergence while recognizing that companies, industries, and nations differ in many ways. As Booraem explained, "We want to focus on the right things, not on everything."

Vanguard is committed to take a stand for all investors, not just for those who rely on it as their investment manager. "If better governance will make a favorable impact—and the evidence is strong that it does—our work will help move the results for all investors up and to the right," Booraem said. "We want to leave the woodpile higher as a result of our work."[6]

Some proxy matters are *event* driven (such as a merger) or *topic* driven (such as gender diversity), and some matters are sufficiently complex to warrant a "strategic engagement" between Vanguard and a particular company. Since most proxy votes—168,786 in 2019—are simple, routine items, any differences on the more important or tougher decisions can seem few. Vanguard often votes the same way "public interest" proxy advisory groups like International Shareholder Services vote, but certainly not always. For example, in 2019, 7 percent of the times ISS advocated voting *for* a proxy item, Vanguard voted *against*, and 9 percent of the times ISS recommended voting *against* an item, Vanguard voted *for* it. Here is how Vanguard reported its proxy votes in two recent periods:

> "If better governance will make a favorable impact—and the evidence is strong that it does—our work will help move the results for all investors up and to the right."

Alignment with our principles	Proposal type	2020		2021	
		Number of proposals	% for	Number of proposals	% for
Board composition and effectiveness	**Management proposals**				
	Elect directors	61,303	92%	64,021	91%
	Other board-related	12,285	91%	13,134	88%
	Shareholder proposals				
	Board-related	4,034	84%	3,869	87%
Executive compensation	**Management proposals**				
	Management Say on Pay	6,757	90%	6,807	87%
	Other compensation-related	10,839	90%	12,262	90%
	Shareholder proposals				
	Compensation-related	113	50%	99	57%
Oversight of strategy and risk	**Management proposals**				
	Approve auditors	10,354	99%	10,812	99%
	Environmental and social			27	100%
	Shareholder proposals				
	Environmental/social	264	7%	269	22%
Shareholder rights	**Management proposals**				
	Governance-related	11,150	88%	11,204	81%
	Shareholder proposals				
	Governance-related	335	40%	292	38%
Other proposals	**Management proposals**				
	Capitalization	30,794	98%	26,444	98%
	Mergers and acquisitions	8,474	98%	7,643	97%
	Adjourn/other business	18,937	96%	19,641	95%
	Shareholder proposals				
	Other	1,063	85%	783	83%
	Total	**176,701**	**93%**	**177,307**	**92%**

Source: https://global.vanguard.com/documents/investment-stewardship-semiannual-report.pdf.

Policies Vanguard recommends to regulators are published, in the hope that other investors will speak up, and all its proxy votes are reported. Moreover, Vanguard governance experts are ready to meet with any corporate leaders who would appreciate a briefing on the recommendations. However, that does not satisfy a cluster of hypothetical academic concerns.

Two schools of concern about index funds and proxy voting have articulated their views that index funds wield excessive power, but the two are in clear disagreement. One is concerned that index fund managers will be excessively deferential to management in their proxy voting, while the other is concerned that index fund managers will excessively exploit the power over managements that comes with their large ownership stakes. Charlie Munger, Warren Buffett's nonagenarian partner, warned against that power in early 2022 when he said of the CEO of BlackRock: "I think the world of Larry Fink, but I'm not sure I want him to be my emperor."[7]

Both groups note the past and projected future increase in the percentage of all shares held in index funds. Neither recognizes the intensity of competitive rivalry between the leading index fund organizations: if any one of them behaved even slightly unwisely, the others would pounce, and surely so would the media. More important, neither school recognizes the difference between strategic capacity and strategic intent. Both leap to theoretical possibilities and raise far-fetched suspicions of potential misconduct.

One academic analysis,[8] apparently confusing correlation with causation and using simplistic data mining as opposed to rigorous statistical analysis, concludes that, as index funds own shares in multiple airlines (as they do in all major industries), this has somehow led to pricing collusion on fares by the airlines. A similarly curious concern is that *if* the three major index managers somehow got together and tried to pressure corporate managements to take particular business strategy initiatives, they might exert undue power in collusion. In a rare foray into a contested corporate vote, in May 2021 Vanguard voted its ExxonMobil shares in favor of two new activist directors who promised to push the oil giant to speed up its transition to renewable sources of energy. So did other large shareholders, including the two other big indexers.

Vanguard's unusual vote to influence long-range strategy reflected persuasive arguments that the company's future was clouded, and of course it required no "collusion" with many others that felt the same. Referring to "the increasing need for ExxonMobil to better align their climate strategy with target setting in line with their global peers and their public policy efforts," the firm explained, "Importantly, Vanguard does not dictate how companies should run their business; rather, we seek to understand how their boards are governing their strategies and overseeing material risks that could affect companies' long-term value. . . . [Vanguard's vote] was intended ultimately to hold the board accountable on their risk oversight processes and to enhance the board's composition and energy sector experience." As index funds and ETFs get still larger, Vanguard might be wise to divide the authority to vote on such major corporate decisions as mergers, acquisitions, and strategy reversals among two or three policy decision-making units.

The Federal Trade Commission held hearings on whether concentrated share ownership damps down new product introductions or competition for customers. BlackRock's long-serving vice-chair, Barbara Novick, wrote, "We do not dictate to companies how they should run their corporate balance sheets, nor do we have the ability to do so."

Harvard Law School professor John C. Coates became a prominent critic. First, he cited the rapid growth of indexing and "quasi-indexing." Second, he focused on the concentration of indexing in a few major firms. Third, he created clever terminology, "The Problem of Twelve," to clarify that in a few years only about a dozen people—members of the small group at each management organization that decides how to vote proxies—would somehow have virtual control over the majority of U.S. public corporations. In dramatic words, he declared this a deeply concerning problem. "A small number of unchecked agents, operating largely behind closed doors, are increasingly impactful to the lives of millions who barely know of the existence much less the identity or intentions of those agents."

Borrowing from antitrust experience with major industrial corporations engaging in price signaling, Coates wrote, "Index providers can obtain strong signals about other index providers' views on management performance and strategy. No explicit collusion is required to send highly aligned signals about what they want to each other." While acknowledging that "index provider managers have very weak [financial] incentives to use their control," he warned: "An announcement by a major index fund provider that it does, or does not, support a given governance position gives greater clout to those [proxy voting advisory services] who tee-up, debate, and form investment community opinion around those issues."

Sounds alarming, but is it a false alarm? While thoughtful observers are increasingly expressing concerns about "short termism"—corporate managements' overemphasis on quarterly results to boost stock price—index fund managers are leading in the opposite direction, advocating long-term thinking. Index fund managers like Vanguard explicitly define their focus: good governance for the long run.

Coates's central concern is clearly stated on his final page: "Unless law changes, the effect of indexation will be to turn the concept of 'passive' investing on its head and produce the greatest concentration of economic control in our lifetimes." These last 10 words certainly try to command readers' attention. Coates declares: "The mere threat of an activist supported by index funds can reduce investment" or "lead to layoffs." He then grandly concludes: "That power creates a legitimacy and accountability challenge."*

Another academic provided a wholly different concern and suggested restricting proxy voting by index funds because they have such weak incentives to learn enough about proxy issues that their votes will be underinformed and so will drive proxy voting away from good governance. But that's why indexers concentrate on broad good governance policies and seldom take positions on other business decisions.

As CEO, Bill McNabb reacted publicly in July 2017 to a similar academic article proposing that index funds should, in effect, give up their voting rights: "The proposal is careless and dangerously misinformed." He went on to say two things about Vanguard's role as investment stewards: (1) "We care deeply about governance." And (2) "We're good at it."

When Jack Brennan was asked whether he saw any risk of a conflict between proxy voting and Vanguard's pension management business, his immediate response was clear: "We're unbending. Life's too short to compromise your principles for a piece of business. And we've never had [a client] say, 'If you don't vote the way we like, goodbye.' We've won a lot of business, and we've voted tough votes that management didn't like. But good companies understand that we're fiduciaries, just as they are. People who run good companies are too principled to politicize something as important as employees' retirement savings."

Another concern, most colorfully expressed in the title—but *not* in the evidence—of a 2016 paper, "Passive Investing Is Worse than Marxism,"[9] suggests that when indexing becomes too popular and somehow drives out active investing, "the process of capital allocation in our market and then our economy will wither and die." Let's look briefly at the reality: well over 500,000 professionals, perhaps as many as a million, enjoy generous incomes as active participants in active investing. To degrade the market mechanism at all meaningfully, at least half and likely three-quarters of these experts would need to quit one of the highest paid and most interesting, engaging lines of work in the world. Even though 89 percent of mutual funds

---

* Coates spent eight months at the SEC in 2021, four as acting director of the Division of Corporate Finance and four as general counsel.

fail to match the market, the number of people entering each year into active investing continues to exceed those leaving, so it won't happen soon. (In 2019, US-focused index equity funds made up about 14 percent of the American stock market and contributed about 5 percent of US stock market trading.)[10]

When Vanguard went no-load decades ago, a shareholder sued, claiming that since he had paid the sales load, he had been unfairly disadvantaged by that cost. Nobody on the Vanguard board thought the complaint had merit, and the suit was taking an enormous amount of time and energy, many days as much as 90 percent of both Bogle's and Riepe's time. Both had far more important things to be doing to advance a then fragile Vanguard. Any simple cost-benefit analysis concluded: *Hold your nose and settle with the SOB—even if it costs us $5,000.* That amount had been requested by the plaintiff's attorney.

Bogle was adamant. "No! Never!"

The lawsuit went on for another year and was eventually settled for . . . $5,000.

One July day in 1996, Vanguard refused to accept a $40 million account that had been intended for the Admiral Short Term Portfolio, a $430 million bond fund. That made the Hastings Foundation's EVP so angry that he sent a message—typed in ALL CAPITAL LETTERS—saying that he would pull all its investments "as soon as possible" and would never again do business with Vanguard.

Why the ruckus? When asked how long the money would be invested in the fund, which was explicitly designed for long-term investment, the answer was "about two months." For Vanguard, that was way too short: the costs to invest nearly 10 percent of the fund and then withdraw that same investment would drive up the fund's expense ratio, and this would penalize all the other investors.

Vanguard was supported in the press. The *Wall Street Journal* ran a story with an arresting headline, "Vanguard Puts Up No-Parking Sign."[11] Bogle was, of course, certain about his decision to reject and had good reasons. If the $40 million were held in the $430 million fund for only two months, it would earn Vanguard some $30,000 in management fees, but buying and selling that amount of Treasury bills—a total of $80 million of transactions—would cost the other investors in the fund about $50,000. When Vanguard offered to help Hastings buy appropriate Treasury securities or invest in a larger money market fund, Hastings refused because that other fund had a lower yield.

The Short Term Portfolio's prospectus stated, "The Fund is intended as a long-term investment [and], consequently, the Fund reserves the right to reject any specific purchase." Brennan tried to explain: "By the time you invest and disinvest, all the other shareholders would pay a significant expense in transaction cost for the benefit of a single shareholder." So Vanguard chose not to accept the account. Jim Riepe, by then at T. Rowe Price, was quoted in the article as saying that putting such a large chunk as $40 million into a $430 million fund for only two months is "just plain nuts." Once again, Vanguard was watching out for its clients.

Governance at Vanguard has many facets, all based on a simple concept: do the right thing. Stories abound about Vanguard's closing funds entirely or to new investors. Unapologetically paternalistic, Vanguard will close access to funds that appear to be attracting unsophisticated investors chasing past performance. Issuing warnings on hot sectors of the market—emphasizing risks—originated with Jack Bogle and has become an important part of trust building. Vanguard's leaders always see it as an investment organization, not a sales or marketing organization.

Most mutual fund organizations, being sales-minded, habitually accentuate the positive. Bogle insisted on reporting to investors the way he would want to be reported to if he were an investor: accurately and candidly. That policy goes way back. In 1991, when health-care stocks were market darlings, Bogle cautioned:

> In recent months, the Health Care Portfolio has attracted a good deal of publicity about its excellent *past* performance. Almost simultaneously, the Portfolio has had substantial cash inflows (totaling $76 million in the past three months) from thousands of new and existing shareholders. As press attention has focused almost exclusively on the strong performance of the Health Care Portfolio (and other mutual funds specializing in this field) we wanted to write this

note to ensure that our shareholders and prospective investors have a balanced understanding of the risks and the potential rewards of investing in the Portfolio.

The returns of the Health Care Portfolio have been very strong. Through February 28, 1991, the Portfolio's annualized returns for the past one, three, and five-year periods were +39.7 percent, +24.5 percent, and +20.4 percent, respectively (compared to +14.7 percent, +15.1 percent, and +13.9 percent for the unmanaged Standard & Poor's 500 Stock Price Index over the same periods). However, it is highly unlikely that such absolute returns—or even the Portfolio's relative performance advantage—will be matched in the future. Experience has shown that such periods of superior performance by an industry group do not continue indefinitely. Indeed, periods of outperformance are often followed by periods of underperformance.

Bogle went on to warn against too much concentration in any one industry. Vanguard closed the Health Care Fund again in the spring of 2005 and kept it closed for a dozen years until the autumn of 2017. (Over the years Vanguard also closed the Explorer, Primecap, Capital Opportunity, Precious Metals, and Mining funds.) When it reopened, the Health Care Fund was available only to existing shareholders seeking to increase their holdings. A reason given for reopening was to have enough new investment dollars to meet modest redemptions rather than having to sell the portfolio's low-cost-basis stocks, incurring capital gains that would be taxable to the funds' long-term shareholders. Jack Brennan was explicit that the fund opening was *not* a "buy" signal from Vanguard. "We consider ourselves the conscience of our industry," said Brennan.

As Jack Bogle had told the Vanguard crew, "There is no mystery about the benefits of candor. Making investors aware of risk is not only ethically essential, it represents wise shareholder relations, and good public relations. In short, miracle of miracles, candor has proved to be a sensational business strategy for Vanguard. We distinguish ourselves by being straightforward rather than strident and understating rather than overstating."

When the financial crisis hit in 2008 and pulverized the stock market, Vanguard knew that with much lower assets, its at-cost operations would require an offsetting increase in the expense ratios of its funds. Believing it would be wrong not to inform investors, Vanguard pleaded with the SEC for permission to tell investors what was coming. The SEC would not allow "projected" fee information in fund prospectuses. So Vanguard sent the same heads-up message in an informal way, by including a note that expense ratios would be rising in its regular quarterly letter to investors. This met both the letter of SEC regulations and the spirit of candor sought by Vanguard. Helpfully, *Morningstar* brought attention to Vanguard's move with a highly favorable article.

> "There is no mystery about the benefits of candor. Making investors aware of risk is not only ethically essential, it represents wise shareholder relations, and good public relations. In short, miracle of miracles, candor has proved to be a sensational business strategy for Vanguard. We distinguish ourselves by being straightforward rather than strident and understating rather than overstating."

In 2015, Bill McNabb wrote "an open letter to all mutual fund investors" that ran as an op-ed in the *Wall Street Journal*.[12] He began: "In the years since the global financial crisis, lawmakers and regulators have worked to stabilize the markets and economy. They identified risks to the financial system and took steps to ensure that Main Street would not be on the hook—again—for bad bets placed by Wall Street. Now regulators might place that burden squarely back on Main Street mutual-fund investors without any solid evidence that the funds or their managers could bring on another panic." The U.S. Financial Stability Oversight Council and the global Financial Stability Board considered mutual fund companies as systemically important financial institutions (SIFIs) like the big banks, imposing the same bailout obligations on them and their 90 million investors. This would, McNabb wrote, require fund companies to hold capital reserves of up to 8 percent of fund assets, significantly reducing investors' long-term returns.

As he explained, mutual funds use zero leverage—they don't buy securities on margin—while banks and securities dealers could borrow up to 30 *times* their equity capital. Moreover, even in times of great stress, fund investors "never redeem shares en masse." Finally, "Even when funds exit the business (and hundreds do each year), the risk is contained. Investors in a fund bear the risk of any losses, just as they stand to benefit from only gains. Since funds operate as separate entities from their managers and other financial institutions, there is no risk of losses elsewhere in the financial system, or any need for a taxpayer bailout. It's not the size of an institution that determines its risk. It's the amount of leverage in play. Mutual funds use little or no leverage." The regulators eventually saw the point.

Vanguard is cautious about seeming holier than thou or strident. As it said in a 2019 report: "Vanguard understands that people have a wide variety of deeply felt humanitarian, ethical, environmental, and social concerns, and that some may want to see their beliefs reflected in their investments. As a fiduciary, Vanguard is required to manage our funds in the best interests of [all] shareholders and obligated to maximize returns in order to help shareholders meet their financial goals. Like other investment management firms, Vanguard understands that some individuals choose investments based exclusively on social matters and personal beliefs. For such investors, we have offered Vanguard FTSE Social Index Fund since 2000. This low-cost, broadly diversified fund seeks to track a benchmark that screens companies on social, human rights, and environmental criteria."

Sure enough, Vanguard was called out on some of the companies held in this fund for not being sufficiently correct. On first complaint, it turned out that the creator of the index Vanguard was matching had failed to do sufficient due diligence. Both index creator and Vanguard moved quickly to eliminate the problem and get back on the straight and narrow. (As described in the previous chapter, a more individualized approach to social index investing may be ahead.)

Indexing is based on disciplined replication—not creativity or judgment calls—so investors should never be surprised either favorably or unfavorably by actual results, particularly *un*favorable results. That's why a deviation in 2002 challenged Jack Brennan to change bond management leadership.

Dow Jones's Richard A. Bravo set the stage: "In this year's second quarter, a period of market volatility in credit and equity markets, index funds reported a wide array of returns, many of them falling below expectations." His article went on to report that Vanguard's Total Bond Market Index Fund in just one quarter had fallen short of the index return by 89 basis points—a 3.6 percent annualized shortfall! The article reported that while some deviation might be expected, to miss the mark by so much in an *index bond fund* was "unheard of." Bravo noted that the $22 billion Vanguard fund had, over 10 years, earned returns before fees and expenses "right on top" of the index *and* that credit rating downslides had been unusually high—nearly 5 to 1 versus upgrades—*and* that WorldCom bonds, with $30 billion outstanding, had plunged by two-thirds. Finally, because the most popular bond index contained 6,873 different bonds—over 13 times as many issues as the S&P 500—"sampling error could become a potential nightmare for bond index fund managers."[13]

Vanguard was forthcoming about the performance disappointment, attributing the fund's shortfall to sampling; an overweight in hard-hit sectors like telecommunications and energy; a corporate substitution policy in which high-quality corporates were substituted for US Treasury bonds; and operating expenses. Vanguard's portfolio exposed the fund to far more credit risk at a time when the bond market was not tolerant of credit risk. While the "corporate substitution" practice had added returns in past years, this time it hurt returns. That was an explanation, but certainly not an excuse. That was not what investors had expected with a bond index fund—and not what Vanguard had promised investors.

Brennan, as CEO, took full responsibility and reached out to clients with Vanguard's characteristic candor. He initiated a flurry of calls and visits to institutional investors to explain. He told investors he was changing the fund's portfolio management team and specified how the bond management process would be changed to ensure rigorous replication of the index. Going forward, he would make sure that such "I'm smarter than the market" actions would be forbidden.

Most of the institutions liked being called on by the CEO, understood what had happened, and admired Brennan's taking "command responsibility."

CHAPTER 19

LOOKING AHEAD

With its ability to raise over $5 billion of capital to finance a major commitment, low-cost, low-margin Vanguard has become a strategic financial powerhouse. As Buckley and his board and management team look ahead, the Vanguard flywheel can generate substantial financial resources that begin with a very small percentage in fees and yield a very large total capacity to invest in new capabilities, services, and products. That enormous financial power will enable Vanguard to disrupt the mutual fund industry again—and again.

One basis point is tiny: a mere one-hundredth of 1 percent. But even something so very small, when multiplied by a very large number, can become quite big. Vanguard now manages over $8 trillion: $8,000,000,000,000! So a tiny 1 basis point in fees equals $800 million *every year* to invest in new, high-impact strategic moves. This gigantic sum could be earned by Vanguard simply not reducing fees quite as much as it might, or by raising fees ever so slightly. If you were Vanguard, what might you do with over $800 million of financing for new ideas and new capabilities *every* year?

Consider for a moment a thought experiment: If Vanguard decided to spend $100 million of that $800 million on carefully collecting and rigorously analyzing the past behavior of its 30 million individual investor-owners, might it achieve a game-changing advantage that would enable it to serve clients better in compelling ways for years to come?

For a small fraction of that annual $800 million, Vanguard could offer 10 million of its investor-owners appropriate incentives to spend half an hour with a well-designed multiple-choice survey asking them to describe themselves with a few financial metrics: income, annual retirement savings, size of portfolio, and major investment goals; answer some questions about their investment behavior (for example, time and interest in investing, past investing behavior and concerns such as retirement security, health-care costs, education for children or grandchildren, home purchase, intergenerational bequests and charitable giving); and indicate where they are most and least concerned on a series of dimensions: saving for kids' college, for a family home, for vacations, or for retirement.

Ask what they wish they had done financially in the past 10 years to improve their present financial position and what past mistakes they most regret, like trading too much, saving too little, trying to time markets, or holding so much in bonds. What do they intend to do differently over the coming year, ten years?

Vanguard could divide and analyze the responses by age in five decades, by five major income levels and by five levels of wealth. With 1 million participants, if the data were divided into five age groups, and each of these into five wealth and income categories, and each of those into five "risk attitude" categories, each "cluster" would, on average, still have a sample of participants large enough for rigorous analysis.

With such a large sample in each cluster, all sorts of analyses could be done, particularly if participants agreed to re-participate—perhaps at two-year intervals or as markets rise and fall and participants live through changing life and financial experiences. Vanguard could organize, analyze, and make valuable information available to investors—perhaps with a follow-up call from a Vanguard adviser to identify specific ways to make fewer, better financial planning and investing decisions.

Could analysts identify important realities that would help 30-year-olds (or 40- or 50-year-olds) see themselves as they will most likely be in 10 or 20 or even 30 years—and so help them make better decisions now? Vanguard investors could quietly observe their own "virtual futures" by seeing what investors just like them but 10 or 20 years further along in their lives have done or are doing, or *not* doing; what they wish they had done differently; how they feel now about their finances and how they might want to improve. What mistakes can I avoid because I'm getting to see my probable personal financial future thanks to Vanguard? Could this exercise help me make better decisions? Could it help me avoid mistakes? Could Vanguard give me a few helpful nudges toward making my own best moves? If Vanguard offered the results of this sort of research, at a modest fee or free to all who participate, would investors feel well served and even more loyal to and likely to use Vanguard even more?

If Vanguard concluded that this survey idea worked well, would it be able to develop more ways to invest other parts of that annual $800 million in developing several other ways to engage the interests and loyalties of its investors? As a consequence, might it increase its "share of wallet" with current Vanguard investors? Might it attract many more investors who appreciate the new services?

Or, to go in a different direction, could Vanguard decide to invest several years of development funds in building up its business in a series of other countries and allow itself five or even 10 years to earn back those costs of bringing the benefits of Vanguard to international investors?

If investing $800 million every year is promising, but not enough to accomplish "everything," could Vanguard invest even more by increasing, or not decreasing, fees by just *two* basis points? That could permit investing over $1.6 billion every year in developing extraordinary expertise and new technology to help its clients—or help financial advisers help *their* clients—pursue custom-tailored investment advice programs *and* "stay the course"?

Every year, Vanguard leadership is now in the powerful position of deciding how best to invest the extraordinary accelerating power of its flywheel on behalf of its many millions of investors. Every year, Vanguard can invest in either further reducing fees or in further increasing the value it delivers—or both. It is able to accelerate the flywheel and increase the value of its services to each investor, and so attract more of each investor's assets—and continue to disrupt the traditional investment industry with innovations.

Advice may recently have opened a major market—perhaps the world's largest future investment market—to the service capabilities of Vanguard: China. In late 2019, Vanguard and Ant financial services group announced the formation of a partnership that would offer to help China's investors select mutual funds from the 5,700 funds now on offer through Ant, which, as a reminder of the potential scale, has 900 million people now using its Alipay service. The Chinese stock market is now dominated by amateur investors. While they will surely give way in the future to expert professionals with excellent research and technology, as in other major markets, at present actively managed mutual funds in China can and do outperform index funds after costs and so can charge high fees.

Ant and its founder, Jack Ma, have recently been under pressure from the Chinese government, which blocked Ant's initial public offering and put its mutual fund operations under the supervision of the central bank. But Vanguard remains committed to the joint venture, which has always been regulated by the Chinese government. Vanguard said, "We continue to invest in the growing venture, which is now providing risk-appropriate, diversified, and high-quality mutual fund portfolios to more than 2 million Chinese investors. That's 2 million clients who are better off in well-managed, long-term oriented funds, in just over one year of operation—a clear testament to Vanguard's mission to improve investor outcomes worldwide."

In recent years, while gaining international business overall, Vanguard has had various disappointments. In October 2020, it returned $21 billion to Chinese government clients to focus on individual investors, then in March 2021 suspended plans to launch mutual funds in China. In addition, it has been withdrawing from Japan, Hong Kong, Taiwan, and other difficult international markets. Going global with financial services has always been hard; only a few have succeeded greatly. One reason is the remarkable reluctance of investors to entrust their investments to "foreign" managers. Another is the protection by regulators in almost all countries of their nation's own financial service organizations—banks, insurance, securities dealers, and investment managers. Regulators know what they *should* do for investors in their home markets, but actually making the changes can be politically difficult.

Vanguard has fallen behind key competitors like Fidelity and Schwab in service to investors. The reasons range from the firm's explosive growth in assets to its long-ago reluctance to automate, compounded by pandemic-era challenges with many representatives working remotely. The problems are multiple. Routine service requests can take hours, not minutes, to resolve. Mistakes are made. Requests for custom service can get a "We don't do that sort of thing" response. The troubles haven't visibly affected growth, particularly in new accounts, and extensive corrective measures are showing some results. While this is a problem that can be solved, it has been a serious error to allow it to become widespread.

Both Vanguard and Fidelity are making major investments in their futures, confident that cost of developing strong client relationships will pay off handsomely over the long run. Vanguard has introduced new contact center technology, reorganized client service teams, and accelerated efforts to redesign and improve clients' digital experience. A spokeswoman notes that one recent evaluation, J.D. Power's 2021 U.S. Self-Directed Investor Satisfaction Study, ranked Vanguard first in self-directed investor satisfaction among investors seeking guidance and among do-it-yourself investors.

Fidelity has been expanding its workforce substantially; in September 2021 it announced plans to hire 9,000 new workers, a 22 percent increase in its staff, taking the total to more than 60,000. This enormous commitment, its third in a year, is in response to the surge in new individual market participants. In the year ended in June 2021, Fidelity added 1.7 million retail accounts, including 697,000 for people under 35. Of the 16,000 new hires Fidelity expected to make, nearly 80 percent would be in client-facing roles. Fidelity is also expanding its technology support staff and adding new services.[1] With a wide variety of services on offer, including the bill-paying service Vanguard discontinued, Fidelity's strategy appears centered on finding ways to add new accounts with the expectation that new customers will decide to add more and more services to their initial relationship with Fidelity.

Vanguard anticipates more focus on advice services in its future international expansion, with particular interest in 10 countries, including the United Kingdom and Australia, with large potential and fewer constraints designed to protect local banks. The still-untapped possibilities for transforming advice-giving at home and abroad remain vast.

Like almost all investment managers today, Vanguard's investment advice is based only on an investor's portfolio of securities—cash, stocks, and bonds. This focus seems too narrow. It leaves out such stable-value assets as the investor's home, future Social Security payouts, and the present value of future earnings and savings—and for some, future bequests—all of which matter financially. While understandable, this blinkered approach can be seriously misleading. One danger is an overemphasis on fixed-income investment such as the old "invest your age in bonds" rule, which would have a 40-year-old with a sizable, steady income choose bonds for a substantial 40 percent of a securities portfolio that won't even begin to be tapped for retirement for 25 or 30 years. Investment advisers should direct clients' attention to all the various parts of their whole financial picture, not just the securities portfolio part.

The business of providing financial advice is driven by scale. The big investments now at Vanguard's disposal can finance breakthroughs in automation, allowing differentiated, individualized services previously unimagined and compelling to investors. Vanguard has made huge changes in the investment business in every decade of its past. In the next decades, it is certain to do so again.

AFTERWORD

"Charley, good morning! I just wanted to say hi," said the woman with a graying pixie haircut and a nice Florida tan. She was wearing a handsome wool suit and a big warm smile, as though we were great friends. She seemed to know me, but I was embarrassed to be drawing a blank.

Then she continued, and I knew exactly who she was: "I'm Jean Dowling, and I just wanted to thank you for your letter."

A few years ago, I'd been so appreciative of the years of superb professional service I'd been receiving from him that I asked my Vanguard Flagship representative, Chuck Dowling, to give me his parent's mailing address so I could write them a short letter, congratulating them on being such wonderful parents. Chuck was always upbeat, consistently professional, quick to give help, and in every instance over many years always delivered outstanding service in an exemplary manner. As I told Chuck, it was my belief that a strong service-work ethic is usually learned at home from parents, and that as managing partner of Greenwich Associates, I'd enjoyed writing complimentary notes to the parents of our newly elected partners and now wanted to write one to his parents. On the third request, he relented.

Now I was meeting Jean Dowling for the first time and had the chance to thank her in person. Then she answered my unasked question: Why was she there? "I was a member of the crew for 32 years."

Readers may wonder where we were and why. Jean and 400 others were gathered in March 2019 to celebrate the renaming of the

Majestic Building on the Vanguard campus for Jack Bogle. I was there for two fascinating days of interviews with Vanguard's senior leadership team as part of my research for this book. I was pleased to be a part of this "family" celebration among many Vanguard veterans who, like Jean, had served as Vanguard crew for over 30 years.

Organizational excellence has been the focus of my long career as leader of a professional firm, as strategy consultant to leading financial service organizations around the world, and as a student of great business organizations. It never "just happens." Excellence, as every Olympic athlete knows, is always intensely deliberate.

While most who aspire to excellence fall short, they know their efforts—their striving for excellence—have been important to them. Not all Olympic athletes win medals, but all great athletes know the hard work and self-discipline that took them to the Olympic Games was well worthwhile; they will enjoy being recognized for the rest of their lives as Olympians.

> **Excellence, as every Olympic athlete knows, is always intensely deliberate.**

When I made the commitment to launch Greenwich Associates to provide a new kind of strategy consulting service based on proprietary research, I knew that in addition to an effective business model, success would depend on attracting, organizing, and retaining first-rate people committed to high professional standards. Looking for books on leadership and management of professional service organizations, I was surprised to find so few. Most were celebratory biographies of remarkable people like David Ogilvy's *Confessions of an Advertising Man* or dull, potted histories of law firms. Hardly any tried to come to grips with the important "how to do it" questions I would face and need to answer in real life and in real time. While some serious magazine articles were modestly helpful, most focused on reporting current events with little explanatory history or analysis.

The only way for me to learn what I needed to know and understand was to engage in my own primary research: ask, and ask, and ask again several hundred partner-level professionals at the leading firms in each professional field, particularly the firms recognized as exemplars. Every lawyer, doctor, consultant, accountant, investment banker, or investment manager I knew or met got asked the same question: "Of all the firms in your field, which are the very best—and *why*?" If asked for clarification of what would define "best," I would respond: "If you faced a major, difficult problem, the one firm you would most like to have in your corner. Or, if someone important to you were pursuing a career in your field, the one firm—other than your own—you would most like to hear had been chosen."

The first surprise was how often the same few firms were cited. Within each field, the best firms were widely acknowledged by their peers: in consulting, McKinsey; in law, Cravath; in health care, Mayo Clinic; in finance, Goldman Sachs; in investments, Capital Group.

The second surprise—mercifully brief—came when the idea of a rigorous comparative study was first put to the leaders of the chosen firms. "That makes no sense. Other firms are not at all like ours." True enough for a leader thinking only about the other firms in the same field. But all agreed immediately that a careful comparison of the best firm in each field to the best firms in the other fields could be useful and interesting.

The third surprise developed during the investigation of how and why each of the great firms had risen to the top of its field—*and* stayed at the top through at least three generations of leadership. (That criterion for inclusion in the winners' circle of great firms was admittedly arbitrary, but it makes sense. The only challenge more daunting than rising through the ranks of the good and then the better firms to recognition as the field's best firm was to sustain excellence over many years of changing leadership, changing environments, changing competitors, changing client needs, changing technologies, and changing laws.) Over time, every organization faces many challenges, and some of those challenges, whether originating internally or externally, can do grievous harm. Resilience—how well each does at identifying and diagnosing difficulties and deliberately overcoming them—is crucial to sustaining excellence. Because they have had to, all great firms have shown extraordinary capability at self-diagnosis and self-correction or self-renewal. The best test of superior resilience is the well-known test of time: sustaining excellence.

The fourth surprise was how few and how consistent—virtually identical—the key factors were from great firm to great firm. The specifics of their fields differ in important ways, and their own implementations differ in details. But the core commitments of the great firms are all profoundly alike:

- **Mission:** an inspiring sense of overarching purpose.

- **Client-centered:** a persistent determination to serve clients more effectively than any other firm.

- **Culture:** a "tribal" commitment to teamwork, the better to serve clients unusually well.

- **Recruiting:** a disproportionate commitment to identify and attract the most capable, committed individuals with the strongest personal need to succeed.

> Resilience—how well each does at identifying and diagnosing difficulties and deliberately overcoming them—is crucial to sustaining excellence.

- **Training:** an unusually strong, sustained commitment to accelerate the professional and personal education of each new joiner.

- **Innovation:** repeatedly searching for and finding new ways to serve clients more effectively in small ways and large.

- **Leadership:** brings all these components together and ensures that the organization excels continuously on all the other vital dimensions.

Of course, simultaneous success on all seven key success factors has always been a lot to ask of any organization, particularly over a long time. But sustained excellence on the full range of factors across many years and for many clients is exactly what makes all the great firms true champions. For them, as Aristotle suggested long ago, happiness comes from performing along lines of excellence, and excellence is what we repeatedly do. That's why this study of Vanguard and how it became the organization millions of investors trust with their savings is so worth pondering.

Readers may ask, "Why in that original study was Vanguard *not* included?" Simple answer: to be sure the success was organizational and not due to one or two great leaders, an arbitrary requirement was set of at least three different leaders over time. And when my research for *What It Takes*[1] began, Vanguard had had only two. Now, of course, it has had four CEOs. Vanguard has proven that it has institutionalized its striving for continuing excellence on all seven dimensions.

APPENDIX 1

Etfs 101

An exchange-traded fund (ETF) trades on a stock exchange like any stock, holds a portfolio of stocks, commodities, or bonds, and uses arbitrage to keep its trading price close to its net asset value. Most ETFs track a stock index or bond index and are low cost and tax efficient. In 2008 the Securities and Exchange Commission began to authorize actively managed ETFs.

ETFs had their genesis in 1989 with Index Participation Shares, a proxy for the S&P 500 index that traded on the American and Philadelphia stock exchanges. A lawsuit by the Chicago Mercantile Exchange successfully stopped sales in the United States. A similar product, Toronto Index Participation Shares, started trading on the Toronto Stock Exchange in 1990. These shares, which tracked the Toronto Stock Exchange's TSE 35 and later the TSE 100 indexes, proved popular. This led the American Stock Exchange to try to develop something that would satisfy SEC regulations in the United States. Nathan Most and Steven Bloom, under the direction of Ivers Riley, designed and developed Standard & Poor's Depositary Receipts, introduced in January 1993. Known as SPDRs or "Spiders," the SPDR 500 Trust (ticker: SPY) became the largest ETF in the world.

Barclays Global Investors (BGI), in conjunction with MSCI as underwriter, entered the market in 1996 with World Equity Benchmark Shares (WEBS) to give investors easy access to foreign markets. In 1998, State Street Global Advisors introduced Sector

Spiders, which follow nine industry sectors of the S&P 500. In 2000, BGI put a significant effort behind the ETF marketplace, with a strong emphasis on education and distribution to reach long-term investors. iShares created the first bond index funds in July 2002, based on US Treasury and corporate bonds. Within five years iShares had surpassed the assets of any ETF competitor. BGI was sold to BlackRock in 2009 (see Chapter 14).

Vanguard entered the market in 2001 with a single ETF—Vanguard Total Stock Market ETF (ticker: VTI).

Advantages of ETFs are:

- **Low costs.** ETFs generally have lower costs than other investment products because most ETFs are not actively managed and because ETFs are insulated from the costs of having to buy and sell securities to accommodate shareholder purchases and redemptions. ETFs do not have 12b-1 fees.

- **Trading flexibility.** ETFs can be bought and sold at current market prices at any time during the trading day, unlike mutual funds and unit investment trusts, which can only be bought or sold at the end of the trading day. As publicly traded securities, their shares can be purchased on margin and sold short.

- **Tax efficiency.** ETFs generate relatively low capital gains, because they typically have low portfolio turnover and an in-kind redemption mechanism.

- **Market exposure and diversification.** ETFs provide an economical way to rebalance portfolio allocations or to "equitize" cash by investing it quickly.

- **Transparency.** Whether based on index funds or actively managed, ETFs have transparent portfolios that are priced at frequent intervals throughout the trading day.

ETF distributors buy or sell ETFs directly from or to authorized market participants in "creation units," blocks of tens of thousands of ETF shares, usually exchanged in-kind with baskets of the underlying securities. Market makers on the open market exchange creation units with the underlying securities to provide liquidity for the ETF shares, and help ensure that their intraday market price approximates the net asset value of the underlying assets. Other investors, such as individuals using a retail broker, trade ETF shares in this secondary market.

BRENNAN'S LEADERSHIP GUIDE*

Do the right thing: Vanguard people are allowed to make mistakes, but they are never allowed to make ethical mistakes. Violate the confidentiality of client information, and you're out. Accept a gift of material value from a client or a vendor, and you're out. Make investments that are forbidden because of your job responsibilities, and you're out. Ours is a "no ifs, ands, or buts" policy. There are no gray areas. We make no apologies for that black and white view.

Lead by example: Our great leaders must:

- Be the hardest workers.

- Be the most client focused.

- Be the most driven to succeed.

- Be the most caring and compassionate.

- Be the most flexible.

- Be the best role models with unquestioned integrity.

- Be the most committed to excellence.

---

* See Chapter 13.

Love . . . our people, our company, and our business: This is a great company in a great business. Among all the competitors in the industry, this is the preferred place to work. We do things right, and we do right by our clients. We never compromise on those fundamental principles.

Foster teamwork: In embracing this premise, the successful Vanguard leader "puts her ego in her pocket." Effective leaders exhibit personal humility, a trait that is vital in the investment management business considering that we ply our trade in the financial markets, an unpredictable environment in which we have very little control over the results. Investment firms that give in to hubris are apt to find that pride leads to their downfall. The dustbin of history is littered with examples of financial firms that failed to stay humble.

Accept paradox: To accomplish our mission, we must be both the highest-quality *provider* of services in our business *and* the lowest-cost *producer* in our business. It is difficult to name a second organization, in any business, that is accomplishing both of these goals. This is why a focus on continual improvement is so important to our current and future competitive success.

Work hard: Why? Two reasons. First, I've never seen, or even heard of, an organization where emulation of leaders by the employees is so critical to success. And we want our crew to work very hard for our clients. Second, frankly, we want a lean leadership, and a lean ship requires hardworking leaders.

We must be a very profit-driven organization to remain vital and growing. Yet our financial statements say that "revenue equals expenses" and that makes no profit. How do we reconcile those two statements? Simple. We're driven by our clients' profits, not the firm's.

We have the freedom to manage our business for the long term because of our unique structure. Yet we are driven each day by service-level standards that we measure minute by minute, hour by hour, day by day, week by week.

. . . But be balanced: While leaders should work hard, they should also lead a balanced life. We all know that staying balanced is sound investment advice and a sound business strategy. It is also the path that leads to personal and professional fulfillment. The need to work hard but be balanced is one of the paradoxes of being a Vanguard leader.

Compete tenaciously: The drive to succeed has been a critical element in our success at both the personal and corporate levels. One of my coworkers said it profoundly some years back on the day after the stock market's worst single-day setback in a decade. At the end of that day, when it was clear that our client service had been splendid and that all client transactions and requests had been handled, I asked, "How does this happen? How do we, alone in the industry, treat a day of surging volumes and great stress as a normal day, even an enjoyable one?" She responded, "Jack, you know as well as anyone, we're the most competitive firm in the world; we simply won't let someone be better than us on a day like today."

Be decisive and accept responsibility: A great leader accepts all the blame and distributes all the credit. Being the leader is credit enough. Decisiveness—particularly when tempered with sound judgment—is an asset that you won't find on our balance sheet but that has helped us conquer many obstacles and lead the way in this industry for years and years.

Value diversity: This is a people business, and we must have the best people working for us in all positions, at all locations, and at all times. It would be foolish for any of us to think that all of those people should look "just like me." Thus, the high-impact leaders of this company understand the power that embracing diversity can bring to Vanguard. Diversity is important at Vanguard. First, I have learned so much over time from those people who *aren't* like me that I consider working with a diverse team a simply fabulous ongoing educational opportunity. And second, it's more fun.

Set high expectations: Well-run departments become exceptional departments when a new leader is installed who has higher expectations for the group. Conversely, when a unit's relative performance has declined, invariably we can trace the problem to a leader for whom "good enough was good enough." There are a number of lessons to be learned here. The great leaders of this organization have unfailingly high expectations for themselves. In fact, high personal expectations are a must for a leader.

Embrace change: For years, I've heard people outside the company say Vanguard hasn't changed much through the years. "Still dominated by mutual funds . . . still owned by the client . . . still focused on low cost . . . still not too glitzy." On the surface, it's true. We haven't changed much. Actually, this organization has changed frequently and the people who have embraced change are the ones who have led us to success and have thrived. Those who have resisted change have slowed our development and—not coincidentally—have hurt their own careers.

Be personal: One tremendous difference between good leaders and great leaders is this: The great ones are personal. By "personal," I mean they work at being more than a boss, more than someone who guides a team. Vanguard's great leaders open themselves up, letting their people in on their personal lives, their hobbies, their families, their likes and dislikes. In turn, our most effective leaders want to be let in on their team's lives, too, so they can know the crew as people, not just employees. The personal can never get in the way of the professional, but it sure can enhance it. We want everyone on the crew to have both a professional relationship and care about you as a person and know about your children—or your partner if you're gay.

Be positive: Face it. Work is work. Most people don't choose to work; they must. Those are the stark realities of life in a business or in any organization. That said, a leader's job is to make work challenging, enjoyable, and rewarding. You cannot do that except in a positive environment. The need for a positive environment places a big burden on our leaders. The great ones recognize one simple fact: they can never have a bad day. Because if they have a bad day, their work unit has a bad day. And if that happens, the client will know it.

Be resourceful: Our great leaders understand what needs to be done, and they get it done, no matter what it takes. When there's a roadblock or unexpected hurdle, Vanguard leaders figure out a different approach. In other words, leading successfully here requires that innate ability to carry out a mission without turning aside or relying on others when things don't go quite as expected. Our most resourceful leaders don't write a memo to someone explaining why something *can't* happen; they just get it done.

Develop successors: We all know who the great people developers are at Vanguard. They touch the entire company; they touch hundreds of crew members. We also can identify managers who subscribe to the "no one too close to the throne" school of thought. The people developers thrive and prosper with us; the others don't work here anymore.

Prize (and demonstrate) loyalty: Vanguard values loyal clients and a loyal crew—both are critical to the long-term success of our company. And, as in any relationship, loyalty must go both ways. A company can't expect to receive loyalty unless it also treats its clients—and its people—with loyalty.

Be in touch: Our best leaders *want* to know how they're doing. They want candid feedback from their boss; from their team; from their clients. They actively seek face-to-face feedback knowing the more you show you're really listening, the better the feedback will be.

Forget glamour: Clearly, low cost is not the glamorous or glitzy place to be in business. Few firms seek it out; in fact, only the winning firms end up in this position. We've had people say to us "Working at Vanguard is an acquired taste." I agree . . . proudly. Our great leaders understand that *low cost* is not the same thing as *cheap*. The Vanguard leader must be comfortable with our low-cost strategy; comfortable with our "no frills."

Minimize politics: Politics have never had a place at Vanguard. We are a mission-driven organization with one set of clients—Vanguard clients—and one overriding goal—to provide the maximum return for each of those clients. In serving those clients, there is no room for self-interest.

Welcome debate: The ability to disagree is important. The willingness to say to a colleague, "You're right" is essential.*

Teach: One of the major privileges of serving in a leadership role at Vanguard is the chance to teach. It's an opportunity that is presented in many ways. People who view themselves as merely "managing" feel no compulsion to teach. Our best leaders can think of *nothing* more fun.

Think globally: We are becoming a better company as we become a global company. The perspectives that crew from various countries and cultures bring to the proverbial table are incredibly valuable. International diversity strengthens the human fabric that has distinguished Vanguard in every endeavor we've undertaken since we began. It's another one of our subtle competitive advantages.

Grow . . . personally, intellectually, and professionally: Not coincidentally, those who succeed most in meeting new challenges do so because they've been preparing for additional responsibilities throughout their entire careers.

Avoid complacency: The facts and figures about our successes are impressive, but as we should always be reminded, that is all "yesterday." What is relevant is our performance for our clients and our crew members as we move into the future. It takes enormous discipline—personal and institutional—to avoid complacency in a successful organization, and very few organizations have done so. Our own scorecard is in fact not perfect. But I hope we have learned from every episode in which complacency hurt our performance for clients and crew. Our focus on continuous improvement provides the motivation to avoid repeating mistakes. And, in this organization, the great leaders are entrusted with the responsibility to keep us focused, keep us sharp, keep us driven to be the best.

---

* Expanding later on this item, Brennan had no interest in holding back: "The willingness to say to a colleague 'That's stupid' is [also] essential."

Have fun: The leaders of this company work hard. Very hard. We have trillions of dollars of other people's money in our care in markets that can be volatile and treacherous. It's a huge responsibility. We cannot control the ultimate product we produce—investment results. That's a humbling prospect. With that as background, the great leaders recognize that you have to have fun when working here. Our leaders don't have to be comics or entertainers, but if they don't demonstrate the humanity and the humility required to have fun, crew members will be less likely to rally around them and follow them through tough times. So have some fun. Demonstrate a lighter side; a sense of humor; a lack of fear of embarrassment. It will pay big dividends. No team wants to be led by a stiff.

SOURCES AND ACKNOWLEDGMENTS

Any history depends on the teller, as we learned with *Roshomon*, and every storyteller has his or her own perspective. Determined to tell the story of Vanguard accurately, I've been blessed with many perspectives: nearly 60 years of deep engagement in the profession and the business of investment management as a practitioner, as a consultant to many of the world's major players, as a writer and teacher, and as a friend of many of the best thinkers and leaders of the best firms.

This fortunate range and depth of sources to understand the wonderful world of investing has been replicated by my good fortune to have known and worked closely with many of the important participants in this remarkable story. At least as important, it has been my privilege to have known these important participants over many years.

Jack Bogle and John Neff, first met in 1966, were both major contributors. Jack and I agreed on many issues, particularly low fees and indexing and the importance of client service and integrity. We celebrated each other's books and enjoyed a long friendship. For this book, Jack devoted two full days to sharing his recollections. John invited me to write the introduction to his book, *John Neff on Investing*,[1] participated regularly in the seminars I led for leading investment managers, and served as a director of Greenwich Associates. We discussed his rigorous investment disciplines many times.

Burt Malkiel, longtime director of Vanguard and expert observer-participant-overseer of investment management firms, has been a special friend for over 40 years. His *A Random Walk Down Wall Street*[2] is everyone's favorite. Together, we wrote a primer for new investors, *The Elements of Investing*.[3] As dean of the Yale School of Management, Burt invited me to teach the school's investment course. We served together as directors of Vanguard, and, with great patience and kind persistence, Burt gave generously of his broad, deep understanding of the many dimensions of the Vanguard story.

Bob Doran, a friend of over 50 years, provided insights and understanding of the difficult years of confrontation between Vanguard and Wellington and, importantly, the reconnection of the two organizations which has become so important to their great and continuing success. Modest to a fault, Bob has been one of the investment profession's great servant leaders, to the benefit of his colleagues and millions of investors.

Jack Brennan invited me to join the Vanguard board 20 years ago and we have, since its founding, served together on the investment committee for King Abdullah University of Science and Technology in Saudi Arabia. Its endowment is now over $40 billion, the second largest in the world of education. In my years as a director, I had the privilege of observing Brennan's leadership as various challenges and opportunities presented themselves and he led the transformation of Vanguard on multiple dimensions.

Bill McNabb and I got to know each other over the several years I represented Greenwich Associates as a strategy consultant to Vanguard while Bill was building up the company's 401(k) business.

Jim Riepe, long a good friend, generously shared the details of his experiences and the core documents of the early years of Vanguard.

Jerry Kenney, one of Wall Street's great business strategists, gave me vital insights into the bidding for BGI. Philip Augar, author of the story of Barclays Bank, helped me understand the various bidders for BGI.

Dean LeBaron has been my friend for over 60 years.

Most of the key contributors to the surging growth and steady development of Vanguard over the past few decades are identified in the text. They gave generously of their time and understanding in a long, long series of in-depth interviews. Each reviewed and confirmed my writeup of our interview.

A surprising number of coincidental connections enabled me to gain insights into specific aspects of the history. Larry Wilson and Bill Crozier were my classmates at Harvard Business School, and Sam Hayes was a new member of the faculty with whom I shared interesting experiences.

Bob Diamond participated in my Yale seminar on business ethics.

Peter Vermilye, Harold Newman, and I were colleagues at DLJ, and before that Peter was my client at both Morgan Guaranty Trust and at State Street Management.

Dick Smith was an SEC commissioner when we met, and he then came to one of the three-day seminars on investing that I led for DLJ.

Paul Miller, Jay Sherrerd, Hazel Sanger, and I were "friends in the profession," and Bill Hicks and I were family friends from Greenwood, Mississippi.

Erin Passen of Vanguard was helpful in many ways, and her steady hand guided the process skillfully. We developed a strong professional bond as well as a friendship. Judith Newlin of McGraw Hill Education added insights and a sharp editorial eye. The book design and copy editing reflect the expertise of Steve Straus and Richard Camp of THINK Book Works.

William S. Rukeyser, as editor extraordinaire, has been my partner, mentor, and friend in the multidimensional challenge of converting draft chapters into a finished book. Sometimes admonishing, always genial, and superbly skillful, he has worked his magic on many levels—therapist, teacher, coach, trainer, cheerleader, and chaplain. We met and worked together when he was establishing *Money* as the best consumer magazine in personal finance and investing. We worked assiduously together on *Inside Vanguard*, as we have on several books over a dozen years, beginning with *The Partnership*,[4] the story of Goldman Sachs's rise to leadership in the global securities industry. All readers have many reasons to be grateful to Bill for making the inspiring story of Vanguard crisper, clearer, and even more compelling. Bill was a genial professional perfectionist and would have taken professional satisfaction in completing his editing, before a celebratory dinner in Manhattan a month before his early death. He was a great friend.

A few books were particularly helpful: Robert Slater's *John Bogle and the Vanguard Experiment*,[5] which tells Bogle's story of the early years of Vanguard; *John Neff on Investing*; and the several books Bogle wrote about investing and Vanguard.

Of course, it was helpful to have written books about Goldman Sachs and Capital Group,[6] to have taught the investment management courses at Harvard and Yale, and to have devoted 30 years to consulting with investment firms and securities firms in North America, Europe, and Asia. These experiences immersed me in the world of Vanguard.

Confession: Vanguard is the investment manager for my beloved wife, my two sons, my four grandchildren, our church, and the Whitehead Institute, where I chaired the investment committee for many years. I know of no other investment management organization so capable and so devoted to delivering, at low cost, such high value.

NOTES

CHAPTER 1
1. Author's interview with J. Bogle at Malvern, April 26–27, 2017.
2. Ibid.
3. Ibid.
4. Ibid.
5. Robert Slater, *John Bogle and the Vanguard Experiment*, Irwin Professional Publishing, 1996, p. 4.
6. Bogle interview, April 26–27, 2017.
7. Slater, p. 5.
8. McGraw-Hill, 1993.
9. Ibid., p. 6.
10. Bogle interview, April 26–27, 2017.
11. Ibid.
12. Author's interview with B. Malkiel at Princeton, summer 2018.

CHAPTER 2
1. Slater, p. 15.
2. Bogle interview, April 26–27, 2017.
3. Slater, p. 24.
4. Bogle interview, April 26–27, 2017.
5. Ibid.
6. Author's interview with R. Doran in Brookline, Massachusetts, spring 2018.
7. *Institutional Investor* (date unknown).
8. Author's interview with J. Sherrerd, Bermuda, 1990s.
9. Doran interview, spring 2018.
10. Bogle interview, April 26–27, 2017.
11. Walter M. Cabot joined the firm from Putnam for 3 percent voting control, which left 29 percent still to be held by outside investors.

CHAPTER 3

1. Slater, p. 39.
2. Ibid., p. 35.
3. Bogle interview, April 26–27, 2017.
4. Robert E. Worden went to MIT on full four-year scholarship, worked for several years at Campbell Soup and then launched a highly successful consulting firm that specialized in modernizing US subsidiaries of European corporations after World War II.
5. Doran interview, spring 2018.
6. Author's telephone interview with J. Walters, spring 2018.
7. Slater, p. 52.
8. Author's telephone interview with J. Riepe, May 8, 2020.
9. Ibid.
10. Doran interview, spring 2018.
11. Slater, p. 63.

CHAPTER 4

1. Philadelphians' pride in their city often surprises outsiders who formed their opinions back when downtown buildings were stunted by a zoning rule that none could be taller than William Penn's hat atop City Hall; who smirked at old jokes like "second prize was *two* weeks in Philadelphia!"; or who had seen the city only from the highway or trains speeding from New York to Washington through the railyards near 30th Street Station.
2. Doran interview, May 8, 2020.
3. Riepe interview, May 8, 2020.
4. Doran interview, May 8, 2020.
5. Author's telephone interview with J. Riepe, October 16, 2020.
6. Slater, p. 84.
7. Seeking and obtaining federal approval was far from easy. Phil Fine, counsel to the fund, worked with Jim Walters in dealings with the SEC.
8. John C. Bogle, "Lightning Strikes," *The Journal of Portfolio Management*, 40th anniversary issue, Fall 2014.

CHAPTER 5

1. Bogle interview, May 26–27, 2017.
2. Author's telephone interview with D. LeBaron, February 21, 2020.
3. https://www.investopedia.com/terms/g/greenmail.asp
4. Paul Samuelson, "Challenge to Judgement" in the inaugural issue of the *Journal of Portfolio Management*, October 10, 1974.
5. Bogle interview, May 26–27, 2017.

6. John C. Bogle, *Stay the Course*, Wiley, 2019. p. 46.
7. Bogle interview, May 26–27, 2017.
8. Doran interview, spring 2018.
9. Slater, p. 96.
10. Riepe telephone interview, October 16, 2019.
11. Bogle interview, April 26–27, 2017.
12. The initial SEC administrative law judge rejected the Vanguard proposal. The civil suit was dismissed with Vanguard paying $85,000 in lawyer's fees and $3,869 in expenses, far less than the $1.1 million sought.
13. Vanguard and Bogle had been beneficiaries of other legal and regulatory changes in many parts of the securities and mutual fund industries. In 1969, contractual investment plans were outlawed. The Investment Company Act of 1970 clarified that fund management companies were corporations and so should have staffs and that fees were a specific responsibility of funds' board of directors. In 1974, ERISA and the fiduciary standard became law. And in 1975, "May Day" brought negotiated commissions to Wall Street.
14. Author's interview with I. MacKinnon at Malvern, May 6, 2019.

CHAPTER 6

1. Julie Roher, "Doing it Jack Bogle's Way," *Institutional Investor*, March 1988.
2. MacKinnon interview, May 26, 2019.
3. Author's interview with J. Brennan at Malvern, May 7, 2019.
4. Author's interview with G. Sauter at Malvern, April 10, 2020.
5. Author's interview with E. Snyder in New Haven, May 5, 2020.
6. Author's interview with J. Brennan at Malvern, April 10, 2019.
7. Ibid.
8. Ibid.

CHAPTER 7

1. John Neff, S. L. Mintz, *John Neff on Investing*, John Wiley & Sons, 2001.
2. While serving on President Ford's Council of Economic Advisers, Burt Malkiel chaired a task force probing the accuracy of the data used by expert units within the federal government; President Nixon had publicly criticized the government for "politically manipulated" data. Malkiel was leading an arcane "insider's study" and was impressed to find Neff knew more about the study's findings than most of those doing the actual work.
3. *Neff on Investing*, page 61.
4. Ibid, p. 64.

5. Ibid, page 239.
6. Newhall studied at Williams College where he enjoyed the important benefits of superb coaching in lacrosse and football. He played on defense and in the line, where consistency is crucial to success. His junior and senior year teams were undefeated. He taught briefly, worked at Chase Manhattan on mortgages, and then earned his MBA at the University of Virginia, where he discovered investing. He got a summer job at Vanguard. When he graduated in 1997, he wanted an investment career (after earning his CFA and taking several investment courses at the Darden School) and decided to work in asset consulting at Cambridge Associates. Nearly five years later fellow UVA alum Jeff Molitor helped get him a job at Vanguard.
7. Author's interview with D. Newhall at Malvern, July 10, 2019.
8. Ibid.
9. Author's interview with Churchill G. Franklin, cofounder of Acadian, in Boston, spring 2019.
10. https://www.morningstar.com/small-blend-funds.
11. Author's interview with G. Sauter at Malvern, April 11, 2019.
12. Brennan interview, May 7, 2019.
13. Author's interview with M. Milias, April 12, 2019.

CHAPTER 8
1. As the first in his family to go to college, Rodney Comegys studied engineering at Penn, joined the Navy ROTC, served on nuclear submarines, and became proficient in Six Sigma programs.
2. Author's interview with R. Comegys at Malvern, May 7, 2019.
3. Telephone interview with Comegys, winter 2021.
4. Sauter interview, April 11, 2019.
5. Ibid.

CHAPTER 9
1. Author's interview with B. Malkiel in Princeton, New Jersey, spring 2019.
2. Sauter was an undergraduate at Dartmouth when John Kemeny, inventor of the BASIC programming language, was president of the college. Sauter then studied under several of the inventors of indexing at the University of Chicago. Sauter and Brennan had been classmates and friends at Dartmouth and were back for their tenth reunion when Brennan asked Sauter's wife what Gus was doing at an Ohio bank. Quantitative investing was the answer, and since Vanguard wanted to expand there, Brennan asked Jeremy Duffield, head of planning and development, to give Sauter a call. The overture was accepted. Sauter,

who habitually worked 12 hours a day, had first bought stock at age 12 with money saved from a paper route he started at 11.

3. Sauter interview, April 11, 2019.
4. Most of the legal work with the SEC was done by Greg Barton's team of in-house lawyers. "As it happens though," Barton recalls, "my first hire when I came to Vanguard in 1997 was a former SEC staffer known for his technical expertise and careful and creative thinking on regulatory issues. He really was Vanguard's ace in the hole, a lawyer who, while working at the SEC, had been assigned to State Street's first ETF application for SPDRS. There was no one better equipped to work with Sauter on getting Vanguard's application approved."

CHAPTER 10

1. Author's interview with J. Gately at Malvern, May 7–8, 2019.
2. Ibid.
3. Ibid.
4. Author's interview with B. Malkiel at Princeton, April 21, 2019.
5. Lewis Braham, *The House that Bogle Built: How John Bogle and Vanguard Reinvented the Mutual Fund Industry*, McGraw-Hill Education, 2011.
6. Bogle interview, April 26–27, 2017.
7. Telephone interview with M. Miller, summer 2019. After law school at Boston College, Miller practiced law briefly but decided he was more interested in business management. He accepted a request from the New York State Attorney General to take over First Investors Corporation and work it out of a high-yield debt fiasco that had put it into receivership. When half the sales force and all the investment management people left, he turned to Wellington for help. Hiring Wellington was, in his view, one of the best decisions he ever made. He liked the people, their professional skills, and the firm's culture. Over three years, Miller had achieved the reorganization he had signed on for. Then the "old guys," who still owned a lot of stock, decided they wanted to come back. Miller was advised, "This is a fight you cannot win and can lose in a major way, so why not fold?" And that's what he did, in a gradual way. He had learned an important personal lesson: he liked management and was good at it, and so could not go back to practicing law. With a rising bond market, Miller was able to work out a "global agreement" with First Investors' creditors and, after three and a half years, was pondering his next career move. Casting a wide net, he discussed possibilities with Pam Dipple and Duncan McFarland, managing partners at Wellington. Dipple recommended Miller to Brennan. Shortly after joining Vanguard, Miller got word from the board of directors: "You will be in charge of managing the transition" from Jack Bogle to Jack Brennan.

8. Brennan interview, April 10, 2019.
9. Miller telephone interview, summer 2019.
10. Ibid.

CHAPTER 11
1. Author's telephone interview with J. Zweig, spring 2019.
2. John Wiley & Sons, 2006.

CHAPTER 12
1. Before heading Alliance Capital, Vermilye had been the leader of Morgan Guaranty's successful business with large corporate pension funds and then of State Street Research & Management's major success in that same growth market.
2. Author's telephone interview with Richard Jenrette, 2018.
3. Standish, Ayer & Wood was the third investment organization invited to compete.
4. Author's interview with R. Doran in Brookline, April 7, 2019
5. Author's interview with J. Neff in 1990s.
6. Author's interview with H. Sanger in Atlanta, 1980s.
7. Doran interview, April 7, 2019.
8. Author's telephone interview with J. Walters, November 13, 2019.
9. Author's telephone interviews with S. Hayes and W. Crozier, spring 2019.
10. The Wellington partnership began with 27 partners, one partner having left just after the partnership was formed to join another who had left just before the change to set up his own firm. Over time it has grown to over 150 partners who come from all areas of the firm. The partnership is now a limited liability partnership, a form not available in 1979, but all the governing principles are unchanged.

CHAPTER 13
1. Hal Lux, "Can Vanguard Stay the Course?", *Institutional Investor*, August 1999, pp. 44–49.
2. Brennan interview, April 10, 2019.
3. Author's interview with J. Brennan at Malvern, May 26, 2019.
4. Miller interview, spring 2019.
5. "The Vanguard Leader," fourth edition, April 14, 2014.
6. Brennan interview, May 7, 2019.
7. Ibid.
8. Ibid.
9. Ibid.

CHAPTER 14

1. TIAA-CREF was later acquired by Madison Dearborn and combined with Nuveen for $6.3 billion.
2. Author's interview with J. Kenney in New York City, July 5, 2017.
3. Author's interview with G. Reed at Malvern, May 8, 2019.
4. Private equity is an alternative form of private financing, away from public markets, in which funds and investors directly invest in companies or engage in buyouts of such companies. https://www.investopedia.com/terms/p/privateequity.asp.
5. Ibid.
6. Penguin Random House UK, 2019.
7. Author's interview with P. Augar in London, July 24, 2015.
8. Author's interview with A. Rankin in New York City, February 20, 2020.

CHAPTER 15

1. Author's interview with W. McNabb at Malvern, May 24, 2019.
2. Ibid.
3. Ibid.
4. Ibid.
5. Ibid.
6. Geoff Colvin, "C-Suite Strategies," *Fortune*, June 14, 2012, p. 60.
7. Ibid.
8. Author's interview with K. Gubanich at Malvern, April 10, 2019.
9. McNabb interview, May 24, 2019.
10. Ibid.
11. Author's interview with John T. Marcante, chief global information officer, at Malvern, April 24, 2019.
12. Dawn Lim, "Vanguard Hits Pause on Fund Ambitions in China," *Wall Street Journal*, March 16, 2021.
13. Julie Segal. "Vanguard Exports Its Low-Cost Model Around the World," *Institutional Investor*, April 3, 2015.
14. McNabb interview, May 24, 2019.
15. "William McNabb, Chief Executive of Fund Giant Vanguard, to Step Down," July 13, 2017.

CHAPTER 16

1. Author's interview with A. Perold in Boston, confirmed by Tim Buckley in Malvern, May 27, 2019.
2. Author's interview with Tim Buckley, April 7, 2021.
3. Michelle Celarier, "Deal Book," *New York Times*, December 4, 2021.
4. American Investment Council, September 2021.

5. Cloud computing is the on-demand availability of computer system resources, especially data storage (cloud storage) and computing power, without direct active management by the user. The term is generally used to describe data centers available to many users over the Internet. https://en.wikipedia.org/wiki/Cloud_computing.

6. "Vanguard Rolls Back Plan to Cut Retiree Benefits," *Wall Street Journal*, October 11, 2021.

CHAPTER 17

1. https://www.ssa.gov/benefits/retirement/planner/delayret.html.

2. Jason Zweig, "The Huge Tax Bills That Came Out of Nowhere at Vanguard," *Wall Street Journal*, January 21, 2022; "Talal Ansari, "Massachusetts Investigates Potential Target-Date Funds Tax Issue," *Wall Street Journal*, January 25, 2022; "Vanguard to Pay $6 Million to Investors Hit With Big Tax Bills," Wall Street Journal, July 7, 2022.

3. Brennan interview, May 7, 2019.

4. Risi earned BS and MBA degrees at Villanova and joined Vanguard in 1996 following two years in investor relations in Sunoco. She currently leads the Planning & Development Group.

5. Author's interview with K. Risi at Malvern, May 27, 2019.

CHAPTER 18

1. Author's interview with H. Stam at Malvern, May 26–27, 2019.

2. Ibid.

3. "Women Were 29% of U.S. Board Directors in 2020, Up From 19% in 2014," *Barron's*, https://www.barrons.com/articles/women-are-29-of-u-s-board-directors-in-2020-up-from-19-in-2014-51626880842.

4. "Does Majority Voting Improve Board Accountability?", Harvard Law School Forum on Corporate Governance, https://corpgov.law.harvard.edu/2015/11/27/does-majority-voting-improve-board-accountability/.

5. For his first 27 years at Vanguard, Glenn Booraem was in Fund Financial Management and more recently has been in the Office of the General Counsel with Ann Robinson. Booraem grew up near Malvern, Pennsylvania, studied finance and accounting at Temple University and later completed Harvard's Advanced Management Program. He had heard of Vanguard and assumed it was in insurance. In 1989, Vanguard was offering members of the crew $250 for each successful hire, and he and his wife had both been given applications. She asked, "Have you filled out yours, Glenn?" So he did. Two weeks after graduation, when he was negotiating for a job in house building, he got a call from Vanguard to come for an interview. In 2001, Booraem got into proxy voting at an early stage with a focus on such nonroutine actors

as Enron and WorldCom. Rather than rotating into a series of new jobs, Booraem's personal growth challenge has been to keep up with a steadily growing area of responsibilities as corporate governance has become increasingly important, varied and international.

6. Author's interview with G. Booream at Malvern, May 7, 2019.
7. Editorial Board, "Calling Out 'Emperor' Larry Fink," *Wall Street Journal*, February 18, 2022.
8. John C. Coates, "The Problem of Twelve," draft, September 20, 2018.
9. By Inigo Fraser-Jenkins of Alliance Bernstein.
10. Dawn Lim, "Index Funds Are the New Kings of Wall Street," *Wall Street Journal*, September 18, 2019.
11. Ellen B. Schultz, *Wall Street Journal*, July 2, 1996.
12. "The Tax Threat to Your Mutual Fund," May 7, 2015, p. A15.
13. "Corporate Bonds Index Funds No Longer the Old Stalwarts," Dow Jones Capital Market Report, July 12, 2002.

CHAPTER 19

1. Justin Baer, "Fidelity to Add 9,000 More Jobs," *Wall Street Journal*, September 1, 2021, p. B1.

AFTERWORD

1. Charles D. Ellis, *What It Takes: Seven Secrets of Success from the World's Greatest Professional Firms*, Wiley, 2013.

SOURCES AND ACKNOWLEDGMENTS

1. John Neff, S. L. Mintz, *John Neff on Investing*, John Wiley & Sons, 2001.
2. Burton G. Malkiel, *A Random Walk Down Wall Street*, W. W. Norton & Company, 1973.
3. Burton G. Malkiel and Charles D. Ellis, *The Elements of Investing*, Wiley, 2010.
4. Charles D. Ellis, *The Partnership*, The Penguin Press, 2008.
5. Robert Slater, *John Bogle and the Vanguard Experiment*, Irwin Professional Publishing, 1996.
6. Charles D. Ellis, *Capital*, Wiley, 2005.

INDEX

INDEX

Beijing, China, 150
Benchmark price, 94
Berkshire Hathaway, 171–172
BGI (*see* Barclays Global Investors)
"Big Money in Boston" (*Fortune* article),
 8
"Big tent" model of management,
 151–153
Bill-paying service, 83
BlackRock, xi, xii, 10, 169, 172–175, 184,
 210, 222, 224
Blair, William, 171–172
Blair Academy, 6–7, 12
Bligh, William, 50n*
Bloom, Steven, 245
Bloomberg Television, 181
Bloomberg terminals, xvii, 77
"Blue water" strategy, 70–71
Board of directors, 191–192, 214, 218
Bogle, David Caldwell, 3, 4, 6
Bogle, Eve, 20
Bogle, John Clifton "Jack," ix–xiii, xvi, 78,
 200, 239–240
 achievements of, 11–12
 Jack Brennan and, x–xi, 117–120
 changeover to Brennan's leadership
  from, 126–128
 death of, 140–141
 departure from Wellington, 29–43
 early career of, 13
 early years of, 3–12, 138
 frugality of, 73–74
 governance under, 226–228
 health concerns, 20–21, 27, 31–32, 57,
  119, 127–129
 hiring decisions, 160–161, 179–180
 legacy of, 137–139
 media interactions, 81–82, 126–127,
  132, 134
 retirement of, 119, 127–128, 132–134
 sacred-cows speech, 70–71, 121
 "Saint Jack" image of, 34, 133
 Vanguard–Wellington relationship
  under, 45–51, 143–145
Bogle, Josephine, 3
Bogle, Josephine Lorraine Hipkins
 (mother), 3, 4, 8, 138
Bogle, Lorraine (sister), 3

Bogle, William Yates, III, "Bud," 3, 5–7
Bogle, William Yates, Jr., 3, 4
Bogle Financial Markets Research
 Center, 137
Bogle on Mutual Funds (Bogle), 8
Bogle Scholars, 12
Bogleheads, x, 12, 138–140, 195n*
Bogleheads Guide to Investing (Larimore
 et al.), 140
Bond fund, 31, 67, 68, 230–231
Bonds, xvi
Bonuses, employee referral, 182–183
Booraem, Glenn, 220, 221, 268–269n5
Boston, Mass., 17, 22, 24, 25, 27–28, 33
Boston College, 158
Boston Company, 159
Boston Consulting Group, 73
Bravo, Richard A., 231
Brennan, Catherine, 159
Brennan, Frank, 158–159
Brennan, John J. "Jack," x–xi, xiii, 81, 105,
 264n2
 advice-embedded products under, 200,
  205
 BGI deal for, 170–172, 175
 Jack Bogle and, 117–120
 compensation under, 84–86
 cost management by, 78, 83
 culture under, 165–167
 "do it yourself first" philosophy of,
  167–168
 early life and family of, 158–161
 governance under, 217, 225, 228,
  230–231
 hiring decisions, 121–126, 189, 191
 leadership style, 120–121, 157–158,
  161–165, 249–255
 leadership style of, 129–132
 legacy of, 134–135
 partnership with Wellington under,
  143, 148–151
 retirement of, 178–179
 transition to leadership by, 126–128
Brennan, Mary, 158
Brigham and Women's Hospital, 31–32
Brown Brothers Harriman, 153, 154
Buckley, Marilyn, 189
Buckley, Mortimer (father), 189

INDEX

INDEX

Facebook, 97n*
Fama, Eugene, xi
Family offices, 199
FAS (Financial Advisor Services),
 208–209
Federal Reserve Board, 192
Federal Trade Commission (FTC),
 223–226
Feedback, for leaders, 253
Fees:
 for active managers, 74–75
 calculating, 74
 management, xii, 40, 50, 65, 75, 79, 91,
 202, 226
 redemption, 78, 215
 trading, 50
 12b-1, 65
 (*See also* Low fees; Transaction fees and
 costs)
Fidelity, xii, 68, 81, 118, 123–125, 145,
 185, 199, 236–237
Fiduciary responsibility, 153, 230,
 263n13
Financial Advisor Services (FAS),
 208–209
Financial Engines, 205
Financial Industry Regulatory Authority
 (FINRA), 214–215
Financial Services Authority (FSA), 173
Financial Stability Board, 229
Financial Times, 79
Fine, Phil, 262n7
Fink, Larry, 172–174, 222
FINRA (Financial Industry Regulatory
 Authority), 214–215
First Index Investment Trust, 59–62
First Investors Corporation, 265n7
First-mover advantage, 59
Fixed-income investments, 237–238 (*See
 also* Bond fund)
Flagship investor specialists, 126
Flywheel 2.0 (at Vanguard), 184–185
Forbes magazine, 71, 81
Fortune magazine, 8
401(k) plans, 121–125, 180–181, 200, 204
Franklin Portfolio Associates, 96
Fraser-Jenkins, Inigo, 225
French, Jim, 14, 60

FSA (Financial Services Authority), 173
FTC (Federal Trade Commission),
 223–226
FTSE Social Index Fund, 230
Fullwood, Emerson, 191
Fun, having, 255
"The Future Structure of Wellington
 Group of Investment Companies"
 (memo), 48–50

Gage, Jesse Witherspoon, 6
Gardiner, Robert "Stretch," 64
GARP (growth at a reasonable price)
 managers, 96–97
Gately, James H., 78, 121–126, 129–130
Gemini Fund, 30
General Electric (GE), 107, 130
Gillette, 39
Girard Bank, 67
Glamour, 253
Global financial crisis (2008), 82–83,
 107–108, 170, 174, 180–182,
 229–230
Global Investment Committee, 191
Global thinking, 254
"Go shop" provisions, 170
Goldman Sachs, 171, 195, 241
Gooch, John, 150
Google, 97n*, 185
Governance, 213–231
 in 2008 financial crisis, 229–230
 alignment of SEC and Vanguard,
 213–215
 under Brennan, 131–132
 communicating unfavorable results,
 227–231
 doing the right thing, 227–228
 as foundational principle, 10
 of FTSE Social Index Fund, 230
 New York investigation of mutual fund
 companies, 215–217
 no-load shareholder lawsuit, 226
 proxy voting, 217–226
 rejecting accounts, 226–227
 transparency, 221–223
Graham, Benjamin, 88
Great bear market (1973-1974), 37–38,
 60

275

INDEX

ABOUT THE AUTHOR

CHARLES D. ELLIS served Vanguard for many years as a director and as a business consultant. Over 60 years he knew and worked with all the principal players in this fascinating story of how, starting with nearly nothing, Vanguard grew to be America's largest and most admired investment organization.

Charley founded and led Greenwich Associates for three decades; taught the investment management courses at Yale School of Management and Harvard Business School; was chair of CFA Institute, the global organization of investment professionals; served for 17 years on Yale's investment committee and on a dozen other investment committees; consulted on strategy with leading investment organizations around the world for 30 years and was for many years chair of Whitehead Institute for Biomedical Research.

This is his nineteenth book. Others include *Winning the Loser's Game, What It Takes, Figuring It Out* and studies of Goldman Sachs and Capital Group. Charley and his wife and best friend, Linda Lorimer, live in New Haven.